QUALITY & PRODUCTIVITY:
THE NEW
CHALLENGE

by
Glenn E. Hayes
Professor, Quality Assurance
CENTER FOR QUALITY AND PRODUCTIVITY STUDIES
Dept. of Engineering and Industrial Technology
School of Engineering
California State University
Long Beach, California

Publisher:
Hitchcock Executive Book Service
Hitchcock Publishing Company
Hitchcock Building
Wheaton, IL 60188

Dedicated to those who would inspire,
promote, and execute the causes of
quality and productivity in the
United States.

Library of Congress Catalog Card Number: 84-62379
ISBN 0-933931-00-X

1st Printing, March 1985
©1985 by Hitchcock Publishing Co.

Publisher: Hitchcock Publishing Company
Hitchcock Building
Wheaton, IL 60188

CONTENTS

PART II: MEETING THE CHALLENGE 140

Chapter VI

THE CULTURAL FOUNDATION 142

Chapter VII

QUEST FOR TEAMWORK 169

Chapter VIII

Chapter IX

Chapter X

PREFACE

The idea for this book has been developing for several years. As professor and consultant in the fields of quality and productivity, it has become apparent to me that a candid coverage of the macro aspects of productivity should be organized in book form.

The problem of improving industrial productivity in the U.S. carries broad implications reaching virtually every facet of society. From the political, social, educational, and religious institutions to industry itself, a number of factors which influence the effectiveness with which products are produced need to be reassessed and brought under control. A growing number of conditions that must be "managed" have markedly increased the complexity of managements' jobs. Concomitantly, some of these variables have had deleterious effects on the effectiveness with which outputs are generated.

The principal purposes of this book are fourfold: (1) to present a "tell it like it is" account of major issues which confront industrial managers, (2) to examine the importance of organizational, institutional, and teamwork factors as they relate to productivity improvement, (3) to reveal some latent paradoxes and deterrents to productivity improvement which generally need to be addressed by institutions and industrial leaders alike, and (4) to suggest methods and areas where improvements can be made.

Part I of the book (THE CHALLENGE) is devoted to status, trends and issues of the productivity movement. It is a frank discussion of productivity factors which continue to confront industrial managers. In the pursuit of improvement, today's executives have to make choices in the midst of complex and often oppositional circumstances. Many of these dilemmas are readily manageable, but others are abstract and elusive, and have become more or less institutionalized barriers. Largely concealed in industrial cultures, these are important challenges that many industrial leaders face.

In **Part II** (MEETING THE CHALLENGE), methods and principles, which have been and continue to be used to generate improvement, are explored. Industrial culture, its influences on productivity and characteristics which support or inhibit improvement are also discussed. Examples of proven problem solving techniques which are used by industrial engineering and quality engineering professionals are presented. The importance of teamwork and how it is being successfully accomplished in companies is also examined. While the entire book is management oriented, the final chapter deals with leadership principles and management concepts which successful companies are using to their advantage.

This book deals with a number of issues which may have sensitive implications to certain readers, but it is hoped that the candor and straightforward style in which it is written will not detract from the importance of the messages contained herein. Throughout the book, analogous concepts are presented in the hope that readers will glean ideas that can be adapted to their organizations. There is no cookbook list of remedies which apply across the board to productivity improvement. The purpose is to contrast situations so that a better understanding of the issues will lead to individual and company introspection, with improvement as the outcome. If ideas for improvement are conveyed or new ones conceived, and if greater determination is generated to execute them, a principal goal of the book will have been accomplished.

ACKNOWLEDGEMENTS

No book of this nature can be completed without the help and patience of others. First, I want to express my sincere thanks to my wife, Marjorie, and daughter, Adrianne, for typing the initial drafts of the manuscript, which only they could interpret. Secondly, I want to thank Olga Poisal and Debbie Smith for their word processing support, and Dee Allison for her creative skill in completing most of the artwork. Also, I wish to thank Editor, John Kendrick and typesetter, Annette Mola of Hitchcock, for their circumspect attention to the project.

My appreciation also goes to quality directors Ferris Bell, Thomas Oldham, and Richard Metzler, for their helpful suggestions on certain segments of the book. Finally, I especially wish to thank Reginald Audibert for his counsel and insightful contributions.

PART 1:
THE CHALLENGE

Can industrial leaders use indicators of historical and modern origin to bring about steady productivity gain? Can these managements muster and apply the wisdom needed to effectuate sustained improvement? Many believe they can. Most agree that they must. Industry in general is on the threshold of integrating productivity factors that will produce these results. But, it must concomitantly unleash hidden talents of the work force and untie the knots that stymie improvement. This is the great challenge that faces executives in this era, and one which will surely continue to exist.

For nearly 100 years, a number of factors have been evolving which have made improvement increasingly difficult. Some of these are summarized as follows:

1. A carry-over of scientific management has left mixed industrial cultures. Some companies have successfully integrated scientific methods with behavioral aspects of work. Others have found this process tedious, time-consuming, and leading to unnecessary conflict.

2. Managements' rights have been uncompromisingly supreme. The management has had sole responsibility for operations and for productivity improvement, and has essentially made all operating and policy decisions unilaterally.

3. Managements' actions and responsibilities to the employees have often been constrained by adversarial relations with labor. In most instances, where unions do not exist, the management has learned to balance the company's needs with employees' needs, and has developed a more employee-centered style of management.

4. Employees have not shared directly in productivity gains. In most cases, profit sharing and perquisites have been awarded to managements, with conventional incentives being offered to employees on the line. Most

1

"middle class" employees have not been included in any sort of monetary incentive program.

5. The culture in companies to a great extent is still not conducive to free expression of ideas. Leadership styles, crisis management, and anxiety still have a high degree of control over the emotions and actions of employees. However, more and more managements are inaugurating policies and organizational devices to systematically deal with the factors that influence productivity. Commensurably, they are instituting measures that will bring about better control of these variables.

6. The concept and scope of prevention have not been sufficiently understood and applied in order to realize potential benefits. A host of areas where prevention can be applied, traditionally have been dealt with only superficially or not at all. In addition to the more conventional categories, these areas include methods and tooling, training, process control, and up front design integrity.

7. Short range planning and attendant anxiety to ship more and more in less time have assuredly resulted in problems for many companies. This evolving process, now essentially a fixed part of company culture, has placed some companies in situations in which the top executives find most difficult to manage. These are considered challenges by the vigorous and the successful, however, and healthy change is being witnessed.

8. An area which is beginning to receive more attention, and being identified as having a large potential for productivity gain is white-collar work. While the myth that indirect activities cannot or should not be measured is being dispelled, improvement of white-collar performances remains a major objective. Albeit, an increasing number of companies are conscientiously attempting to measure white-collar work, significant improvement in this area will probably remain one of the greatest productivity challenges in the years ahead.

9. For several decades, quality has been a latent and misunderstood dark horse, but this appears to be improving. Both managements and employees are seen demonstrating greater commitments to quality, with improvement as the outcome. An increasing number of seminars and discussions on the subject of institutionalizing quality improvement are also evidences that yester tenets about quality are changing for the better.

CHAPTER I

Productivity: An Overview

Little is more important on the American industrial scene than productivity improvement—increasing the rate of output per input dollar invested. Higher productivity can be converted into higher wages as well as a better competitive position for companies. On a national scale, it also means a higher standard of living and a better selection of products for consumers. Even more subtle, productivity is a means of securing a better national economic image, and a better position in the international market. When productivity is high, the nation, as well as constituent companies, receive reciprocal benefits because it is integrally tied to generic economic health.

When productivity gain is accomplished, employees and consumers alike enjoy the excitement and benefits of this progress. Innovation and creativity not only are at work, but feelings of company spirit and individual pride are experienced as well. Most agree that people are the most happy when they accomplish things. Both individual and company achievements are integrally tied to productivity improvement.

Meaning and Scope

Fundamentally, productivity is most often defined as simply the ratio of output to input (output/input). This definition is inadequate however, if one wishes to know something about the variables and influences that affect this ratio.

The Bureau of Labor Statistics measures and reports national productivity statistics in terms of the gross domestic product (output) divided by the number of paid hours worked by all employed persons. This is an example of labor productivity. There are usually other inputs to any production process, including capital, materials, and energy. Also, questions about quality levels, whether the organization is

3

producing the "right" outputs for the market, and influences these outputs have on users, customers, and society in general should be addressed. Questions have also been raised about the *effectiveness* of the less measurable factors which have more macro significance than simply efficiency.

There are essentially three ways in which productivity can be increased.

1. Reduce or eliminate hinderances of output.
2. Increase the rate of output by working faster or smarter.
3. Technological advances.

The aforementioned hinge considerably on the indirect factors described in Figure I-1 in the productivity equation. Inputs in the equation are divided into two major segments—direct resources and indirect factors. Those which are relatively easy to quantify and often referred to in the context of productivity are the direct resources. However, factors which have even greater influence on productivity and are more difficult to measure are those which have indirect connotations. These have very important meaning when understood in the deeper context of American corporate culture.

In general, responsibility for the content and performance of the indirect factors rests with the management. Although many of these factors are beyond management's control, these influences and how they interact with the direct inputs are profoundly important to productivity gain.

Productivity Status and Influences

American workers produce more per employed person in thousands of U.S. dollars than other countries, but the trend is weak. The growth trend in labor productivity per hour in the nonfarm U.S. business sector is shown in Figure I-2.

The U.S. experienced a steady decline in industrial productivity during the years between 1955 and 1980, albeit beginning in 1981 the picture began to improve from approximately 0% to about 1%. A *trend* however is established over a longer period, and there is some question as to whether all the elements will be in place to constitute a steady gain. If a trend is established, productivity rates of increase by France, West Germany, and Japan could also be comparable. This is shown in Figure I-3 where the lines tend to run more parallel, beginning in 1983. If the U.S. is unable to maintain or increase this rate, and if France, West Germany, and Japan stay on their courses, the U.S. could be

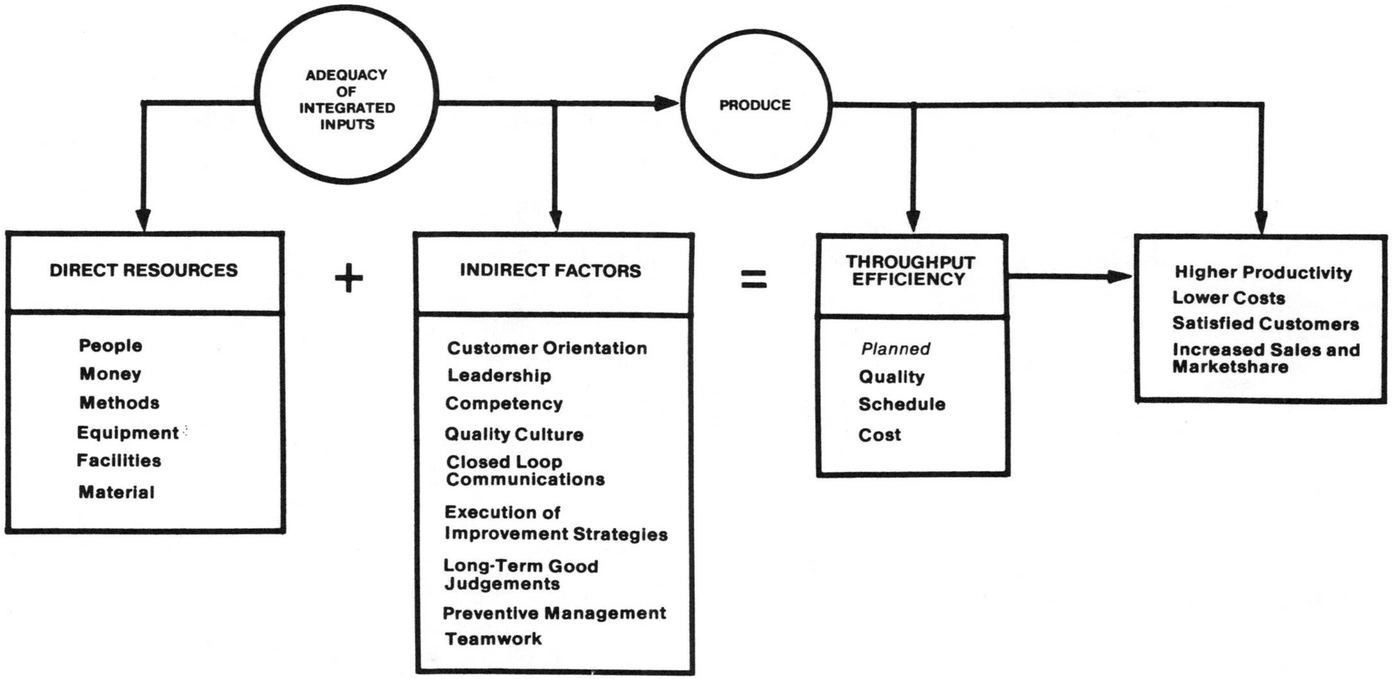

FIGURE I-1. THE PRODUCTIVITY EQUATION

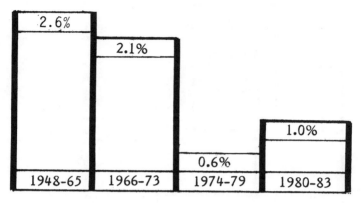

FIGURE I-2. U.S. NONFARM PRODUCTIVE RATE

overtaken by one or more of these countries by the end of the 1980's. For the past decade, Japan for example, has been holding at 2.9% average annual growth rate of real gross domestic product per employed person.[1]

Many reasons have been attributed to U.S.'s productivity difficulties. Those having strong historical bases include: lack of capital investment in state-of-the-art technology and research and development work; disregard for quality; adversary relations between labor unions and management; government regulations and attendant bureaucratic strongholds on industry; short-term planning by executives; declining number of hours spent at work by the workforce; internal inefficiencies; the decline in the ratio of products industries to service organizations; and world competition for the market share on the basis of delivering products of best values to customers.

When increasing demands for higher wages are added to the aforementioned issues, it is not surprising that the U.S. witnessed a decline in productivity during this era. On the subject of salaries alone, statistics from the U.S. Department of Labor in 1983 indicated considerably higher salaries for some U.S. industries compared to other countries. For example, presented in Figure I-4 are approximate cost figures for steel workers in the U.S. compared with five other countries (these figures include benefits and are rounded off to the nearest dollar.)

During the 1970's, the productivity issue was being complicated by a growing number of quality problems. Consumerism was the number one topic during this decade. Consumers had become conditioned that some failures were "normal" and could be expected and manufacturers

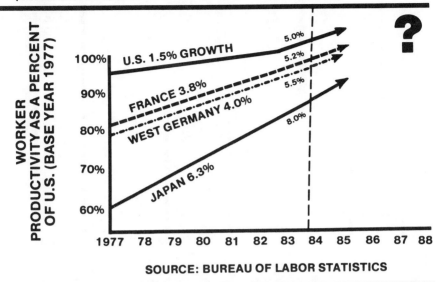

WORKER PRODUCTIVITY PROJECTIONS
(BASED ON PROJECTED GROWTH RATES - ALL INDUSTRIES)

SOURCE: BUREAU OF LABOR STATISTICS

FIGURE I-3. THE PRODUCTIVITY RACE

covered such inconveniences with sundry warranties. In some cases, the consumer even became the "final" inspector. But, consumers began to ban together to fight back against buying products that did not live up to *their* standards of quality.

Historically, manufacturers and dealers have had success with advertising campaigns that *inferred* quality. However, beginning in the early 1970s, there was growing concern (perceived and real) that consumers did not receive the level of quality they believed they purchased. In an era in which sales are increasingly made on the basis of competitive quality, advertising "quality" on the basis of warranties and guarantees has lost some of its sales appeal. Consumers would rather receive quality the first time without having to resort to the secondary inconveniences of delay and having to "negotiate" reimbursements or replacements.

This general concern about quality was indicated in an extensive study conducted by the American Society for Quality Control in 1980, in which 10,000 questionnaires were mailed to American households. Several significant conclusions were drawn from the 71% return.

According to the study, people who were better educated, better paid, and between the ages of 25 and 49, were most negative about American-

7

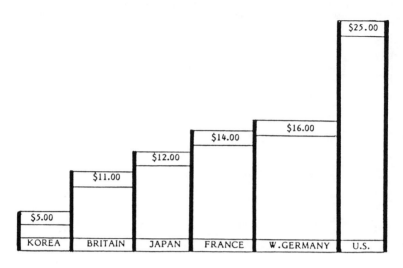

FIGURE I-4.   EMPLOYEE COSTS IN THE STEEL INDUSTRY

made products. This group includes the most active purchasers of goods and services on the American scene. To a large degree, this segment of the population will shape future buying decisions.

More than a third of the American public thought that U.S. automobiles were poorly made. Quality of cars was ranked "high" or "very high" by just 17.6% of the respondents, while 36.5% ranked it "low" or "very low." (Since this study was conducted, however, American automobile sales have turned upward, and there are signs that the public is perceiving higher quality from U.S. auto manufacturers.)

According to the study, quality of household appliances was considered "high" or "very high" by 39.1% of the public, with 16.7% ranking their quality as "low." Drugs and pharmaceuticals were even more well thought of, with 67.3% of the respondents giving that group favorable marks.[2]

The managements of every company have the power to control and manage the most significant sources of productivity improvement; namely, those that involve general marketing and business strategies, quality issues, budgeting practices, investments in capital equipment, systems efficiency, diversification options, staffing practices, the

2) Copyright, American Society for Quality Control, Inc., reprinted by permission.

leadership philosophy, and priorities for maximizing progress in a dynamic business culture. Those who have been able to meet these challenges are demonstrating success.

While many U.S. companies are enjoying an increasing market share, others are finding productivity growth to be a goal filled with uncertainty and complexity. Executives feel the need to change some of the values that have been adopted by managers and employees that appear to be counterproductive, while at the same time retain those which are perceived as making the company uniquely qualified to build for a better tomorrow. Ironically, even some of these executives have stilted adherence to past practices, and give their allegiance to methodologies that will no longer keep them competitive.

In a study of 236 companies, Arnold Judson concluded from reports from top executives that over half had less than 5% annual productivity gains and 25% had no meaningful index of measurement.[3]

This study and similar studies indicate that productivity improvement energies tend to focus on day-to-day problems and have little concern for how the internal organizations affect each other. Most productivity programs apparently are geared to react superficially to wherever companies are hurting at the moment. Subjects for quick fixes could involve industrial accidents, absenteeism, excessive scrap and rework, and even abuse of work breaks. Dealing with such issues with a very short time horizon increases the likelihood that symptoms rather than real causes are being addressed. As a result, lasting solutions to productivity problems will escape much of the effort.

The Improvement Challenge

The most challenging question facing industry in this era is finding the right recipe to effectuate improvement. Consultants are utilized to instill awareness of need, provide stimulus and energy releases of commitment, and to present a "telling" message of philosophy, principles and tools that might be applied. Also, there is no dearth of ideas generated by professional societies on how to improve productivity; thousands of reports and data are continuously amassed on the meaning of productivity and generally what needs to be done. The question which is uniquely company-oriented is how best to *carry out* the assignment. How can the quest for improvement become an integral part of the organization and woven into the fabric of day-to-day operations? What works best for one company, another may not be ready to attempt.

There is general consensus that appreciable increases in productivity

9

will be accomplished through appropriate actions taken by the management. This involves the planned, systematic control of inputs and the effective integration and transformation of these inputs into expected and worthwhile outputs. This means that the management needs to first recognize if certain changes need to be made, are willing to make them, know how to institute them, and finally be able to correlate improvement with a known baseline to assure that improvement did indeed take place. While effective productivity measurement indicates where improvements are taking place and gives direction for further improvement, measurable improvement in *indirect* factors, where substantial gain can be found, is frequently difficult to accomplish. In companies where good working conditions exist, effective leadership is exercised and where the general company culture exemplifies quality values, system and human effectiveness is seen.

New high tech companies are in excellent positions to deliver efficient outputs. Benefiting from substantial investments in equipment and from the position of being able to adopt successful attributes and reject undesirable features of old established firms, it is likely that these industries can contribute substantially to a better productivity posture for the U.S.

Some of the large established corporations are facing more difficult problems in the improvement process however. A company may wish to implement a well conceived productivity improvement plan, but the culture which has matured for many years may not be conducive to easy change. Also, just as a program for improvement is launched, sales have been known to drop sharply, causing a general layoff and taking employees by surprise. Under such circumstances, efforts to effect improvement or motivate workers will meet with difficulty.

These situations should not detract from the importance of embarking on a long-term productivity improvement program. If morale does decline, the senior manager should be even more persistent at generating resources to continually improve quality of work life. When senior managements find themselves in short-term predicaments which force the company into layoff positions, they should strongly resist the tendency to cut back resources for such activities as research and development, planning, training, quality circles, and quality of work life programs. Such activities provide the foundation needed to sustain long term improvement.

In some instances, productivity improvements also have been inhibited because first line supervisors and employees have seen no clear commitments to this end by the top officials of the firm. If there is no clear enterprise expectation of improvement, employees will lack personal commitment to carry out this mission. An improvement *value* needs to be set in motion in most companies, starting first with the senior management, then inculcated at lower levels.

A firm that would do nothing else than substantially reduce the quality associated costs of rework and scrap would in all likelihood experience a significant improvement in productivity. But, even in accomplishing this, executives continuously encounter new obstacles which negate these efforts. These are indeed challenges that go with being a senior manager in this transitional era.

Ambiguity and Perspective

In the midst of change, communication gaps, inconsistency, and conflicts of interest exist. People who make good decisions for the future are able to mold the best of the past with visions of the future in carrying out missions. However, in the pursuit of this objective, it is found that managements and workers as well as department heads tend to differ (sometimes considerably) as to courses that should be followed, with interests sometimes interfering with agreement. This is illustrated in the following examples.

(Supervisor) "I'm not sure, but try it and see—but if it goes wrong, I didn't tell you to do it," or, (Employee) "The drawing shows that I must hold a ±.002 tolerance. Why are parts sometimes acceptable at ±.005?" or, (Employee) "Why do I get reprimanded for going over my boss' head when the plant manager made it very clear that his door was always open to anyone who wanted to see him?" or, (Employee) "Why is it that I am supposed to be given assignments from Mary, but Bill insists that I do what he says? I wouldn't mind so much, but I can't seem to please either of them," or, (Employee) "Why do I have very little to do the first week of every month and get paid overtime the last week of the month?"

In the quest for productivity improvement, companies are also dealing with another kind of issue which historically has had a deterring effect on productivity. Increased efforts are being made to alleviate certain internal adversarial situations that have tended to exist between organizations. For example, companies are devoting more attention to improving teamwork between design engineering, production, and the quality organizations.

While this objective is receiving much attention, many paradoxical and ambiguous situations still are commonplace. The following examples illustrate the traditional problems that have existed and continue to occur.

1. *Statements from the frustrated middle-manager*
   a. "I want to know how that shipment of parts got out of here without the latest design change."
   b. "There is simply too much red tape to work against. I'm fighting it 50 hours a week."
   c. "I can't get direct answers from the senior management."
   d. "I've been here 20 years; I have seniority and I don't care anymore—the work usually gets done, one way or another."

2. *The quality dilemma*
   (Quality Assurance Managers, I, II, III) "These units do not meet specifications. I must reject them."
   (Production Manager) "So what, if they are a little off from specifications."
   (Marketing/Sales Manager) "Don't worry, I can sell them!"
   (Plant Manager) "We cannot afford to reject all these units; they are too costly—let's get them shipped!"

3. *Quality Managers reactions to the above situation*
   (Quality Assurance Manager I, *The about face*) "You're right—the customer won't know the difference."
   (Quality Assurance Manager II, *The protectionist*) "I will document to you (Plant Manager) why these units should not be shipped and suggest ways to avoid problems like this in the future."
   (Quality Assurance Manager III, *The martyr*) "My department is the only one which really understands quality, but no one ever listens to us."

These are but a few examples of situations confronting employees and management which lead to low productivity.

Viewed from society as a whole, a host of perspectives can be identified. Some view American industry, for example, as going through a phase in which it needs to regroup, stabilize, and muster resources to launch into a new high productivity level not yet reached by any country. Others have the perspective that a dramatic reawakening must take place in society at large as well as in American management before industry can regain world leadership. Others have the view that American industry is alive and well, and there is no cause for alarm or negative thinking . . . the free enterprise system has a built-in cooling out characteristic in which those who can be reasonably competitive will survive.

The perspective that has been gaining momentum, however, is one in which the U.S. position is described in terms of the international market and competition. When the facts about productivity are understood and one grasps the full meaning of losses in sales to foreign competition, complacency soon turns to apprehension, and apprehension turns to commitment and sometimes anxiety to find solutions.

As W. Edwards Deming pointed out, some executives are seeking "instant pudding" to cure their ills, while others are seeing the need to effect long-term strategies for success.[4] Some employees are insecure and must depend on an equally insecure management for answers, while others feel very confident because their companies have been built on confidence. Managements which have had long-term visions of excellence backed up with sound quality and management philosophies, and undergirded with a loyal team of workers are on a course of continuous improvement. Those built on the soil of inertia to change and incompetence will be washed away by a high tide of competition.

United States industry comprises among other things, a complex mixture of methods, strategies, attitudes, and styles of management. These factors combined with countless other ingredients have been "managed" effectively by successful companies. These companies have been run by visionary and provisionary managers who have been able to discard past ineffective practices, and continually execute decisions that have helped their companies enjoy a healthy market share.

Other companies continue to search for that magic formula which will yield for them acceptable profit margins. Leaders of these companies have tended to resist change and adhere to past technologies, methods, and styles of management that are no longer effective in a network of world competition.

Illustrated in Figure I-5 is a scenario of the past, present, and future expectations for U.S. industry. While many companies have passed through this transformation period, the general complexion of U.S. industry is shown by the figure. Based on research findings and trends, the late 1980's and 1990's should carry a better productivity posture.

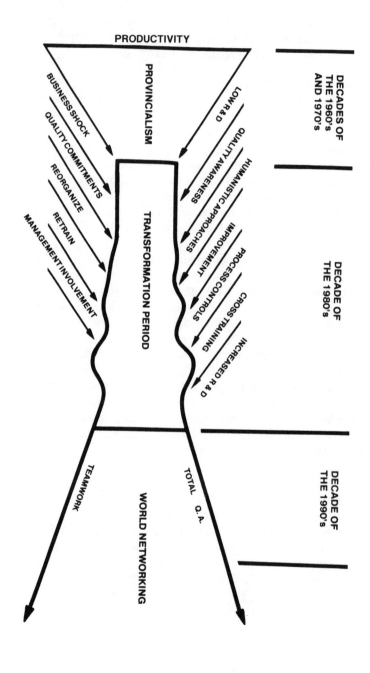

FIGURE I-5. FALL AND RISE OF U.S. PRODUCTIVITY

14

UNITED STATES' FRIENDLY
COMPETITOR: JAPAN

U.S. managers have reportedly become weary of hearing about how the Japanese have been so successful at taking away some of the market share that historically has been held with pride by Americans. There is growing optimism now among U.S. leaders that Japan will not be able to dominate indefinitely any industry they wish to "target." Only those companies which choose to hold on to outdated practices will continue to be vulnerable. It is now generally accepted, however, that international competition will remain a strong force with which U.S. industrial leaders must contend.

Japan's Success Story

After World War II, Japan needed help to get its economy moving again. As part of the rehabilitation process, teams of American specialists went there to help them rebuild, begin new industrial strategies, and to capitalize on cultural factors that were uniquely Japanese. With virtually no natural resources, who would have believed that in 30 years a country in its war torn state could progress to where it is now, one of the most envied and respected competitors in the world?

Ironically, American technology has played a significant role in the emergence of the new Japan which now challenges the United States for economic supremacy. Much of the early credit for their success in revolutionizing Japan's industries goes to W. Edwards Deming and J.M. Juran. The Deming Award remains a coveted prize by Japan's companies even today.

Between 1950 and 1982, Japanese companies acquired much of the world's available advanced technology by signing at least 30,000 licensing or technical agreements with western companies, mainly American. The price paid by Japan in royalties and fees has been about $10 billion, less than one-fifth of what is spent in the United States for research and development in one year.

In 1982, Japan's Gross National Product (GNP) was third highest in the world and, if one extrapolates current trends, it would be first by the year 2000. A country the size of Montana, Japan exports $75 billion worth more goods than it imports, and has an investment rate as well as a GNP growth rate which is about twice that of the United States.

In *Megatrends,* John Naisbitt explained Japan's position this way, "Japan has seized from us the position as the world's leading industrial power. On a per capita basis, Japan's GNP has the growth edge. We are ahead only because of the sheer size of our economy."[5]

The impressive productivity gain in Japan has been conveniently attributed to factors such as Government subsidies, higher capital investment, and a labor force impregnated with cultural values stressing disciplined hard work and cooperation in group endeavors. There are two other factors which have contributed to Japan's success. These are, particularly in large firms, permanent employment and the bonus system. These encourage productivity by meshing the worker's self-interests with organizational success. Base pay in Japan is less than in the U.S., but bonuses bring total compensation up to nearly the same amount. Bonuses are tied to a firm's profitability, so the greater the productivity gain, the higher the bonuses.

Japanese — United States: A Comparison

Culture. It is well documented that Japanese management is structured primarily around people, and is strongly influenced by culture and tradition. Family, group, rank consciousness, and vertical interpersonal relations are characteristics of the Tokugawa legacy which dates back to the 17th century. That members of a group are motivated to work in the best interest of the group is a resultant trait.

Japanese workers have an abundant amount of curiosity about their work. One spokesman pointed out that, "If any single factor explains Japanese success, it is the group-directed quest for knowledge, irrespective of rank, they believe they can learn from anyone." This has a lesson for American managers. Workers respect and appreciate supervisors who have empathy, technical know-how, and are able to continuously exemplify these attributes.

On one hand, the traditional Japanese system begets cooperation, but historically has stimulated less individual creativity (albeit this appears to be changing), while the traditional American way has lended itself to more individual creativity (although this too seems to be changing). In Japanese industry, strength and direction comes not from the individual, but from group processes. A deep sense of loyalty, team spirit, and company image are the driving energies. Tens of thousands of quality circles are the vehicle by which group processes operate. Consensus is more or less a way of life for Japanese workers. Decisions are sometimes slow, but they are certain to manifest team effort and promote both national and company causes.

It is a well established theme in the literature that the Japanese pay close attention to detail as part of their quality ethic and inherently apply this value with team spirit. However, some believe Japan's success with teamwork in industry originates not so much from the *country's* culture, but from a style of management which produces a highly dedicated and committed team of employees. If this is the case, this "style" can be learned and applied directly in the United States. If on the other hand, Japan's ability to achieve teamwork in the industrial environment is rooted in country culture, their method of generating teamwork will not be so readily transported.

John Warne, President of Omark Industries, pointed out that managements have the power and the authority to control the environment within the company and that teamwork is largely a product of their specific efforts to achieve it.[6] In any case, American management is structured essentially around work performed by "specialists." Culturally, the American is influenced by individualism, independence, and making it on his or her own. Implicit in this pattern is the tendency of Americans to be motivated to work in their own best interest.

Japanese industry is inextricably tied to their culture, characterizing a number of features such as consistent management practices and a relationship of trust between the management and employees. Shein pointed out that a look at the Japanese management philosophy reveals a paternalistic and holistic approach to employees, a tendency to employ people for life, and a supervisory staff which takes care of the personal as well as the work needs of subordinates."[7] Japanese culture and management styles have resulted in a high general degree of trust between management and employees. Conversely, building trust is not regarded as a principal American achievement. In most instances, it cannot be placed high on a list of fondly regarded attributes in industry or society as a whole. If the number of lawyers in a society is an indication of mistrust, the U.S. probably would get first prize. Reports indicate that on a per capita basis, there are approximately 10 times the numbers of lawyers in the U.S. than Japan, with this ratio climbing.

American industry has developed methods of operation which manifest the "us and them" attitude, not only between the employees and quality control departments, but also between employees and the management. The only "us and them" characteristic having appreciable significance in Japan is performance vs. defects. Grilled deeply into the Japanese value system is the concept that defects and inefficiency are their adversaries. Historically, neither the workers, the management nor the Government has been regarded as adversaries in Japan. One might be tempted to believe that U.S. industry could rather easily turn an adversarial climate that has matured for a number of years into one of harmony and teamwork. This is not now, nor has it been an easy task for U.S. companies. The "us and them" environment found in most U.S. companies is only part of a much broader cultural characteristic in America. The win/lose ethic and the confrontal value are deeply ingrained in the way Americans do things. (For example, Republicans vs. Democrats, Government vs. Industry, and Taxpayers vs. the IRS). It is difficult for industrial communities to chalk up dramatic improvements in teamwork when they function in a general culture which contains and seems to thrive on forces which are antithetical to teamwork. Nevertheless, many leaders are challenged by this goal and are making great strides. Their effectiveness appears to be correlated with the degree of commitment they are willing to give to this end.

The Change Factor. Both Japanese and American industries are undergoing change—some planned, some unplanned. Companies in Japan are experiencing more and more of the complexities that have been encountered in the western part of the world for many years. Although cultural patterns are heavily entrenched, individualism, free thinking, and rivalry are causing some "movement" in Japan.

For example, movement away from concensus management is beginning to occur in Japan. *General* agreement in a maturing, competitive culture begins to be cumbersome. In an international marketing situation, plans need to be ready for deployment; they cannot always wait for the last nod of approval. Those who are not responsive to the need for timely change will find great difficulty in remaining competitive. There are indications that an increasing number of Japanese firms are finding themselves in this dilemma.

To a large extent, Japan is also at the mercy of the status of the world market. Sales of their products is significantly dependent on other countries. Import regulations of trading countries, for example, are an important and somewhat uncontrollable factor with which Japan must reckon. Japan's position, although culturally stable and conducive to current high productivity, possesses problems unique to its situations and inherent limitations. Being a country almost totally dependent on outside sources for its raw materials, and one which is irreversibly geared to international sale of its products, Japan cannot afford to begin making poor business decisions.

On the other hand, while the U.S. is blessed with a wide variety of resources, in many instances it needs to sharpen its business strategies. A burgeoning number of variables that must be managed, together with a long history of opposing interests, have made constructive change slow for many U.S. companies. For example, there is growing concensus that companies without unions, are better able to keep pace with needed changes in technology for modernization, and can accommodate the need for general change better than those that have had a long history of management/union confrontation, strikes, etc. Attitudes formed over a long period of time in a negative quality culture are much more difficult to change than can be modified through cursory training programs, attention getting posters, and instituting quality circles as a panacea. It has taken one to three decades for some industries to gradually reduce their output per input dollar invested, and in order to show substantial improvement, it may take this long to reverse the trend and stabilize.

Companies which have not been encumbered by a long history of management/employee conflict, and whose managements have strategically dealt with the controllable factors, appear to have the edge and are doing quite well. Firms that have been and continue to be productive, have recognized and pursued the following objectives.

1. All employees need to have some degree of freedom of expression of ideas—in the atmosphere of not only a listening management, but demonstrated *belief* that employees have good ideas.
2. The concept that doing the job right the first time transcends the need for inspection oriented quality departments.
3. Quality has both people and system-wide connotations, and must be well imbued in the company.
4. The management of successful companies believes in the total value of quality and is committed to eliminating deterrents that exist in both direct and indirect activities.

It is neither feasible nor practical for U.S. industry to attempt to *match* what the Japanese have done so successfully. Methodology, culture, and government involvement are uniquely Japanese. However, smart U.S. executives are learning that a portion of Japanese methodology can be adopted in the U.S., much like they learned from the U.S. soon after WWII.

Other Trends

Patents and Capital Investments. While the cultural bond of teamwork remains strong in Japan, individual creativity appears to be on the increase as well. One way this is evidenced is by the increasing number of individual patents applied for in the U.S. by the Japanese. As illustrated in Figure I-5, the trend is upward for the Japanese; after a 10 year period of decline, an uptrend is now being recorded in the United

States. While not all applications are approved, patent applications are an indicator of "technical activity" of a nation.

	United States	Japan
1970	72,343	6,093
1972	65,943	6,831
1974	64,093	9,163
1976	65,050	9,365
1978	61,441	10,189
1981	62,404	14,009
1983	63,100	17,312
TOTAL CHANGE	−11%	+138%

Sources: World Intellectual Property Organization and the U.S. Patent Office

FIGURE I-6.   APPLICATIONS FOR U.S. PATENTS

Capital investments in the U.S. have also fallen behind its competitors. There is a high correlation between manufacturing output and capital investment. Statistics from the Department of Commerce indicate, for example, that during the period from 1960 to 1982, the United States capital investment was 9.1 (average annual percent) with a growth of output per employee hour of 2.8 (average annual percent increase). During this same period, France invested 19.2% with a 5.5% growth in output, while Japan invested 28.8% for an 8.2% growth in output.

Competition for High Technology Products. Can the Japanese with their high degree of cooperation between Government, financial institutions, industry, and labor continue to accelerate their technology and productivity at the pace they have in the past? A sufficient number of U.S. executives are betting that they will, to cause considerable concern.

High technology fields which involve robotics, integrated circuits, computers, communications equipment, and machine tools are said to be areas which the Japanese are targeting for dominance. In robot manufacture, for example, Japan already has in place a greater number of robots than the United States, and is far ahead of most countries. By 1982, they had installed over 67,000 robots compared to 44,000 produced in the United States. The greatest edge held by the Japanese is about a 3 to 1 ratio in the programmable type of robots. Shown following is a comparison of the U.S. with other leading countries in robot manufacture.

	Mechanical (Not Reprogrammable)	Programmable	Total
Japan	53,189	14,246	67,435
U.S.A.	40,000	4,700	44,700
West Germany	10,000	1,420	11,420
France	38,000	620	38,620

Source: Robotic Institute of America

Another area of growing concern is the computer and ancillary components industries. Visitors to Japan are continually impressed with efforts under way there to develop a new generation of powerful and high speed "thinking" computers, which will compete even more strongly with similar U.S. manufactured products. Some industrialists are concerned about the *secondary* effects. Carmelo Santoro, President and CEO of Silicon Systems, Inc., pointed out that while the Japanese may not directly target U.S. manufacturers of components, they do compete strongly with U.S. producers of systems which require these components. (For example, disc drives and computers which require integrated circuits.) "If U.S. customers who use our integrated circuits are unable to compete with the Japanese in the computer market, sales of U.S. integrated circuits are more apt to decline due to this indirect competition unless companies in the IC business are able to develop markets with Japanese firms." [8]

Historically, U.S. manufacturers of components have had great difficulty breaking into the Japanese market. Japanese quality standards are not only very high, but a kind of protectionist national attitude tends to exist which has made business dealings with Japanese firms slow and difficult.

On the other hand, an increasing number of Japanese managed companies are springing up in the U.S. Reports indicate that the Japanese style of management of U.S. firms with American employees has turned sinking U.S. companies around.

Sharp Manufacturing Company of America for example, a Japanese-owned firm and formerly an unsuccessful U.S. plant, apparently has been very successful at applying the Japanese style of management. Open since 1979, the management has turned around the company which was besieged with labor unrest. Still a union plant, morale is reportedly high with worker complaints low. [9]

High technology industries form the foundation for a considerable part of the future of U.S. economy. But, United States industries,

21

having experienced development which spans over a century have encountered many forces, which transcend a company's ability to successfully analyze and plan for the future. Institutional, cultural, and governmental factors coupled with the development of organized labor and cyclic economic conditions, have interacted to make the job of industrial management a very complex task.

CHAPTER II

Quality Quandary

The Evasive Term — Quality

Quality has become a household word; but it continues to have varied connotations and diverse meaning. While quality represents the threshold and finale of improvement, the frosting on the cake of sales and the coffer of profit, those who apparently understand it the most are the consumers who deal directly with it, knowing if and when the purchases they make meet their expectations. As producers and originators of quality, manufacturers should be the experts, but based on results, provocative questions and doubts have been raised.

Some misunderstanding about quality is undoubtedly rooted in its lack of definition consensus. Quality professionals for many years have attempted to win universal acceptance of a single definition that says it all, but without total success. People have read and heard cliches about the meaning of quality so often that some have accepted these abbreviated expressions as complete truths without looking further into the purposes and implications of quality. Although authors of quality definitions generally understand each others' intended meanings, confusion exists among those who are entering this field and even among those who must produce a "quality" product. Ironically, axiomatic statements can divert attention away from foundation issues and diffuse the meaning of quality even further.

To illustrate some of the differences in the way quality has been defined, a few have been gathered and are quoted as follows.

- The degree of conformance of an item to governing criteria. A composite of characteristics that satisfy an expectation.

- The highest level of excellence with which one would deliver a product and still be competitive.
- Efficient production of the quality the market expects.
- The establishment of, and adherence to, specifications that enable a manufacturer to earn a reasonable profit on his investment by fabricating and selling a product that equals competition in price and customer satisfaction.
- The totality of features and characteristics of a product or service that bear on its ability to satisfy a given need. (ANSI-ASQC-A3, Quality Systems Terminology)
- Fitness for use (User) and conformance to specification (Manufacturer).
- Conformance to requirements.
- The ability to satisfy the customer.
- Possession of some measure of value defined in terms of its performance, its appearance, and its unique ability to satisfy a specific requirement.
- The composite of all the attributes or characteristics, including performance of an item or product.
- Innate excellence.
- Highest value to the customer.

In a dynamic industrial culture, the real problem is to convey an unmistakably clear meaning of quality and at the same time, bring about the unlearning of biases that are antithetical to quality, which have matured through decades of conditioning. While quality professionals offer oblique versions of quality, those who must directly manage, design, build and market quality products should have an even better appreciation of the total value of quality. These people need to be girded with a sound quality philosophy and have a clear comprehension of the relation of quality to productivity and profit. Definitions, per se, fall short of providing these important macro concepts.

The problem of defining quality is that it has multifold parameters. Some *expectations* of quality relate to reliability (i.e., how well the product will perform for a given time in a given environment) and others will emphasize conformance to specifications. A comprehensive definition of quality will cover parameters of appearance, specifications, reliability, maintainability, availability, and whether or not these generate customer satisfaction.

Customer expectations should always be a primary consideration. How do customers define quality? What do they expect in the products they purchase and what service, etc., do they expect after purchase? A customer driven quality program addresses these questions by constantly seeking answers through customer surveys, interviews and feedback from the marketing department and the field. No matter if the customer is the Government or the consumer, the buyer will ultimately drive quality.

Customers are sometimes fickle, however. Their "satisfaction" may be based on a brand name or on a perception that is subjectively based. Especially in the consumer market, at least on a short run basis, clever marketing strategies can sell low value products over those that have been scientifically proven to be better. Subjective quality values sometimes take precedence over objective characteristics.

In any case, whether it be hi-tech, industrial or consumer products industries, the customer is all important. If a purchase order is written for an electronic component which requires a high reliability, the buyer has the right to expect that this minimum level of quality will be shipped. Or if a person purchases a new automobile, he or she should not have to experience a major early failure with the added distress and haggling that sometimes occurs (even during the warranty period) between the dealer and the customer. In such cases, consumers are weary of not only the implication that they must bargain for something they believe they have already paid for, but also of having to deal with the uncertainty that an item saved for and representing a substantial investment may turn out to be a "lemon."

Another aspect of quality definition which deserves more attention than it often receives, and one which always helps to build good relations with customers, is the attention firms give to educating and serving customers. Everything else being equal, excellence of service not only prevents loss of customers, it is becoming the number one factor in building customer confidence. Service should be planned by the seller as an important part of the marketing strategy and a way of gaining the competitive edge—without leaving the buyer with the impression that service is a costly necessity that should be minimized. Active and genuine attention to service is an indication of commitment to excellence by a firm's management, which will render increased profit for the company in the long run.

At a minimum, quality involves meeting all customer expectations of product performance, longevity of service, attractive appearance if appropriate, *and* rendering good service. The *spirit* of quality, however, means this and more. Quality needs to be regarded as a dynamic goal, carrying the connotations of challenge and continuous improvement. This involves developing as well as manufacturing better products than competitors, and simultaneously even surpassing customer's expectations of quality. With top management's commitment to this kind of excellence, long-term profits, productivity and customer satisfaction all can be maximized.

Further Implications of Quality

In a world market where a great amount of emphasis is placed on producing "high quality" at a competitive price, a higher quality ideal needs to be engendered and manifested by executives and employees in general. Until recently, evidences appeared to be accumulating that a general contentment with mediocrity was replacing pride of workmanship. Today, there appears to be a national awareness and movement toward taking quality more seriously. A revival of the attitude which associates quality with superiority and an attendant pride for having achieved this goal is gradually replacing the attitude that something is "good enough."

Industries which were first to imbue this meaning of quality have not only remained healthy and competitive, but have built a foundation which gives them a significant edge over those which have not. Firms which have difficulty with quality (viewing it superficially) have allowed other factors such as cost and schedule to predominate in decision making. Paradoxically, efforts to keep costs from rising and productivity from lowering without due consideration for quality will produce high cost and low yield. But, short-term thinking has such a hold on some businesses, that when quarter-end reviews of balance statements are made, costs still become the overriding short-term *emotional* issue.

The preconception that any amount by which quality surpasses acceptable levels is reflected in loss statements is a notion held by managements who have short time horizons. This concept is regarded as fallacious by visionary managers who think in the long term. Even in the short run, quality is costly only if it is inefficiently conceived, produced and marketed. If in the pursuit of quality objectives, the company experiences excessive design changes, sluggish throughput, scheduling delays, proliferation of paperwork, overtime, scrap and rework, customer disinterest or dissatisfaction, costs will indeed rise. Sometimes so much energy is devoted to making certain that just enough quality is produced *quickly,* that attention is directed away from producing the required quality *effectively.* Herein is found a major cause of lowering productivity.

Making the Quality Commitment

The Quality Policy. A clear, definite statement of quality policy should be enlaced with top management's commitment to quality. The policy statement is a formal statement of upper management's interest in quality. Commitment without such supporting statements lacks the driving force needed to inspire confidence. An example of a good policy statement is as follows:

> "Our policy is to supply products and services of unmatched value to our customers; we are committed to world leadership for quality in our industry. In meeting these objectives, we have an obligation to our customers, employees and stockholders to manage quality well."

A commitment is a pledge; when upper management makes a quality commitment and formulates a policy statement, they pledge their support by not only honoring the philosophy contained therein, but by providing active leadership to implement the intent of the policy as well.

This task is normally more complex than it appears. Awareness of the need for and implementation of a consistent quality policy are basic; knowledge of customer expectations of quality is essential; choices between alternatives, each having important merit and quality impact have to be made; both macro and micro quality perspectives need to be examined; both long-range strategic and short-range tactical quality planning need to be completed; belief that education and training are necessary to gain and keep the competitive edge is needed for continuous improvement; top management involvement needs to be a way of life; and especially important, is the realization that commitment to quality can reach full maturity only through *people.*

Gaining and Keeping a Satisfactory Market Share. The design, manufacture and attempted sale of a product which has little or no sales appeal or customer need is a costly management error. Maintaining sensitivity to customers' needs, then responding and translating these expectations into deliverable units, are tasks which sometimes elude even the most highly respected companies. In order to be effective, business strategy must incorporate a means of monitoring changes in customer attitudes and needs. This includes an alert marketing group which maintains constant awareness of changes that are occurring in the field, as well as what the competition is doing. Marketing people can become so enamoured with sales, per se, that they fail to accomplish these important missions.

Usually the best information research and development engineers can accumulate is from sales personnel, or people in the field who deal directly with the customer. Just as the sales staff must stay close to customers, so do research and development people need to stay close to sales and field personnel. Development engineers should have ready access to field data relevant to product performances as well as be apprised of new areas for development. This enables the engineering team to be effectual at improving current products or developing new ones.

Products and services bring profit only to the degree that they serve customers' needs. The IBM Corporation is an example of a company whose business strategy is to make every attempt to stay close to the customer. "We must (1) know our customers' needs and help them anticipate future needs (2) help customers use our products and services in the best ways and (3) provide superior equipment, maintenance and support services." [1]

Gaining and keeping the market share has even broader implications. It means that the entire company is committed to delivering (with pride) products that *exceed* the value sold by the competition. This requires system-wide cooperative efforts, low tolerance for error, cost consciousness and a pervasive dedication to quality. Gaining and keeping the market share requires cradle-to-grave efficiency. From the time that research and development personnel embark upon a new design configuration, until the units have served their useful purposes at the hands of a customer, quality is a driver of profit. If the systems of design and change control are efficient, the profit picture cannot help but improve because of greater production efficiency. Accordingly, if high yield can be achieved from production operations through optimum utilization of resources and low corrective action, profit increases will also be experienced. Long-term profit, customer confidence and repeat business are all built on delivering products that meet customer expectations of reliability and maintainability, on time and at competitive prices.

Organizational Implications of Quality

Traditional Methods of Organizing. The organization chart reveals much of the true character of a company. Among other things, it reflects what top managements believe has greater or lesser importance. As a "picture" of how management expects a system to function, organizations are shown in positions where the power structure and peer relationships are described or inferred. Everything else being equal, departments will be effective according to how they are designed and articulated into the overall organizational matrix.

Quality organizations are a good example. If they are camouflaged by other organizations such as design engineering or production, giving them token acknowledgement, there is strong indication that the top management either does not comprehend the importance of quality, or has allowed strong leadership of design or production managers to influence the decision to subjugate quality functions to others. With the power structure "opposing" quality, outgoing quality will likely be sacrificed, especially if cost and schedule already are given precedence. Viewing quality as a principal function—giving it equal status on the organization chart with engineering and production departments—will strongly suggest that upper managements are serious about quality matters.

Although organization charts are somewhat fluid, they tend to have more permanence than people and have greater longevity than the people who comprise the organization. When the organization structure was conceived, a certain orientation may have been deemed appropriate at that time, based on the people affected. But, both people and conditions change. Where major quality authority is subjugated to design or production functions, both strong and weak quality directors may come and go, while engineering and production functions perform their charters—designing and building products to meet delivery promises. If a strong quality culture has not been established, and if a quality "authority" has not been built into the organization, there is high probability that quality will ultimately be sacrificed. Until quality mindedness and concomitant teamwork are real and functional in the company, it is folly for the plant manager to believe that organizational compromises can be made against quality and achieve long-term success. A quality leader may be strong and even possess charisma, but be forced to succumb to overpowering decisions that are neither in the best interest of quality, nor the long-term good stance of the company. On the other hand, placing principal quality functions on a par with design and manufacturing organizations, may also result in situations adverse to productivity. With the quality organizations in a safeguarding role, an atmosphere is sometimes created which hampers the smooth flow of units and causes excessive conflict. In an adversarial climate, together with the exercise of power by quality officials, the plant manager too often becomes the quality referee. Some maintain that this is desirable because it is believed that in the long run, there will be more confidence that delivered units will meet all quality standards. Substantial productivity losses can be incurred because of conflict, however. Without a degree of teamwork which will transcend sporadic differences of opinion, energies of those directly and indirectly involved will be misdirected or diffused.

Historically, the way industrial organizations have been designed, quality departments have been pitted against other functions, or have been subordinated to direct functions. (The latter case has been viewed by quality managers as a way to strangle quality problems.) Once the company culture is exemplified as being a place where quality is the source of turmoil, productivity becomes the loser. For more than 20 years company officials have been groping with the issue of what to do about quality organizations. Should they have separate identity, or should they be merged with other organizations? U.S. industry is now in an era in which quality organizations and attitudes about quality are even more the focal point of attention. This decade is witnessing countless reorganizations of quality functions—some on the basis of quick fixes that are politically expedient for an ambitious V.P., and others which are attempts to correct a long standing problem with which quality functions have been identified. Still, there is considerable lack of consensus about what to do with quality organizations.

Most of these efforts have focused largely on short-term customary views of quality which frequently repeat themselves every few years with little real improvement. For example, history tells us that for a number of years companies have wrestled with quality organizational questions like: Should inspection report to manufacturing? If so, which ones? Should reliability be split between the design and quality assurance departments? Should there be separate quality control and quality assurance organizations? Should all quality functions maintain separate organizational status? What functions should quality engineering encompass? Who should justify and release capital monies to purchase "quality" equipment?

Changes in quality management are sometimes the result of brief encounters during executive staff meetings or lunches to find quick answers to "quality predicaments." A frequent consequence of such meetings is for an influencial member of the senior staff to embark on a venture which nearly always involves a new perspective of quality, and a campaign to reorganize the functions. The extent of the eventual change will be a measure of his or her influence over the organization. Compromises are usually made, but the net result frequently will be some new organizational concept.

The question is not whether a certain change is or is not necessary; when quality organizations are regarded as adversaries or bottlenecks to "progress," they will always be the focal point of controversy and a subject for change. The real issue is how to institute a quality climate in the company such that the quality organization will be respected as part of the leadership for quality.

During this era, at a time when executives are discovering secrets to productivity improvement and those which work best for them, there does not appear to be one best way to organize quality functions—one that will satisfy every situation and meet all company needs. Albeit, improvements in systems, quality of work life, and teamwork are the thrusts in most companies, establishing the right priorities in concert with organizational changes which will bring about lasting improvements seems to evade management action.

Company culture is a mixture; most companies are comprised of heterogeneous groups, each generally attempting to do the jobs that have been assigned. Departments usually consist of the "old timers" mixed in with the new breed. Values often differ. When quality is the question, some are prone to have traditional beliefs—"build it the best you can, turn it over to an inspector, keep your mouth shut, and go on to the next job." Others who are products of the new era are impatient for change. "Let's set-up quality circles, train operators to control their own quality, do away with time clocks and speak to everyone on a first name basis."

Some companies are encountering indecision about the direction changes should take. At one extreme, one will find the hard line manager who takes the simplistic view that organizational lines should be clearly drawn with management giving orders and employees simply carrying them out. At the opposite extreme, others believe that if the company is one big happy family, people will somehow desire to work harder, and thus produce more.

U.S. companies comprise both extremes. Some can be characterized as leaning toward one or the other—strong vertical hierarchical lines of authority, or the increased use of horizontal networking. Though managers are somewhat divided on which is the most effective, there is movement toward a better balance of horizontal relationships with the vertical power structure. The only answer to these issues is to educate both managements and employees on the value of quality, so that *it* is brought into focus. Gains will occur when the inherent discontinuities in organizational design are cleared up and when the control of quality can be achieved by the process itself, or pushed up front where it is created.

Realities of Quality Control. In seeking answers to the quality/productivity dilemma, the quality organization can be a part of the solution or a contributing cause of the problem. Since the quality organization has among its charters, quality and productivity improvement, one would assume that quality control personnel would always be a positive influence. This is sometimes not the case; they are real people too. Purposes and goals of quality functions can become distorted by organizational conflict and self-interests. When work of any sort is presented for review, appraisal, or approval, there is a built-in "assignment" of the appraiser to modify, find error, suggest change and/or reject. Personality, charter and method can and do interfere with harmonious relations between the appraiser and those being appraised. It is hoped that productivity will win from such conflict, but this is not likely if the problem is rooted in confusing quality standards or inconsistency between inspectors.

When dual standards exist, an inevitable consequence is conflict between the organizations in question. The quality manager may honestly believe that his or her organization must safeguard quality and that some lower level conflict is "inevitable and good," and thus, the inspectors are doing their jobs if material is pondered over and rejected.

On the other hand, manufacturing personnel become bewildered and ambivalent if certain quality rules exist, but are not made known to operators, and inspectors in turn, use these as an "I gotcha" gimmick. Meanwhile, production supervision is under pressure to deliver the goods, and seek ways to meet schedule deadlines. In the process, an air of emotionalism finds its way back to upper levels of management and finally to the heads of the two departments. These people now find themselves in weekly staff meetings with less than cordial feelings toward each other in the presence of the plant manager or the vice president.

If the inspection department is organized as a separate hierarchical line of authority outside production, quality organizations typically feel they must in some way demonstrate their control over quality. People in quality organizations are made to feel that they are *responsible* for quality, instead of administering a quality system in which the design and production aspects of quality are accomplished economically, and through their leadership and assistance to those who have a direct responsibility for quality.

Some quality problems are said to be caused directly by the lack of cooperation between design, quality and manufacturing departments. Insufficient knowledge about each others functions is said to be one factor. In any case, these departments are members of the same quality team, each having a specific responsibility toward meeting quality objectives, with progress being directly proportional to the amount this team is pulling together. (This triad of teamwork is illustrated on page 175).

Quality Systems are in Transition

Early Rejection of Statistical Methodology. Several decades ago, both W. Edwards Deming and Joseph Juran admonished U.S.

executives of the impending and creeping problems that lie ahead. Many of their cautionary statements were directed at quality issues, warning that the U.S. was falling behind because it was not taking quality as seriously as it should. In 1964, in his book *Managerial Breakthrough,* Juran cited a number of the areas where breakthroughs were needed to turn U.S. industry around.[2] Some took his points seriously; others were either naive about, or unable to effect needed change. As early as 1932, Walter Shewhart wrote about how statistics should be applied to manufacturing processes in his now famous book titled, *Economic Control of Manufacturing Processes.*[3] This subject has taken over 40 years to achieve more than token acceptance in most U.S. plants. Statistical applications were rejected by many because the concept was not understood. Statisticians made the subject so formidable that many who had a relevant and strong need to understand statistical process control learned only enough to cause its rejection. Many could not believe such principles could be applied to their situations. Some were intimidated by the symbology and mathematics of the tool and dismissed it as something too complicated for their employees to comprehend. As a consequence, this field has had very slow adoption in the U.S. Ironically, the real values of statistical quality control surfaced in the United States only after Deming and Juran found receptive ears in Japan three decades ago. Where Americans had many years to develop a resistance to the subject, the Japanese did not know statistical quality control would not work. They simply applied the principles and made them work with outstanding success.

Recently, there has been more activity in the U.S. to train employees at all levels in the use of statistics as a tool for controlling processes. W. Edwards Deming has led this movement, while hundreds of other consultants have jumped on the bandwagon. In spite of these efforts, managements of many well established companies still find themselves struggling with statistical approaches.

Quality Back to the Source. For many years, an over emphasis on *control* of quality has tended to mask where the responsibility for its achievement should reside. Considerable emphasis has been placed on safeguards and after-the-fact fixing things, and as a result, attention has been drawn away from those who originate characteristics of quality.

Prior to the 20th Century quality, per se, was essentially uncomplicated. People sold products which conformed to requirements without the legal complications, logistical difficulties of suppliers, complexity of large systems and the myriad other diversionary factors with which modern day industrial executives are confronted. Proprietors were originally the designers and fabricators as well as salespeople. Closing information gaps between company personnel, procurement sources, and even the buyer was more or less a "natural" process for those in manufacturing businesses.

Complications began to develop as industry expanded and technocracy started to creep into industrial life. Whether or not the industrial culture as it is known today had its roots in Frederick Taylor's theories of scientific management, as some writers proclaim, is relatively unimportant. No one who has studied technological and cultural trends can argue that the scope of managements' problems has not increased correspondingly with industrial development.

From individual proprietorships to conglomerates, from single function businesses to multifaceted organizations, from simplistic activities of direct personnel (designers-fabricators), to an increasing number of indirect personnel (management, secretaries, quality control, safety, marketing, security, finance, and so forth), the number of variables which need to be managed has vastly increased. This expansion of the industrial organization has led directly and indirectly to the proliferation of "control" groups which are identified with providing order and integrity to an unwieldy network of functions. On the surface this does not appear to be profoundly significant; safeguards are certainly needed, based on the present state of the technocracy.

This burgeoning network of controls, however, has left productivity scars on a number of companies. While it would be inappropriate to insinuate that the aforementioned growth factor is a primary cause of declining productivity, this must be included as part of the overall issue. During the period from approximately 1910 to 1980, the U.S. witnessed a creeping shift of quality responsibility. With the expansion of control functions (in this instance quality control), responsibility for quality gradually shifted from where quality was created to those who controlled or safeguarded it. Long-term results have indicated three situations that are now in question, and being changed in a number of companies—(1) adversary relations developed between operators and inspectors, and between quality departments and producing departments in general, (2) operators became less knowledgeable about the end use of products and even the quality of their work, and (3) scrap and rework as well as general inefficiencies increased.

For quite some time, the question of who has the responsibility for quality has been raised. Should it rest with the owner of the business, with the top manager, with the first line manager, with a resident customer who witnesses activities, with the quality department, or should the quality responsibility reside with the designers, operators and assemblers?

Wherever quality responsibility has been in the past, strong commitments now are being waged to move it back to the source (source in this instance means the point of origin of quality characteristics). This cycle is illustrated in Fig. II-1. Companies are demonstrating that pride in quality (workmanship) can be restored to the people who have the initial encounters with quality more easily than through secondary or indirect routes, with the result of lower quality associated costs.

When attempting to shift the quality responsibility back to operators, designers, buyers, etc., a sudden and all-encompassing change is usually

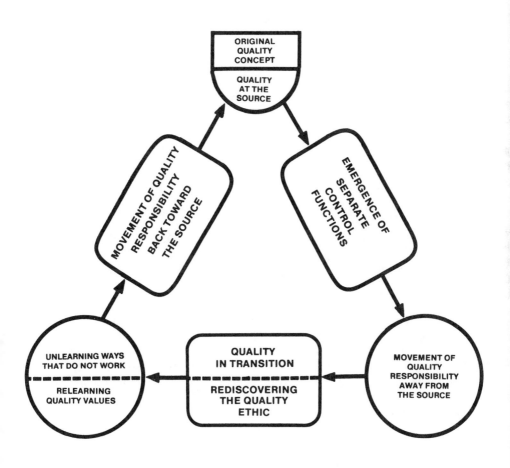

FIGURE II-1.   RETURN TO QUALITY AT THE SOURCE

not desirable, however. Among the factors to be considered is the organization itself. Based on past experiences of dealing with manufacturers, some customers want to see proof that manufacturing personnel can handle the responsibility for quality.

The Department of Defense (DOD), for example, may want to have the confidence and assurance that "inspection" as an independent function has given its final verification that quality indeed conforms to requirements. Such customers are very uneasy about any sudden change that might jeopardize the quality of delivered units, and may insist on more assurances that units meet all specifications. Especially when companies are in the transformational phase of trying to become more productive, the user of the product should not have to be the final inspector. A parachutist, for example, must have the confidence that the parachute will function properly *before* he or she uses it.

Several questions should be raised and satisfactorily answered when decisions are being made to give manufacturing more responsibility for quality.

1. Can process control of the machines be achieved? If 100% inspection is required, an independent function of inspection may be necessary. If process control can be accomplished, operators trained, and provided the necessary tools, the inspection function can be reduced to various sampling or audit techniques, while operators monitor running quality. If this is possible, it can be much more efficient because operators can make firsthand adjustments without necessitating other information and authority loops.

2. Does the manufacturing management sufficiently understand and believe in quality to take on this new responsibility? Will cost and schedule continue to be, or become primary concerns at the expense of quality?

3. If operators do take on the new inspection responsibility, performance standards will more than likely need to be changed. It would be unfair to increase the scope of an operator's cycle without adjusting the standard to accommodate the extra time needed for inspection. Even though more time is given to an operator to inspect his or her work, this cost will be more than offset by savings that are gained by not having the second party confusion.

4. Does the quality staff possess the technical competence, and the problem solving and prevention knowhow to assure that the transition is founded upon facts, so that informed choices can be made about

opportunities for improvement? These are very important questions that should be carefully analyzed and addressed. The transfer of responsibility back to the source should be done so that outcomes will be measurably better, not worsened by upper managements' anxiety to make quick and drastic changes.

Are Managements Really Serious? During the past ten years there has been no dearth of verbage proclaiming the importance of quality. The profundity of the cliche, "quality must be built into product—not inspected in," is resolutely clear, and has been used repeatedly by both upper managements and quality professionals. Yet, in many companies where such espousals are expressed, there are well established incentives and objectives which preclude the realization of this objective.

Substantive rewards (those that result in promotion, etc.) are frequently found to be based on performance pertaining to matters of quantity, schedule and cost effectiveness. In the midst of pronouncements to "do it right the first time," a person can become a charter member in the hero of the month club by demonstrating that larger quantities have been shipped in his or her unit or that unit costs have been appreciably lowered. These of course are desirable feats and nearly always carry quick recognition; management can anticipate that billing goals will be met or exceeded, and the persons responsible will be looked on with favor. However, would the production unit which was responsible for these achievements be equally rewarded if he or she significantly reduced the number of defectives in the operating unit by taking quality more seriously but without increasing output? Probably not. In many companies *output* achievements which surpass goals, irrespective of quality, are much more likely to be rewarded than if a department substantially reduced nonconformance costs and merely met delivery promises.

That managements believe quality really is inspected into a product is also evidenced in a number of ways. Some examples are presented: the large ratio of inspectors to production line people tends to persist without a strategy to reduce it; a ten to one ratio of measurement accuracy of inspectors' apparatuses to machine operators is advocated so that inspectors *can* inspect quality into the product; and redundant inspection stations are frequently observed to *ensure* quality is inspected in. If managements are serious about such postulates as doing the job right the first time and building quality into the product, they should take more deliberate and systematic measures to remove incentives and mechanisms that produce antithetical results. A transitional period will normally be needed to upgrade skills and equipment and perhaps unlearn old ways, but repeating slogans alone will not produce desired results.

Communicating the Quality Message. Quality assurance managers are frequently heard to complain that upper managements will not listen to the real quality message—that the senior staff continues to push for more production with little regard for quality. Circumstances for such communication barriers are not always clear. Management may have listened in the past, but based on what it heard, decided that the alternative, namely more "quality," was worse than driving for more units out the door. Signals received by production, in turn, were more units per hour, and the message heard by the quality organization was inspect or test the bad units out. There is growing concensus that quality leaders need more skills at negotiating and selling quality. If the quality manager has been unsuccessful in the past and has lost credibility with upper executives, it is especially difficult to convince top officials now that proper and up front attention to quality will positively impact sales, cost and schedule.

A national awakening of the importance of quality is indirectly helping quality assurance managers to influence others about the importance of quality. One method that has worked in recent years to win upper managements support and attention to quality is the "two by four" method. Loss of sales, rising costs and diminished profits—all because of quality—have gotten upper managements' attention. Where quality managers have been unable to effectively compete with the prevailing mentality that quick delivery and short cycle planning are all important, a review of the balance statement may be all that is needed to reveal the quality message without the anxious advice of the quality leader. Knowledge and political savvy on the part of the quality leader are always fundamentally important. The quality leader must not only "study" upper managements to determine how best to get their attention, but also develop a selling strategy. Since managements almost always respond to effective ways to reduce cost and improve profit, this is an area that successful quality managers are pursuing.

The Systems Approach to Quality. An increasing number of industrial managers are recognizing that quality is a *team* effort, as well as a key factor in increasing the company's efficiency and sustaining a healthy marketing position. The systems approach to quality, which is gaining impetus, reflects these changes in attitudes. Illustrated in Figure II-2 are the eight key links to quality which are in turn, "linked" to the quality assurance organization. Starting with management at the top of the figure, education, commitment and involvement in the quality process are generally on the increase. Design engineering departments with their technical knowledge of products, together with data from the field, create the quality of design with increased effort to minimize change action. Purchasing functions are taking a more active part in working with suppliers to assure that the proper quality of units and

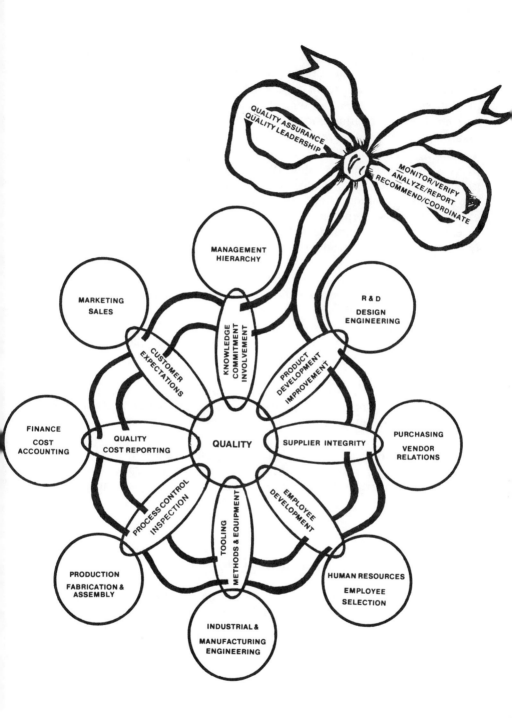

FIGURE II-2.   THE EIGHT KEY DIRECT LINKS TO QUALITY

materials is delivered into the plants. Personnel and training departments are sharpening the focus on employee screening and development programs, recognizing that incompetence is an enemy of quality. Industrial and manufacturing engineering people are devoting more attention to manufacturing planning in order to more effectively produce the required quality, and set up better tools, methods, and machines to produce the quality right the first time. Production personnel are becoming more knowledgeable about quality and are assuming more of the responsibility for manufactured quality. Cost accounting departments are becoming more involved in the quality process by broadening the quality cost reporting network, thus giving greater visibility for decision making. Finally, marketing/sales departments are increasing their sensitivities to customer needs and expectations and reporting such information back to quality and research and development organizations so that these data can be translated into better products.

As the figure also illustrates, quality assurance departments provide the necessary quality system leadership and technical assistance to make the system work effectively. This involves such activities as analyzing and solving quality problems, monitoring and auditing system activities, verifying product quality levels and recommending changes that are needed to make or keep the system efficient.

Variations of this integrated quality concept are being used. For example, Harrington and Shaw gave a list of developments that make quality assurance integration possible at IBM:

1. Management acceptance of quality assurance principles—All levels of management have embraced the quality assurance principles and each manager holds employees responsible for implementing these principles.

2. Personnel appraisals—By establishing accountability for quality and narrowing the responsibility to one person, it is possible to include a quality factor in individual merit salary changes.

3. Escalation system—A rapid escalation system is established to provide upper management with quality-risk assessment. Problems to be escalated must be carefully selected, be important and have a high impact on basic business decisions.

4. Quality assurance manuals—A quality assurance manual defining the total quality system is an essential ingredient required to make integration work. The manual must be complete enough to assure that each area knows what is expected of it.

5. Quality project files—Each area integrated prepares a project file defining how it will implement a portion of the quality plan for each individual program.

6. Process qualification—Qualification of manufacturing processes before first customer shipment results in all employees feeling accountable for the product's quality.

7. Product quality measurement—The quality measurement program ensures the qualified process remains qualified. This is not an acceptance sampling audit, but a measurement of outgoing quality.

8. Job improvement—The integration of standard quality control activities into other functions reduces the amount of duplication and provides stimulation and job enrichment to the individual.

9. Reduced cost—Integration reduces product costs.[4]

Managements have the authority to implement organizational change and set up the system so that expected quality goals can be met, but sometimes do not have good quality information. Top executives who are the steering arm of the company must have timely, accurate and specific facts from the quality organization. It is incumbent upon quality management to *sell* and apprise top management on the following matters:

1. Need for a quality consciousness and continuous quality improvement program in the company.

2. Budget needs for training, equipment, etc., to move the company to quality goals effectively.

3. Status of quality both in-house and in the field.

4. Present a *true* picture of the costs of quality in an understandable form.

5. Involvement of other departments in *system* quality.

True quality assurance requires a much deeper involvement than an organizational unit called "quality assurance." The highest order of quality assurance is a quality philosophy engendered in every employee and manifested in the desire to perform with excellence. The traditional second order of quality assurance is much more costly. It involves setting up safeguards, monitoring, inspecting, auditing and correcting wrong work. If the quality assurance and control departments become the mechanism for shifting the responsibility away from those who create it, economic quality can never be achieved. Quality organizations have been and still are being kept so busy devising better ways to safeguard and inspect for poor quality, that little time is left to plan and institute ways to prevent problems from recurring. Meanwhile, three consequent situations persist.

1. Top managements see quality costs of inspection, rework and scrap increasing.
2. Morale becomes lower; quarreling between departments is more commonplace; tensions increase.
3. Sales go down because competitors are producing and marketing similar products at higher values.

Quality of Design

Recently much more attention has been devoted to the various aspects of design quality. More people are realizing that "up front" attention to quality (namely, better definition of the requirements, complete and accurate design releases, and producibility of design specifications) will produce substantial savings when fabrication and assembly phases are accomplished. Products are developed to meet contracted or expected performance criteria, delivery schedules, and price. The direction the design will ultimately take may not be clear beforehand, but will become known as development work progresses. After design parameters and details have been confirmed and tested, it is up to manufacturing departments to "build it like the design."

If high reliability requirements are involved, they usually require critical operating characteristics of components and systems which, in turn, may involve space restrictions. Out of this complex process, *producibility* problems sometimes arise. In efforts to "move" a design, engineering departments have been known to release design packages with insufficient attention to production capability and methods. Drawings are also sometimes released with design uncertainties. This margin of uncertainty embodies such factors as incomplete information about certain performance characteristics of components, unqualified vendors, specifications not totally documented, and anticipated changes that do not materialize and are not communicated. The degree of uncertainty is related to the cultural tolerance for error that has developed in the company, and accompanies an unwittingness about the high cost consequences of incomplete or unclear designs.

If there is a high tolerance for error in the company and design difficulties are frequently encountered by production departments, there is a greater tendency of operations departments to take on the spot corrective action by either writing a change on the drawing, or calling and obtaining verbal approval from a design engineer. This procedure is known to have very high cost consequences. The shop foreman in charge was able to "build it like the design," move the parts from his or her department, and meet schedule deadlines. But, if errors have been made, departments which subsequently receive these units, not apprised of the situation, continue to work on parts that are already defective.

Design-oriented problems not only have latent repercussions in the manufacturing department, but have long-term customer impacts which do not surface immediately. Products built and sold with design deficiencies have shortened lives, unnecessary maintenance costs, or unsafe features, which sooner or later generate unhappy customers. Sales people may attempt to stay close to customers, but if the products they peddle develop a pattern of failure, there is usually little they can do except to promise improvement. Guarantees, warranties, and promises mean little under most failure situations; a customer is not likely to accept the solace of a replacement if the original one caused down time, injury or other costs and frustrations.

Making the Quality Manual a Living Document

The quality manual describes the technical and administrative controls required to accomplish or insure quality system integrity, valid analytical results, maximum productivity and cost control. Someone once said, "Today I have a plan, I may not follow it exactly, but I do have a plan. I will thus save myself from one important time thief—indecision."

Without a quality plan, customers and clients will likely perceive both the quality organization and the company as being casual about quality, not having a sense of direction, and perhaps even unprofessional about matters affecting quality. The manual of quality policy and associated operating ground rules has a two-dimensional value:

1. It sets forth the direction that the management wishes the organization to follow toward meeting quality objectives of the company, and

2. It conveys an explicit message of the top management's interest in quality.

In addition to specifying quality related activities and requirements to efficiently achieve quality standards, there are several additional benefits of the quality manual.

1. An effective manual will provide a common base of understanding

for achieving quality objectives.

2. If the manual is up-to-date, understood, and in use, it will reduce the tendency of short circuiting the system and creating open information loops.

3. If the manual is a "living" document, it will become known and accepted as providing uniform and consistent quality methodology, and thus the operating basis of quality.

Several important conditions need to be satisfied, however, if these benefits are to be realized.

1. The manual must be *used* by the people who need it.
2. It must be *available* to those who need it.
3. It must be *accurate and up-to-date.*
4. It must be *understood* by the people who need to know.
5. Information in the manual must be *coordinated.*

Every supervisor whose activities are addressed in the manual should have a copy. Also, any department which is directly or indirectly responsible for quality should have ready access to the document. This means that copies should be immediately accessable to supervisors of departments such as manufacturing, purchasing, design engineering, cost accounting, marketing, and tooling, as well as all quality departments.

While there is no guarantee that a manual will be used, there are several steps that if taken will help to increase the probability of its effectiveness.

1. Once appropriate people have the manual in their possession, they should be educated about its contents, particularly in the sections that directly relate to them. Design change control procedures are vital to the design department; supplier controls will be especially important to the purchasing department, and so forth. One of the greatest mistakes made is handling the quality manual as if it contained classified information which only the quality organization has the need to know.

2. An educational seminar covering critical subjects in the manual should be given to all holders of the document every six months or at least once each year. The purposes of these sessions are to, (1) explain new or revised information, (2) acquaint new people with the urgency of following its contents and (3) solicit ideas and reveal areas that should be better covered.

3. Manual accuracy and completeness should be assured. This can be

done by setting forth in the document itself how it will be controlled and reviewed for accuracy. It is important that a person or persons be specifically assigned to the task of maintaining a log of changes as they occur so that revisions can be regularly scheduled. It is also important that whomever is assigned the responsibility for updating the manual, he or she is able to communicate effectively with personnel of other departments. This is important because at the first sign of obsolescence, the manual will begin to lose its effectiveness. The task of re-educating people is considerably more difficult after they have lost confidence in the document than keeping people updated as changes are required. The final version will be only as good as the information it contains. Without the cooperation of affected departments, and making the document a "living" and active reference, its utilization factor will be small.

Quality manuals are frequently found in the quality manager's office and essentially inaccessible to groups or individuals who need them. They are also often in the quality engineering department supposedly being updated but side-tracked for long periods of time. Meanwhile, operating personnel who have the need to know, have forgotten there is such a document and have drawn their own conclusions about a certain quality policy. Every so often when a quality question arises, someone is heard to say, "doesn't the quality assurance department have a quality manual that covers this question?" After some search, the manual is located but found to be so much out of date, it is considered unuseable. This message finds its way to a member of quality management, and someone is then assigned to update the document which by now takes a considerable amount of investigation. Meanwhile, key people have already established a "workable" method of dealing with quality issues and resist new rules drafted by quality personnel. When the new edition is issued, the task of unlearning poor habits of those who have exercised individual creativity in developing a "satellite" quality system of their own, can be a difficult task indeed.

Ladder of Maturity of U.S. Firms

Productivity postures can be defined in terms of how companies have matured in their outlook on quality. Summarized in Figure II-3 are the five maturity stages (steps of the ladder) which describe U.S. firms. While most companies have some characteristics which cut across more than one, they essentially fall into one of these levels of maturity. Which step most closely characterizes *your* company?

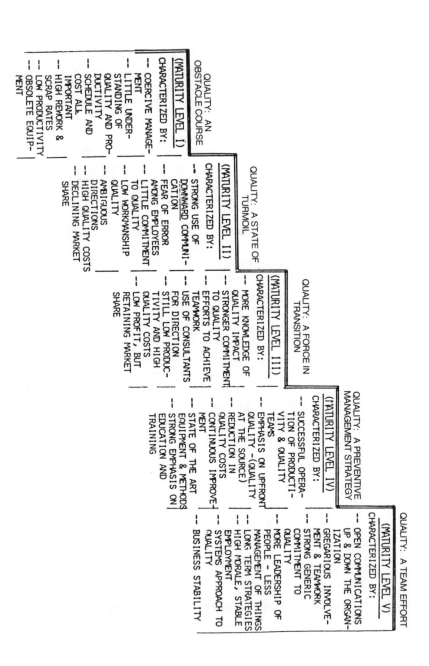

QUALITY: AN OBSTACLE COURSE

(MATURITY LEVEL I)

CHARACTERIZED BY:
-- COERCIVE MANAGEMENT
-- LITTLE UNDERSTANDING OF QUALITY AND PRODUCTIVITY
-- SCHEDULE AND COST ALL IMPORTANT
-- HIGH REWORK & SCRAP RATES
-- LOW PRODUCTIVITY
-- OBSOLETE EQUIPMENT

QUALITY: A STATE OF TURMOIL

(MATURITY LEVEL II)

CHARACTERIZED BY:
-- STRONG USE OF DOWNWARD COMMUNICATION
-- FEAR OF ERROR AMONG EMPLOYEES
-- LITTLE COMMITMENT TO QUALITY
-- LOW WORKMANSHIP QUALITY
-- AMBIGUOUS DIRECTIONS
-- HIGH QUALITY COSTS
-- DECLINING MARKET SHARE

QUALITY: A FORCE IN TRANSITION

(MATURITY LEVEL III)

CHARACTERIZED BY:
-- MORE KNOWLEDGE OF QUALITY IMPACT
-- STRONGER COMMITMENT TO QUALITY
-- EFFORTS TO ACHIEVE TEAMWORK
-- USE OF CONSULTANTS FOR DIRECTION
-- STILL LOW PRODUCTIVITY AND HIGH QUALITY COSTS
-- LOW PROFIT, BUT RETAINING MARKET SHARE

QUALITY: A PREVENTIVE MANAGEMENT STRATEGY

(MATURITY LEVEL IV)

CHARACTERIZED BY:
-- SUCCESSFUL OPERATION OF PRODUCTIVITY & QUALITY TEAMS
-- EMPHASIS ON UPFRONT QUALITY -(QUALITY AT THE SOURCE)
-- REDUCTION IN QUALITY COSTS
-- CONTINUOUS IMPROVEMENT
-- STATE OF THE ART EQUIPMENT & METHODS
-- STRONG EMPHASIS ON EDUCATION AND TRAINING

QUALITY: A TEAM EFFORT

(MATURITY LEVEL V)

CHARACTERIZED BY:
-- OPEN COMMUNICATIONS UP & DOWN THE ORGANIZATION
-- GREGARIOUS INVOLVEMENT & TEAMWORK
-- STRONG GENERIC COMMITMENT TO QUALITY
-- MORE LEADERSHIP OF PEOPLE - LESS MANAGEMENT OF THINGS
-- LONG TERM STRATEGIES
-- HIGH MORALE, STABLE EMPLOYMENT
-- SYSTEMS APPROACH TO QUALITY
-- BUSINESS STABILITY

FIGURE II-3.   LADDER OF INDUSTRIAL MATURITY

46

The lowest possible maturity level at which a company can be is when quality standards or functions are perceived or treated as an obstacle around which work continues. Quality functions are regarded as road blocks to making quick deliveries and are viewed as obstructions to progress. Supervisors/Managers at this level are frequently heard to make statements that clearly indicate disregard for quality.

Examples. (1) A new operator who is running parts explains to his or her supervisor that the parts do not appear to be right and suggests they be checked before the operation continues. The supervisor's reply is, "Run 'em! We don't have time to bother with inspectors; besides, if the parts are wrong, someone else will fix them later." Afterward, the more seasoned operators explain to the new employee that complaints about quality have only led to problems for them and that the new employee will learn soon enough that such complaints will only lead to trouble. (2) A foreman explains to the superintendent that he or she has a machine being used that will not produce the required quality. The superintendent's reply is, "I've heard that story before—we've got a deadline to meet so get out there and get things moving." The superintendent is now forming a negative opinion about the foreman, thinking that he or she is becoming uncooperative. (3) The vice president calls in the quality control manager saying, "What's going on here? My department heads tell me that your people are trying to hold up production—you surely must be aware that profits cannot be reported until invoices are sent, and invoices cannot be mailed if parts are not delivered. I'd like to see your department show a little more cooperation with the other departments by not holding up production."

The reader should not conclude that these examples imply exemption of quality organizations from a share of the responsibility for a company being at this maturity level. Quality is a criterion for company maturity, and this responsibility encompasses all functions which have a quality mission. The top management establishes quality policy and energizes the philosophy under which functions operate, but does so in concert with the leadership and influences of functional organizations. Companies remain at this level because their managements have somehow failed to comprehend the quality message. They are clamped in the jaws of yesteryear, giving little thought to prevention, leadership, collecting quality costs, and long range planning. Companies on this step have a very low quality culture, and poor long-term prospects for prosperity because the forces that created the problem also resist change.

If a company at this maturity level is marketing a unique product which customers want and are willing to pay for, sales will probably continue until the company encounters competition. Eventually, internal quality oriented costs will deprive them of profits in a competitive market. These companies may lose as much as 30% of their potential profits through quality associated costs and other internal inefficiencies. On a long-term basis, these companies are destined to failure unless there is sufficient change in management attitudes about quality to allow the company to progress higher on the maturity ladder. A change of leadership in top echelons may be necessary to effect the desired turnaround.

Maturity Level Step II — Quality: A "State of Turmoil"

Companies on this step of the ladder experience confusion about what to do to improve quality. Where at Step 1 quality was essentially disregarded, now quality has enough identity to result in dual standards, erroneous assumptions, and other causes of confusion. Customer complaints about quality are common and sales are usually declining. Internal management reactions are "finger pointing"; placing blame is the usual practice, instead of identifying problems and solving them. The management is more or less bewildered by the controversy that takes place. Certain people in the quality assurance organization may be the only ones who know what needs to be done, but are unable to get cooperation to institute needed change. When others in the organization have strong, but opposing views, further complications set in. Some senior managers recognize quality as a growing problem in the company, but either do not know how, or take infelicitous actions to effect solutions. Some mention is made about quality costs, but little actual reporting is done except in the forms of inspection and scrap costs. These companies have had a long history of internal conflict and the culture manifests mediocrity. These companies also experience production and quality crises near the end of every month. Month-end overtime to meet delivery schedules is common practice.

Marketing people attempt to increase sales, but competitors' products continue to out-perform those of the company. The vice president pressures marketing to sell more products, but does not heed warnings from the field that quality is becoming inferior to the competitor's. Eventually the plant manager blames production for poor workmanship and quality control for allowing defective units to be shipped. In top level staff meetings, the quality assurance manager blames design engineering for incomplete or conflicting design criteria and being unable to inspect accurately; production management blames the sales department for agreeing to delivery dates that cannot be met, the purchasing department is accused of ordering wrong or substandard materials, and the quality control department is labeled as a bottleneck to production. The top manager acts as a referee during these disputes and receives "side" information from the managers after the meetings. The same kind of issues again dominate discussions at subsequent staff meetings; questions continue to go unanswered because the wrong ones are asked in an atmosphere of turmoil.

Before this company can progress upward on the maturity ladder, more knowledge and commitment to quality by the top officials must take place. Quality responsibilities need to be understood and fixed in the organization. The system also needs to account for the proper reporting of quality and attendant costs. Equipment and people unable to perform adequately must be identified, reasons attributed, and solutions found. Management task forces charged with specific responsibilities in these areas may need to be organized for a period of time to accomplish the aforementioned tasks. Surviving against a strong competitor will be indeed difficult for these companies unless such dedicated and systematic actions are taken.

Maturity Level Step III — Quality: A Force In Transition

The next step upward on the ladder of industrial maturity is the position in which quality is given more credibility and recognition. Unlike Steps I and II where the value of quality was either unknown or had camouflaged identity, it is being unveiled as a driver of profit at this step. History tells the management here that other issues have long been placed higher on the priority of importance than quality. Meeting month-end delivery schedules at the expense of quality, getting the most out of a machine before adjusting or repairing it, cost reduction campaigns which lead to quality compromises, and purchasing parts at the lowest price without adhering to quality standards are examples of quality related issues which are being recognized and addressed by companies at this level.

Although quality at this stage is in transition and companies are on the threshold of further advancement, a strong corrective action philosophy still exists. Remedial work predominates in production departments although there are periods of relief. Preventive measures, if reported, would be approximately 5% of total quality costs, with inspection and failure costs at about 95%.

Quality costs are about 15 to 20% of sales in these companies, but they may not know it. Supervisors conduct occasional meetings with their employees to discuss department progress, new events and so forth, and managers strive to accomplish more advance planning, realizing its importance to productivity improvement, but corrective action activities predominate. It is recognized by most of the management that scrap and rework rates are higher than they should be and quality engineering people are assigned to investigate and solve quality problems, but the customary attitude that quality can be "fixed later" still prevails. Equipment capability studies are conducted in an effort to best utilize machines and establish statistical controls, but considerable resistance is encountered. Most supervisors and midmanagers at this level have been promoted from within, function in a comfort zone and have had little experiential latitude to develop and express creativity. Delivery problems are normally encountered at the end of each month.

Some managers in these companies express the desire to inaugurate quality circles. The concept is considered desirable by some top officials, but with not enough enthusiasm to give circles a very high priority. The majority view such programs as being better applied elsewhere and not a viable alternative in their companies. Circles can be found in companies at this level, but most have difficulty surviving. Schedule priorities and a tendency toward an authoritative management network inhibit circle success. On the other hand, where there is a committed top management and sufficient training, circles can demonstrate great success, and yield substantial benefits at this maturity level. These companies are shown on the left side of Zone II in Figure VII-2 on page 185.

Companies on this step are on the verge of achieving higher productivity rates, and have a good perspective of what needs to be accomplished. Some management personnel as well as employees have had specific training such as quality and productivity awareness to aid them in their jobs and perform more harmoniously with peers. While total cooperation between inspection and production people is not ongoing, more mutual respect is being generated between these functions, and efforts are made to build quality into the products. Also, while most quality associated costs are probably not reported, there is sufficient data about prevention, inspection and corrective action costs to enable the management to make good judgments.

Companies at this maturity level experience a variety of roadblocks that seem to keep reappearing. A new executive may have been brought in to help get the company "back on track." If the new executive has attended a few of the countless seminars offered on quality or productivity, he or she may be tempted to institute certain quick fixes, which can take several forms: superficial training programs without behavior change; inaugurate quality circles without laying the groundwork; issue directives to focus attention on quality without sufficient commitment; or adopt slogans and place posters throughout the plant designed to motivate workers to do their jobs right the first time without attempts to change the cultural base. There is the tendency among these managers to ignore the fact that real quality improvement takes more up front planning and time than expected. They are vulnerable to making short-term decisions that have compromising effects on quality and which lead to further complications.

Albeit at this level of maturity, upper echelons of management may be fully committed to and understand the need for quality and productivity improvement, they may not grasp the full meaning of the problems and consequently take impulsive actions.

The following is a scenerio that might occur at this maturity level:

The top executive in his or her weekly staff meeting brings up the issue of quality and productivity and expresses the desire to implement an educational training program for lower management and employees. After some discussion, specific questions begin to surface. How much training is needed? Which departments need it the most? How many resources are available for such a program? During this meeting (or perhaps the next), the production manager points out that his or her people already produce good quality but could do better if schedules were relaxed a bit, and if the design drawings were more accurate. The production manager goes on to explain that another training program would take good people away from the job and might result in additional scheduling problems.

The quality control manager comments that the inspection department is quite capable of performing its functions, but if they had the proper tools, gages, equipment, etc., and were under less pressure to buy off marginal units, things would run a lot smoother. The quality control manager might also question the value of such training for his or her people, and imply that production people need to have a better understanding that "inspectors cannot inspect quality into *their* work." Meanwhile, the design manager is aware that a large number of change orders are being generated by his or her department, which causes confusion on the production floor, but accepts this practice as normal operating procedure and unavoidable. The top executive now knowing the dilemmas being experienced by the key directorates, points out that quality costs must be driven down and that more cooperation and teamwork between functions will be necessary. He or she holds a series of convincing discussions about the need to change attitudes about quality at all levels in the organization beginning at this senior level.

Many of the companies at this maturity level are turning the corner to a better productivity posture. Unproductive habits are being unlearned and new stimuli introduced. A change of attitude about quality among the general management including production and quality departments is seen.

Companies at this maturity level are becoming quality leaders in their industries. The top managements are dedicated to having their companies become world leaders and regard quality as a dynamic factor in reaching this goal. This level of maturity is distinguished from lower maturity levels by the *up front* attention quality receives. Quality is fully recognized as a predominant factor in not only maintaining the competitive edge, but a leading criterion for productivity improvement. Quality receives a high priority in all eight key areas shown in Figure II-2, page 39.

While companies at this level tend to be non-union and usually promote from within, some have unions and hire outside talent. Many have profit sharing programs for management, and some employ a variety of financial incentive plans for hourly employees. Some of these companies have been able to structure multi-function jobs for employees and create internal organizational units to build the necessary teamwork to achieve satisfactory workmanship and high performances.

Executives, realizing that quality is a long-term driver of profits, are devoting more attention to achieving customer satisfaction. They are careful to consider customer expectations of quality, reliability and field data when planning improvements. Directives and procedures are released that manifest the top management's commitment to quality, and set forth quality criteria; advance planning and budgeting for quality oriented outcomes rank high; these companies not only plan well, but execute effectively to achieve desired results; preventive maintenance programs are strengthened to keep machines in proper working order; industrial engineering and quality organizations consolidate efforts to be knowledgable of and take action to replace obsolete or worn out equipment; these functions also cooperate to provide the best possible work methods for efficient quality output; procurement personnel recognize that purchased items must be bought on the basis of the required quality, *in addition* to the best delivery and price.

Top managements recognize that internal quality costs are a significant source of profit drain and are taking measures to increase employee knowledge in the areas of quality and productivity. These companies are strongly supportive of education and training which is a readily observable characteristic. Quality and productivity awareness campaigns are waged, and outside consultants have been utilized to provide direction. Programs to involve management are active;

mechanisms to enhance participation are established; management circles, task forces and councils are utilized to solve interorganizational problems, increase knowledge and effectuate teamwork between functions.

A variety of successful quality circles can be also found in companies at this maturity level. Company philosophies, management orientations and the preventive environment that are common to companies at this level help to make quality circles more or less a *natural* addition and successful. This is not to say that some companies in this category do not have difficulties. Measuring circle benefits and overcoming some resistance to the circle idea are not unusual. These firms did not achieve this level with the use of circles; they did so primarily as a result of placing quality in the proper perspective and exercising management policies, strategies and prerogatives that reinforce their commitment to quality. Companies at this level would be generally classified at the far right of Zone II in Figure VII-2 on page 185.

Loyalty among the employees is also found in companies at this level of maturity. Enriched experiences gained from sharing ideas, the employment of fair management practices, stable employment and good opportunities for advancement. The value of creative expression, and the opportunity and time for conceiving ideas are also evidenced.

Some companies in this category, having risen from a lower maturation level, retain certain traits carried over from the past. For example, while a good preventive maintenance program has been established, equipment is sometimes found in use which is in dire need of replacement. Also, implementing a truely effective statistical quality control system still meets with difficulty in these companies. There is an everpresent danger of an overemphasis on cost and schedule, but the quality philosophy is sufficiently strong to hold its own. While work methods and tooling could be better, and while some departures from procedures which cause poor workmanship to occur, united efforts to make further improvements are clearly manifested. Though some supervisors and managers do not possess the leadership qualities that produce best results, on balance, quality work is completed on schedule at the targeted cost and productivity continues to improve.

Maturity Level Step V — Quality: A Team Effort

This level of maturity represents a *goal* for most companies. Operating businesses with the countless number of variables that must be controlled and managed, only a few companies can reach this goal; even fewer maintain this level of proficiency very long.

Companies in this category have a savvy management, unconstrained by the past, and energized for the future. These managements not only fully comprehend the importance of quality in improving the company's competitive position and productivity posture, they have instilled these values in the employees as well. Recognizing quality as a driver of profit, these companies are totally committed to improvement in all areas affecting quality. Set in motion by the top executives, managers build camaraderie and mutual respect in their organizations.

Avoiding static fixations of the past, the search goes on unceasingly for better ways to manage than anything known in the past. They do not reject good past practices, but use these to build for a better tomorrow. Education, constantly on the march, provides new skills, concepts and insights, and introduces new possibilities which whet appetites for further improvement. A loyal, productive and thinking environment is practiced in which creative energies of all employees are summoned. The environment that sets this process in motion is inspired by an empathizing management, sensitive to employee needs, yet committed to excellence.

Although waves of controversy sometimes flow through these organizations, the missions of the companies, gregarious involvement and enthusiasm transcend negative consequences, and convert conflict situations into building blocks for improvement. Company loyalty and dedication supercede and most often replace antagonism. Teamwork at all levels in the organization is apparent; cooperation is an unwritten but living principle. Dynamic balances are obtained in all vital areas of concern. Some examples are as follows:

Employees are given flexibility in work assignments and attendant training, but controls are applied and output monitored; organizational mechanisms for participation by employees are established at all levels in the organizations, but objectives are set and performances are reviewed; promotions are made from within, but people with special qualifications occasionally are brought in from the outside; the management at all levels practice a consistent, fair and democratic style of leadership, but exercise power and control when needed; quality costs are reported and used to achieve optimum preventive measures against inspection, scrap and remedial actions; and top executives are truly committed to quality and *actively* support activities that indicate this commitment.

The top management in these companies have long-term visions of success, establish commensurable goals and effectively execute plans to reach these goals. As a result of top management strategies, they have been able to avoid layoff situations even in low business cycles.

The position a firm has on the aforementioned maturity ladder is also determined by how effectively the management has met the challenges of the myriad dilemmas with which they are faced. Fourteen of these are discussed in the following chapter.

CHAPTER III

Challenges for Industrial Managers

Someone has said that dilemmas and predicaments are challenges for improvement. If this is true, there is no dearth of such opportunities for the modern-day plant manager.

This chapter is devoted to some of these challenges that are being experienced by senior executives. Successful companies are demonstrating that to the degree these are addressed and brought under control, sustained improvement is being realized.

Dealing with Company Culture

While the subject of industrial culture is covered in greater detail in Chapter 6, it is included here as an important issue with which a majority of industrial executives are confronted. Company culture either supports productivity improvement or inhibits progress. The culture that has developed in a firm is an abstract evolvement of learned values that reflect a firm's "personality" at a given time. Characteristics of business culture are both dynamic and static; dynamic in that it is a continuously developing process, and static in that it resists sporadic efforts to change its direction once a set of values have become well entrenched.

Company values, which essentially make up a company's culture, should be a matter of great concern to top executives. Values provide a sense of common direction and guidelines for employee interaction and behavior. Companies succeed because the employees can identify, embrace, and act on the productivity values established in the organization. Conversely, companies will find it increasingly difficult to be competitive where employees have learned values which oppose improvement and workmanship.

Successful firms have a clear and explicit philosophy about how they aim to conduct business. The management pays a great deal of attention to shaping values that will identify the company with the quality ethic and a genial, but productive environment.[1] These leaders make certain that these values are known and shared by all employees. If employees are certain about standards they are to uphold and what the company stands for, their actions will more likely support these values, and they are more likely to believe that they are worthwhile contributing members of the organization.

Examples of such values which are implicit in organizational processes are: (1) a pervasive attitude of quality, with the desire to do a job right the first time, (2) a sense of loyalty to the company, speaking for and upholding the company's good name, and (3) team effectiveness, manifested by enthusiasm for getting a job done.

The momentum of a well established company culture will transcend minor disturbances to change its course. Yet, it gains energy as beliefs and patterns of doing business become more permanently integrated with past doctrine. The direction of this culture will be changed positively or negatively by an amount based on the intensity and frequency of influences it encounters.

This characteristic has relevance to productivity improvement. Established firms, having had decades to develop insensitivities to the human side of business, tolerance for error, procedural ambiguity, and habits of corrective action have great difficulty in effecting improvement under the stronghold of these established values. The covert energy of motion of company culture can best be changed by the dedicated and persistent efforts of the senior managements, supported by long-term commitment, involvement, and energized cooperation of lower ranking managements.

New companies which can begin with these approaches and the opportunity to originate new values have the edge on established firms that have inculcated creeping undesirable habits which now resist stimulus for change. New companies can profit by the mistakes of established firms and institute systems and leadership styles that are congruent with building values of quality, efficiency, and teamwork without having to unlearn confirmed habits that oppose productivity improvement.

Established value systems also give a strong direction to new employees. People tend to adapt themselves to the pace, group energy levels, and other patterns that characterize a company. If the culture in which a new employee enters is one that exemplifies a high spirit of achievement, the new employee will tend to adapt to this work ethic. Conversely, if the work atmosphere does not manifest a sense of caring about workmanship, and is accompanied by low expectation levels, the entrant will soon identify with these values. It is a fallacy for a supervisor to believe that he or she can hire a high-energy, self-starting person, use this person to set an example, and be the instrument to "pull up" the performance level of a work group which has a well established norm of low output. In a curious way, employees take on the traits of the value system in existence, and the power of the group and company culture will overwhelm one person's efforts to effect change unless this person is in a position of power. Beginning with the CEO, top officials of a company provide the basis for the kind of values established by setting examples. If the top officials are perceived as being quality minded and having the welfare of the employees at heart, lower levels will adapt this "value" giving it more impetus.

There is evidence, however, that self-perceptions of CEO's are sometimes at variance with how others perceive him or her. Findings indicate that what top executives perceive as occurring in their organizations is often not what is actually taking place. For example, studies indicate that while most CEO's believe their organizations are guided by highly ethical standards, a substantial percentage of people at lower levels in the organizations believe "they are pressured to compromise personal standards to meet company demands." [2]

If a strong downward power structure is exercised, and if communications going back up the organizations are motivated by fear, feedback will invariably contain important omissions, leaving the top officials with inaccurate perceptions about internal operations of the company. It is only through commitment and exemplary efforts of these officials that the employees of the company will feel and identify with expectations that are compatible with productivity gain.

Seeing the Whole Picture

Industrial systems have become so large and complex that a knowledge of the parts taken separately is no longer sufficient. Each person or department of a company may be meeting objectives and viewed by both the department head and employees as doing well, but the company as a whole may still be moving backwards in the marketplace.

Some managers cannot see how industrial experiences deal with the same materials, equipment, systems, and human influences—all representing variations of the same macro-system. Unfortunately, little help may be found in the literature. Because former practices lack relevance to today's issues, there is even hazard in having too great a hindsight!

Contemporary experiences also may not prove to be very helpful. Many managers still believe their problems are altogether unique. A discussion amidst present day managers in the context of helpful suggestions often elicits the reply, "Yes, but my company is different" or, "That does not apply to my department."

How do key organizations dovetail in a harmonious network while maintaining maximum effectiveness? How does the leader of a large plant, or a large division of a major corporation assimilate the needed resources and energies to effectively carry out corporate missions?

Successful CEO's possess a common attribute—*wisdom.* Wisdom is more than knowledge; it is what one does with what is learned as well as how it is applied. Rabbi Edgar Magnin once described wisdom as "the ability to discriminate between good and evil, what is sensible and foolish, and between what is important and trivial."[3] With wisdom and effective listening, decisions with greater synergism can be made.

Understanding the Quality/Productivity Connection

Quality and productivity are integrally bound and share common goals. Quality influences productivity by its effect on profit, and drives it two ways: (1) quality influences sales and consequent income from such sales (this translates into customer satisfaction and repeat business); and (2) quality increases internal efficiency and *capacity* (sometimes significantly) by the degree that sundry corrective actions are prevented. These include the release of unfinished design packages, vendor quality problems, unqualified operators, ambiguous standards, and marginally capable equipment, to name a few.

If quality associated costs are 15% of gross sales (which is not unusual) and if gross sales average $150 million/year, it would take only a 5% reduction in quality associated costs to produce a 7.5 million dollar savings. This sounds large and it is; yet, companies fail repeatedly to capitalize on this potential.

The quality movement is having the effect of opening up broader avenues for quality analysis and productivity improvement. For example, more and more about the *psychological* aspects of quality and productivity are being heard. Quality matters will increasingly involve people and their interaction with the work place, and the psychology of quality will undoubtedly receive more attention. Everything else being equal, employees' attitudes rank among the strongest influences on the effectiveness with which quality and productivity goals are reached. As the roles of quality personnel shift from "policing" quality to assuring quality, more human relations skills will be required by quality personnel. As the responsibility for quality shifts back to those who create it, an important quality mission will be to address the relationship of the worker to his or her environment and to the management, and vice versa. Safeguarding roles of quality personnel will gradually be reduced to audit form, with the quality management devoting more time to working with attitudinal and behavioral aspects of quality and productivity improvement.

These trends imply that upper managements will recognize that quality and its management are in transition, and that quality must indeed take its position in a *real* way among all other high ranking factors.

Responsibility for Quality and Productivity Improvement

Another important issue which is being addressed by an increasing number of modern enterprises is getting both employees and various managers to fully comprehend the scope of responsibility for quality and productivity.

Initial responsibility for quality and productivity improvement must rest with the top executives of a company. Only they can establish the foundation on which quality and improvement values take root. An improvement value can be infused in company systems only if the top management team undergirds, nourishes, and is a living testament of quality values. Given this basis, it is much easier to get people to strive to do their best work.

One lingering and serious mistake of top management is to build a climate in which quality organizations are placed in positions of implied responsibility for quality, where they feel accountable for quality, while having no authority or control over the conditions that affect it. Someone has defined quality as, "the authority to ship"; this serves to point out the plight of quality managers.

There are several ways to describe the total scope of responsibility for quality and productivity, any one of which would be insufficient to cover the total meaning.

Responsibility for quality and productivity rests:

- *primarily* with the top management,
- with those who have a direct influence on their outcomes,

- with those in management who are at the level where control of the variables that influence doing things right the first time is achieved, and

- with those in quality organizations who plan, establish, monitor and guide systems so that outgoing quality will meet customers' expectations.

For a number of years, the aforementioned responsibilities have been discussed, but apparently have been only superficially understood. In some companies, the responsibility for quality still stops at the boundaries of the quality organization, and for productivity, the responsibility is lost in the maze of organizational networking. Quality and productivity effectiveness is influenced by every employee. The implication that the responsibility for these rests solely with isolated organizations, is a belief conditioned by time and misdirected effort.

Failure of industrial personnel to sense their responsibilities for quality and productivity is coupled with divergent interests of managements, employees, and governmental agencies.

Productivity Improvement — A Bifurcation of Interests

Management. Some authorities believe that a substantial change in American management needs to occur before a sustained rate of improvement can be realized. W. Edwards Deming, for example, emphasized that nothing short of a major transformation in the American style of management must take place in order to generally improve the U.S.'s competitive position.[4] This will involve changes in the philosophical as well as the human side of running businesses. While some companies have begun or are already well into the transformation process, many others are just becoming aware that they must change.

That managements hold the key to the greatest productivity gain, most agree. The question that executives often raise, however, is which functions, policy changes, or strategies offer the greatest opportunity for improvement? The number of options is bewildering. Subordinates and others who would not be held accountable for these changes usually have ready suggestions. If a change is perceived by those lower in the hierarchy to be positive for their organizations, maximum cooperation can usually be expected. If it is perceived as having negative consequences, counter suggestions may be offered which will confuse the issue and have the effect of shifting the responsibility to another person or organization. Top executives of the more successful companies recognize such finagling as more or less a normal part of managing, but deal with it decisively. Inability of upper managements to effectively communicate the messages of quality and productivity to subordinate managers will be reflected in increasing ambiguity and indifference as delegation processes are set in motion down the hierarchy. An executive who "goes along to get along" will ultimately learn that his or her organization will be likened to a ship without a sail. It will go on and on without a sense of direction with outcomes left to chance.

Questions have been raised about whether or not such admirable qualities as unselfishness, teamwork and loyalty can mature in an atmosphere in which intense competition and strong desire for *individual* fulfillment exist. Pursuits which require coadjutant behavior seem to be fashionable and worthwhile only if they are perceived not to be in conflict with personal ambition.

Employees in lower hierarchical positions are more adept at observing and even understanding the political maneuvering that takes place in higher echelons than is often believed. Employee reactions range from, "I wonder if John Doe will make it this time" to "I wonder who my boss will be tomorrow." Seeing the examples that managements set, coupled with self-interests of their own, and numerous other outside distractions, workers find themselves in climates of paradox, inconsistency and uncertainty.

Employees. Workers, too, have interests that are often at variance with company goals. Given that most of the direction and responsibility for improvement must come from the management, employee behavior either lightens this load or adds to its complexity.

While it is up to the management to mold heterogeneous employee values into an effective working environment, employees need to be sensitized to the fact that they also have a role in shaping the company's future. Evolving American industrial culture has produced a "wait and see" or "wait to be told" employee attitude that afflicts most companies. Some employees could do a better job, but are reticent about stepping forward to take advocative positions for their company. It is generally agreed that past and present management styles and policies have largely contributed to such attitudes. However, one's leadership style does not evolve unilaterally; employees constantly affect the leadership techniques that a superior deems necessary to produce desired results.

Government. Much is also being said and written about Government agencies becoming more sensitive to the needs of business and industry. When comments are made that quality and productivity awareness and improvement need to start at the "top," the top may be indeed higher than that which can be readily controlled by company executives.

Many producers of goods and services are confronted with burgeoning regulations that are deemed necessary for certain work. This is not without cost consequences. Maintaining records and the removal of obsolete documentation have become knotty chores for companies. The question is not whether the Government should carry some of the responsibility or not (this would probably only compound the problem). The issue is that a sizeable amount of information and rules are on the books, not knowing to what degree they are active, outdated, or which exceptions can be applied to which law. As a result, an inordinate amount of time and paperwork are required to be "safe." More companies could win the battle of increasing productivity and become more competitive if it were not for losing the war against red tape and paperwork.

Governmental agencies have also conveyed the message of "more for less" to contractors. If this means that all concerned should increase efficiency, most would agree with this notion. On the other hand, if more is defined or perceived to mean more quantity without due quality considerations and less is interpreted to mean the lowest bidder, this is sufficient motivation (law in some instances) to remain on the course which emphasizes price, quantity and schedule, leaving quality without essence. Some companies need to receive stronger signals that higher *quality* will carry an incentive without having it overshadowed by on-time delivery and cost reduction incentives. Ironically, if high quality standards are expected, yet perceived by contractors as less important, late delivery and cost overruns will occur *because* of quality issues. Until this message is fully understood, late deliveries and cost overruns will continue to occur.

Income From Sales vs. Profit

A modern-day dilemma which faces most chief executive officers is finding and maintaining the proper perspective on sales and profit. A source of mistaken emphasis which originates at the top, is the gradual diversion of attention toward sales, and away from the effectiveness with which products are produced.

Since the company supposedly is in business to *sell* products, this becomes the cutting edge of management purpose: Build an aggressive sales force, keep service areas sharp, conduct large promotion campaigns to expose new products to the public, and perhaps even sponsor intensive advertising blitzes designed to impress buyers and overwhelm competitors. Further, immediate attention of the management is usually captured because sales of products tend to wax and wane. All this is not new; one is conditioned to expect strong and persuasive sales strategies in a competitive system.

However, other factors which influence *profit* often receive less attention. On the surface, it is illogical to find profit being placed secondary in importance, since this is the ultimate purpose for which a business is created. Monthly and quarterly sales are nearly always closely monitored, and income from sales is well documented. But arriving at a clear picture of all the factors that affect profit is much more complex. Few business managers would trade high sales volume with low productivity for low sales volume with high productivity. (The latter in the long run would generally lead to a better entrepreneurial posture.)

Emphasis on sales is also revealed through attitudes about quality. There is substantial evidence that top managements' prime interest in quality is its importance to increasing sales, and less to its relation to the internal effectiveness with which products are designed and built. These managers express more concern about how field failures will impact sales than how internal failures, system deficiencies, and corrective actions will impact productivity. While this does not lessen the importance of sales, if the company's strategy depends on increased sales to offset rising internal inefficiencies, the company will be in financial trouble sooner than top officials believe.

Correlating efficiency and productivity factors with profit is an ongoing task replete with fact and fantasy. Sluggishness of "throughput" is real, but often evades accurate analysis. Costs of goods sold lose identity in systems where reports beget more reports, and where control of the variables that affect productivity is lost. Such difficulties are compounded by organization change, business cycles, changes in personnel, and market and product line dynamics. While system inequities are subtly created internally, emphasis is placed on generating more sales to show profit.

That profit is the result of both sales and internal effectiveness is a truth not only well understood, but woven into the fabric of the most successful companies. Although there is no magic formula one can use to render balanced attention to marketing, financial, and productivity matters, a better understanding of the negative impact of "unproductivity" on profit margins and how much *additional* income from sales must be generated to offset declining productivity is generally needed by executives. Some CEO's have been accustomed to dealing in "visible" matters and championing causes that have been deemed important to meeting short-term goals, and have devoted less attention to managing the more recondite variables that affect long-term productivity.

Overcoming Deterrents to Long-Term Planning

In early industrial economies, the necessary decision to operate simple factories affected production and consumption two or three years later. Today, key decisions relate to time for research and development, facilities, and then the market. The span from primary research to consumer reaction has risen to 20 years.

Some believe that too many managers are now under pressure to concentrate on the short-term in order to satisfy the owners of the enterprise—the stockholders. Beginning with the stockholders, pressures for quick profit are exerted. While it is possible in certain instances for chief executive officers to improve this situation by convincing stockholders that their demands for short-term profit may not be in the long-term best interest of the company, this problem tends to persist. Capital investments for modernization and research and development work, for instance, must continue, but capital outlays for such projects may appear unreal to stockholders who are anxious for increases in dividends.

While stockholder interest is a factor, this seems to be superimposed with other motivations to show short-term profit. Naisbitt, for example, asserted that business people are willing to make a current quarter look better in order to make this year's bottom line a little more attractive or less embarrassing.[5] Others have taken this a step further, pointing out that short-term profits are not really increased; still others claim that only short-term cash availability is increased by neglecting to recognize certain economic costs and then calling them unpaid cost profit.

Some also believe that productivity will increase only when executive bonuses are linked to long-term profit. Top managements typically receive bonuses based on current profit. Thurow pointed out that boards of directors should stop giving chief executive officers a bonus based on current profits, but on earnings over, e.g., a ten year period.[6] The assumption is that if CEO's were paid based on long-run profits, the internal structure of companies would soon change to lengthen time horizons of the market.

Financial perquisites are also substantial in many instances. Studies show that about three fourths of manufacturing companies have executive bonus plans with the average for the three top executives at 45% of their base pay. In 1978, for example, the two top executives at General Motors and Ford were paid annual salaries of about $350,000 and additional perquisites of approximately $650,000, or 185% of their

65

base pay. In 1983, record profits of Ford earned Chairman Caldwell the salary of $520,534 with the bonus of $900,000. Ford's president, Donald Peterson, earned a bonus of $700,000 during this same year.[7]

High union pay scales (which affect wage levels of nonunion employees) also play an important part in this scenario. In some firms the total salary and bonus structures place a heavy burden on the revenue system. Strong motivation to increase pecuniary benefits, beginning with the stockholders and ending with the front line worker, leads to the *need* for quick turn around profit. Correspondingly, operations departments feel the pressure to increase output so that invoicing goals can be met.

Woes of Business Cycles

If a clear potential for profit exists, keen minds go into action to convert this potential into reality. Pressure is exerted to quickly lay the groundwork to realize as much of this profit as possible. No one in a free enterprise system can argue with this objective; the profit motive is quintessentially American. It is not *if* companies should attempt to maximize profit; it is *how* it should best be accomplished. Herein lies an ominous challenge for the modern-day executive.

When business is good (increased sales and anticipated continued growth), concerted effort and even anxiety are evidenced by stockholders and senior managements to increase output quickly to take advantage of the potential market. As a result, growth in facility and equipment acquisitions together with expansion of human resources, can be faster than management's ability to utilize these resources and stabilize programs with sound judgment.

If such growth is faster than the company's ability to integrate and accommodate the growth pattern, this process will take its toll on internal efficiency. The real danger is even more subtle. Without taking the time to construct the necessary building blocks (e.g., good quality plans, methods, procedures, tools and training), poor habits are learned, inadvertent errors will multiply and the culture will take on negative characteristics. A point can be reached when the rate of growth produces more uncontrollable variables than the system and management in place at a given time can effectively handle. Attention is directed toward sales, while systems become clogged with extraneous information, inconsistency and a burgeoning hidden factory of unwanted costs.

Under conditions of rapid growth, organizational development also becomes a continuous process. People jockey for better positions, and organizations are in a constant state of flux. Rapid growth in management *layers* is also commonplace. An organization can gradually become top heavy with disproportionate growth occurring in the number of mid management people. New organization charts are often posted before people can adjust to the previous situation. Still, the business has an excellent outlook; the sales picture is good, and there is a high spirit and enthusiasm for growth.

Meanwhile, however, companies which find themselves in this exciting position sacrifice their flexibility and responsiveness by adding superfluous elements which are foreign (and sometimes incompatible with) the parent system. The number of employees and machines also increase with creeping underutilization. A result is the expansion of an environment which is conducive to inefficiency and one where preventive functions such as training are overwhelmed by the dynamics of growth. Sometime later (three to ten years) the company will either stabilize with a healthy posture and continue to hold onto a good marketshare, or witness declining sales.

Answers to the following questions will largely indicate the health of the company at this future point.

1. Did upper managements view quality and productivity as evolving bases for growth? Were these factors given ongoing priority during the buildup?

2. Did the company plough back sufficient funds into research and development work including alternate product options? Through new options was the company able to strengthen or capture a different market?

3. Were officials able to avoid unnecessary levels of management? Did they keep the complexity of organizational networking at a minimum, thus reducing bureaucracy and organizational distance?

4. Did the managements keep their sights on building a quality culture during the period of growth? Did the company invest in its people to strengthen teamwork?

5. Did the managements build upon problem prevention techniques, knowing that in the long run these would make the difference between whether the company would falter or thrive?

The way these questions are answered will largely determine if companies are holding their own in the marketplace.

Changes in Upper Management

The average life of a modern-day plant manager in a given company is only about four or five years, and for many it is even shorter. Movement in the ranks within and between companies makes this period equally short for mid and upper managements. This can be attributed to general mobility of the population, ability of employees to move up, inability to hold onto a position, and top management's initiative to find managers who can keep their companies on a profitable course. After several years managers seem to run out of ideas and lose sight of key objectives, and this also can be a factor.

This mobility tends to have adverse effects on long-term efforts to improve productivity. Quality methodology and productivity improvement goals can be compromised in the midst of changing managements. A deep and lasting foundation of quality values are needed to sustain a company, but ironically, the reason for a change in upper management may be to create this base. A new manager is sometimes brought in to improve productivity, but because of a different philosophy, and pressure to change things, progress may be set back. If the person who has the final say about the choice of a new manager does not have a sound understanding of quality, effects can be even more severe. Good recommendations of consultants, or well conceived projects which will improve productivity (given sufficient time) are sometimes suddenly stopped in the throes of management change.

Most managers attempt to institute change when coming into new positions, and there is a logical basis for this. Changes in the organization may be needed to give it a new sense of direction and leadership. If the new manager has any doubts about this charter, he or she will soon discover that such changes are not only desired, but results can be expected quickly. The urgency of the matter may not be totally detected by the new manager at the time he or she begins the new assignment, but in a few weeks or even in a matter of days, an appreciation of the extent of the new assignment will likely be realized.

Under pressure to implement change that will bring about cost reduction or quality improvement, quick changes often produce results which are at variance with the desired goals. A company's structure may involve a long history of promotions from within, and while this offers opportunity for advancement without outside competition, it is characterized as inbreeding and may lead to concomitant status quo thinking. There is some risk that over a long period of time, all levels of management will create and adapt to a stagnant climate in which mediocrity predominates. This is usually recognized by corporate officials or the plant manager and eventually he sets out to correct the situation. For example, changes are sometimes made in operations vice presidents, the senior quality manager, or the head of manufacturing. This new executive now must work out new strategies and diplomacies, not only with other senior staff members, but also with subordinates with whom he or she must function.

The new executive brings with him or her knowledge of what has worked in the past. But circumstances are not the same; team players are different and the company philosophy and dynamics create new challenges. Yet, the new executive is charged with the responsibility to make improvements and sets out to implement changes that he or she believes should be made.

In the case where a new V.P. of operations has been brought in to "clean house" but must work with the veteran managers of Q.A., finance, procurement, engineering, marketing, etc., his homework is soon made clear. The conditioning process of other departments brought about by longevity of service and promotion through the ranks is sometimes manifested in parochial ideas and striving to make outdated equipment and methods work at a time when competitors are modernizing. These can be formidable obstacles for a new executive.

Battle lines are intuitively drawn between the old guard and new thought. Resistance to change may be the real enemy, not the new executive. Good leadership, diplomacy, and humanistic approaches used by the new V.P. can be the basis of productive teamwork; on the other hand, coercive methods and compelling forces to perform beyond capacity will ultimately polarize departments.

Being too anxious to make changes without building confidence and proper groundwork will place additional burdens on the system, even under the best of circumstances. When a new executive first comes in, there is a "wait and see" attitude among peers and employees. Everyone expects that changes will be made. The grapevine flourishes. Will there be a reorganization? Is my job vulnerable?

Employee values and company culture in most instances have evolved over several years and may not be appreciably altered by an immediate change in the organization. But, when a change in an upper management position is being motivated by a corporate executive or the plant manager, a quick fix is the hope and frequently the expectation. *Real* progress, however, may be very slow if negative values have become well entrenched throughout the organization. It is probable that many managers who have been previously discharged recognized the need for more rapid progress, but were unable to do so, gradually losing credibility with the chief executive officer.

A change in executive personnel and a reorganization may be the only way to redirect the course of a company to one which is more profitable. If a current senior manager is unable to articulate strategy and lead the company effectively toward its profit oriented goals, activate quality oriented policy, and inaugurate corrective measures to keep the company on course, a CEO is left with no other choice but to bring someone in who, in his or her best judgment, is the kind of person who can bring about needed changes.

Schedule Fever

Another condition which has crept into many U.S. companies is "month end shipment fever." This contagion has spread over American industry to the point that the first week of each month is regarded as a period to relax from last week's crisis.

From the stockholders to production operators, pressure is felt to "move products out the door." If output targets are not reached, income from sales cannot reflect increases, and if increases cannot be shown, stockholders want to know why.

Such pressure originating at the top has the predictable outcome of panic situations at lower levels. As indicated in Figure III-1, pressure applied in the front offices without the necessary provisions will cause separation and chaos on the shop floor. Applied constantly and uniformly, this affliction will encourage or generate additional hidden costs of manufacture; hence, productivity losses will be experienced. The expanding nature of this development is shown in Figure III-2. Problems A and B need the attention of management in January, but they are put off because of other "emergencies" that must be dealt with in order to meet month-end delivery deadlines. In February, problems A and B again are highlighted, but now their significance has grown, resulting in additional corrective actions and allied costs, which in turn place greater pressures on the system. By March, continued toleration of the problems has produced a third problem C, which adds further to schedule costs and quality issues. By the end of the second quarter, additional roadblocks E, etc., have been created.

Pressure and anxiety to meet schedules tend to become a part of the value system of a company and override logical and systematic actions. The CEO and those to whom he or she reports are the only people who can commission a more realistic, planned, and systematic order of events. Setting month end or quarterly goals is certainly a desirable practice, but if they supersede abilities and capacities to reach them, damage to morale, quality, and productivity will be experienced.

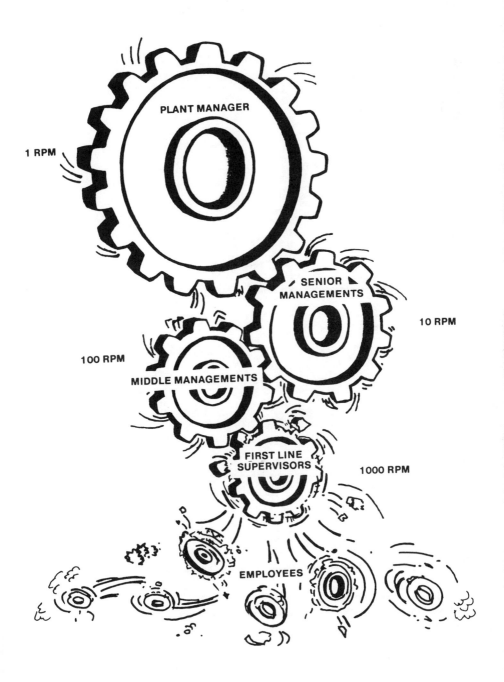

FIGURE III-1. THE HIERARCHICAL BREAKDOWN UNDER PRESSURE

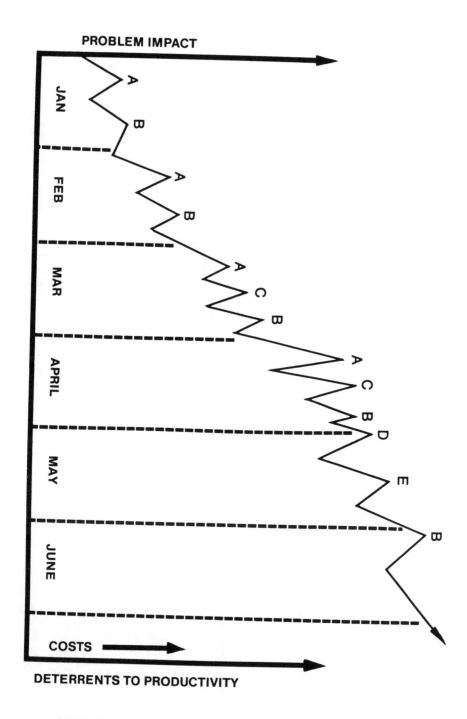

FIGURE III-2.   EXPANSIVE EFFECTS OF PROBLEMS RESULTING FROM
SCHEDULE PRESSURES

Illustrated in Figure III-3 is the typical way U.S. firms regard cost, quality, and schedule during any given month. (In some companies this could represent a quarter period, but the message is the same). The amount of *attention* given to cost, schedule, and quality varies systematically with each week of the month. Given that these factors begin each month at a common starting point, by the end of the month, schedule can dramatically affect this balance. There is usually noticeable inattention to schedule during the first week of every month, but growing to great intensity by the last day of the month. This has the effect of drawing everyone's attention away from pursuing preventive strategies.

Illustrated in Figure III-4 is the impact of schedule pressure on cost, quality and productivity in companies where high quality-associated costs are experienced. If a company has made a strong commitment to safeguard quality (ensuring that all quality standards are met) while facing high inspection, scrap and rework costs, curves $quality_1$ and $cost_1$ will apply. In order to ensure conformance throughout the month, costs will increase as the end of the month approaches because of quality problems and creeping concerns about meeting schedules. If the work atmosphere has a high tolerance for error and systems are not geared to uphold quality standards, schedule concerns will grow even stronger and take their toll on outgoing quality, as shown in Figure III-4 by curves $cost_2$ and $quality_2$. Productivity in either case will be low because of the adverse combination of schedule stresses, and the demonstration of concern for quality only when it becomes an after-the-fact issue. These conditions will push operating costs upward and outputs downward.

Long-term productivity will be worse in the latter case, unless stronger commitments are made to quality. In this example, high quality costs already exist because complacent attitudes about workmanship are prevalent. This, together with delivery anxiety, will reduce the effectiveness with which outputs can be generated. If nonconforming units are delivered, external failure costs not only will increase, but systems will become burdened with customer returned units and attendant paperwork.

De-institutionalize Corrective Action

Increasing efforts are afoot to institutionalize quality improvement, and there is good reason for this; any progress made toward institutionalizing quality improvement will help to de-institutionalize corrective action. (The subject of institutionalizing quality improvement is discussed further in Chapter VI.)

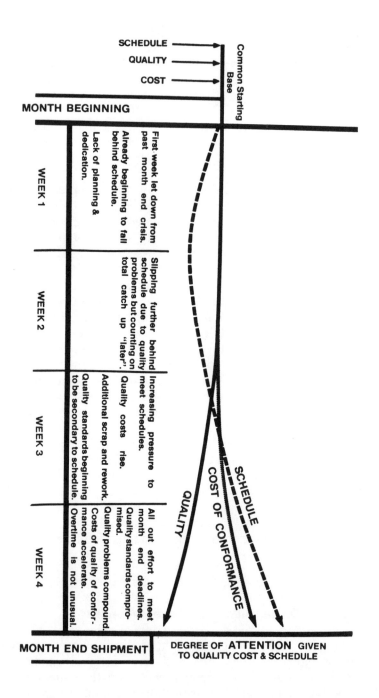

FIGURE III-3.   WEEKLY ATTENTION GIVEN TO COST, QUALITY AND SCHEDULE

74

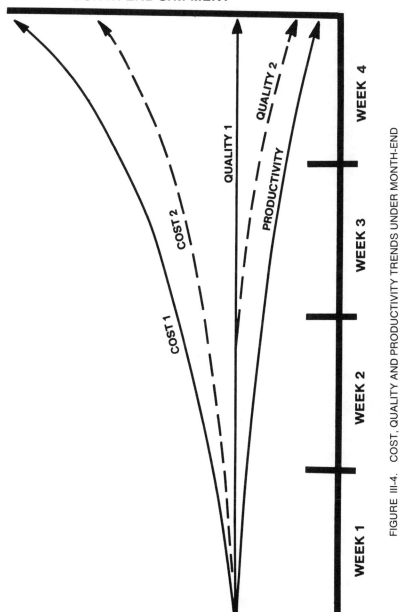

MONTH END SHIPMENT

QUALITY 2

QUALITY 1

PRODUCTIVITY

COST 2

COST 1

WEEK 4

WEEK 3

WEEK 2

WEEK 1

FIRST OF MONTH COMMON STARTING BASE OF QUALITY, PRODUCTIVITY, AND COST

FIGURE III-4. COST, QUALITY AND PRODUCTIVITY TRENDS UNDER MONTH-END DEADLINE CRISIS SITUATIONS

75

Corrective action must be counted among the most serious deterrents to productivity improvement (corrective action is used here as a generic title for "doing things over." It therefore encompasses rework and ancillary activities). While it is normally thought of in terms of production departments where scrap and rework are expressions commonly heard, a much more general problem of corrective action exists. Doing things over is woven into the attitudes and habit patterns of people in all departments.

Corrective action is so much a part of industrial mentality that people in administrative, as well as manufacturing areas, expect it, are conditioned to have little concern about its effects, and even plan for it. Moreover, it is often camouflaged so that people are not aware that most of what they do is a result of prior work done wrong or left unfinished by someone else.

Willingness to accept and tolerate doing things over is the first step toward long-term productivity problems. Physicians do not intentionally provide medicine that will nourish cancer. Ironically, some managers intentionally provide nutrition to make corrective action become very healthy. How does this happen? Management's acceptance of the condition that sundry errors and rework are unavoidable.

Focus on week to week quantity goals draws attention away from the creeping system anomalies and burgeoning "band-aids" that are used to temporarily fix situations. The long-term result is the growth of activities and reliance on functions which are believed to be essential, but are actually parasitic and have snowballing characteristics. This is accomplished by a tolerance for such activities, not realizing cost implications.

In shop environments, rework and scrap are believed to be inevitable and managers make sure that sufficient equipment and people are supplied to adequately handle the problem. A material review board is established and ample rework centers are provided to correct salvageable parts. These activities, in turn, are specifically dealt with in fiscal budget planning. For example, "Last year, we spent a little over $400,000 for rework in this department. It looks as if we will have the same problems next year, so we had better put a little more into the budget to make certain we are covered—say $450,000. Our last year's report shows $700,000 lost in scrap. On the surface, this appears to be a high figure, but we must remember, it would have been much higher if the parts reworked had not been salvageable!"

Positive or Negative Reinforcement?

Existing in U.S. firms are also some very strong stereotypes and parochial notions about jobs, which are associated with specific talents for these positions. Job definition and the scope and content of performance objectives are not always in line with productivity improvement goals. Without knowing it, managers sometimes perpetuate behavior that drives wedges further between organizations by establishing objectives that indirectly lead to undesirable outcomes, then cinching the transaction by rewarding the performance. A person may be indirectly rewarded for *not* extending oneself beyond customary organizational boundaries.

An example of this is the design-production interface. Design people frequently have the knack for designing certain items with needless or complicated features which cause production departments a great deal of difficulty. In other situations, production departments are very clever at "making something like the drawing," knowing that certain design dimensions are incorrect or highly suspect, but choose to remain silent about the matter. The design engineer, meanwhile, is rewarded for doing a good job; conceptually on the design board, and by means of preliminary test data, the new design met all product engineering parameters and as far as the design department is concerned, this was an excellent job. The only problem is the item could not be reliably built the way it was designed. Correspondingly, like the designer, the production operator is rewarded for making it like the design even though it was recognized at the time that the part could not be assembled properly, leaving considerable doubt about the reliability of the deliverable unit.

Both the designer and the production operator have done their jobs; the expert designer was able to create a new design concept, and the production operator was able to finish 1,000 parts ahead of schedule. Meanwhile, the inspector is rewarded for an outstanding job, having inspected and passed all of the parts as conforming to specifications. Quality problems may not be disclosed until after the product has been placed into service by a customer.

Another kind of example is where the top executive makes a commitment to improve the quality of work life in the company, but without the proper provisioning. His or her *expectations* are driven downward through the organization, but are "imposed" without the necessary building blocks of equipment, training, and methods for producing a better quality of work life for the employees. Pressure to produce more and more with less and less can only be counter-productive. As such pressure increases, employee emotions as well as the systems in which they function, begin to break down.

Need for New Organizational Concepts

The formal organization is a relatively inflexible structure which depicts authority, lines of communications, and accountability. It also reveals managements' intentions about how they expect departments to "work together" and relate to one another. Without such a "plan," the execution of assignments would be chaotic and little control could be expected.

The Traditional Organization. Organizational creativity is needed. In most cases, one cannot detect directly or by inference that productivity and teamwork are dealt with organizationally in industry. These objectives are left to the creativity and leadership skills of the manager, who must somehow effect and control organization cross links that will accomplish these purposes.

Shown in Figure III-5 is an example of a traditional industrial organization chart. It sets forth the divisions in which *specialty* functions operate and how the power structure is to function. While details vary, these eight key functional units are usually found in most large companies.

Traditional organization structure inherently supports the "us and them" dichotomy, and by *design,* sets the scene for provincialism and interdepartmental conflict. Industrial organizations are characterized by classifying functional units into departments or subdivisions which have similar tasks or missions. This reinforces the notion that each department has special and unique talents which "should" be surreptitiously utilized. While a degree of specialization is needed, it is also important to provide an organizational scheme which will highlight productivity factors and illustrate means by which teamwork can function. The organization predetermines interaction, and it is among the most important factors to be considered when functional or cultural change is the objective.

Some companies are continuously making major organizational changes, with questionable motives and results. Reorganization can be a quick and dramatic way to illustrate managements' intentions for improvement, while sending shock waves throughout the organization.

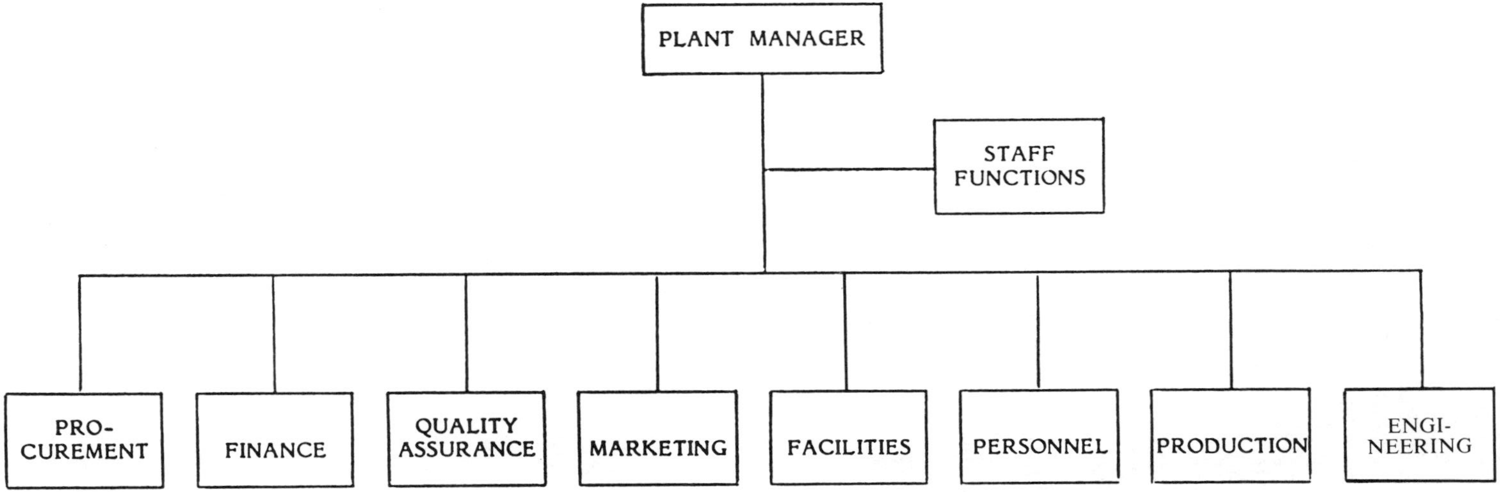

FIGURE III-5. GENERAL DIVISIONS IN INDUSTRIAL ORGANIZATION

The chart shows the following organizational structure:

- PLANT MANAGER
  - STAFF FUNCTIONS
  - PROCUREMENT
  - FINANCE
  - QUALITY ASSURANCE
  - MARKETING
  - FACILITIES
  - PERSONNEL
  - PRODUCTION
  - ENGINEERING

More long-range thought should often be given to plans before an organization is structured or before a reorganization takes place. One company brought in a new operations vice president in an attempt to improve productivity. At his arrival, design engineering, procurement, quality assurance, reliability, and production were separate departments reporting to him. He decided to make some changes; he moved quality assurance under the control of design engineering and production without realizing the need to improve a conspicuously low quality culture. Quality problems increased; productivity decreased. Making no effort to improve the quality of work life for the employees, he soon became overwhelmed by negative cultural factors that were growing faster than his ability to make improvements. Within one year, the organization went through one complete cycle; it ended like it began, except that he and two managers were no longer with the company— and so the cycle continued.

Organization-reorganization issues are revealed in numerous ways. Ever since the responsibility for quality was removed organizationally from those who created it, difficulty has been experienced in how to best organize "quality" functions.

To remove quality as a control function in a company where there is current mentality to ship without taking quality seriously, would be a mistake. On the other hand, over-control of quality in an improving quality culture can also thwart gain. Conscientious efforts made by operators to demonstrate quality improvement, need to be built upon by increasing cooperative efforts between inspection and operators, and by the systematic and commensurable reduction of inspection tasks.

A wise management will vigorously attack any condition that opposes harmony and workmanship and institute organizational changes that support meeting quality standards with less resources. Productivity issues could be made easier in most instances, if they were brought under control and given credence by the organization itself. Creation of a productivity management unit is a good place to start. Such a function would cut across all major lines of the organization and utilize the expertise of quality, industrial engineering, safety, finance, procurement, and sales. This will help to identify and focus on the need to improve productivity as well as assign responsibility for action.

A Modified Matrix Approach. Another organizational prospect for improvement is the *matrix* type of organization. Matrix management is an integrative management technique for sharing a common pool of specialists across product lines. Effectively administered, it can substantially reduce duplication of overhead functions and at the same time reduce the conflict that typically exists between organizations. Illustrated in Figure III-6 is a variation of the matrix/organizational concept. It shows how a productivity unit might be integrated into the functional line type of organization by classifying "productivity type" groups under a productivity head. The make-up of this unit will vary from company to company.

As a company grows, the top down concept usually leads to communications, delegation, and execution difficulties. Companies have found the matrix concept to be beneficial when a strong need for multiple support functions exists and, when it is necessary to process large amounts of information simultaneously. It also sets forth cross links and shows how teamwork can be achieved.

On the other hand, the matrix method is viewed by some to have the disadvantage that dual authority is imposed on the pool of specialists, and eventually it can create *less* cross functional teamwork if allowed to run out of control. Companies which have tried matrix techniques, however, report that advantages outweigh disadvantages.

Achieve Greater Information Efficiency

Paperwork Design. One of the greatest sources of white-collar inefficiency comes from the inanimate system of paperwork which dictates to the human what he or she must do. Paperwork can essentially "act" like a manager and be received as if it were a living authority. A form, for example, "requests" certain information and people tend to accept this without question. "Someone must need this information; the form says so."

Forms design involves two basic rules: (1) information requested should be needed and (2) provisions should be made on the form to accommodate complete descriptions. Some forms are so "busy" that needed information is concealed in the maze of irrelevant data.

As a result, an analysis is delayed, or certain information is omitted from the analysis. Under urgent situations, if needed data are not obvious, there is proclivity to guesstimate what appears to be omitted with the attendant risk of drawing erroneous conclusions.

The kind of paperwork used (forms, computer printouts, correspondence, etc.) and the reason for its existence should be continuously challenged. Principal purposes of paperwork are to

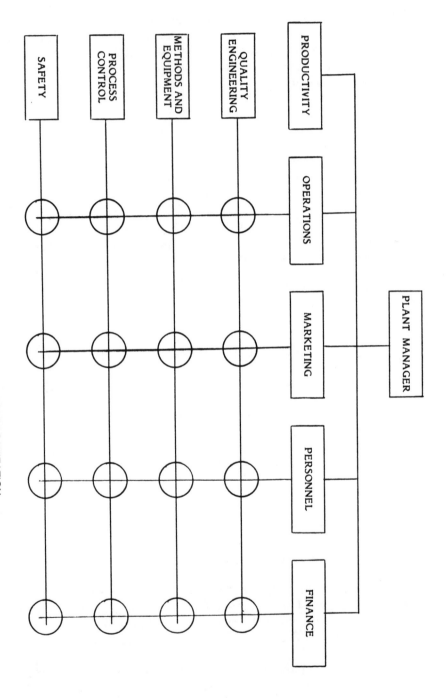

FIGURE III-6. PRODUCTIVITY IN A MATRIX ORGANIZATION

communicate a message, make a decision, and get effective results. Plans are messages for action, and results are gleaned from information feedback. If messages are clear and understood (given that other factors such as willingness are in place), plans most likely will be carried out. Conversely, if plans are incomplete, difficult to interpret or inaccurate, actions will not meet expectations. Correspondingly, reporting reports (forms, nonconformance reports, progress reports, etc.) need to be properly designed to convey action language for decision making.

An essential part of any planning process is having information on which to base and support decisions. Both the quantity and quality of information are important; the lowest quantity, consistent with the highest quality needed for decisions is the goal. Quality information means that it is not only relevant to the planning process, but also in a readily useable form. Executives usually need to see trends, overviews, or specific problem areas highlighted. The need for detail will generally decrease at the higher levels of management. Except under special circumstances, reports submitted to upper management should be brief, action oriented, with exceptions highlighted.

Most organizations generate mountains of information—more than they would ever use or ever need. Before defining any input information to be collected or maintained, one should always ask, "What kind of outputs are required for the successful operation of the organization?" and "Which input data are required to produce such outputs?" and then proceed to collect and maintain only the relevant information.

Computer Influences. Information technology is advancing so rapidly that only those that produce computer products have an in-depth understanding of its applications and characteristics, and even they have difficulty. Managements are sometimes perplexed by the number of choices available to them.

In recent years, a bewildering variety of computer oriented equipments and languages have been introduced onto the market, and some firms now have the problem of getting their computers to "talk" to others that have been purchased earlier. While constant progress is being witnessed, it seems that one purchase leads to another, while the number of open communication loops grows. Those who are well into the computer age are seeing millions of computer printouts being produced daily—often depicting data only. Some companies are demonstrating success at converting these data quickly into useful information, but others are toiling over mountains of reports, attempting to prioritize data, construct charts, and draw accurate conclusions.

The introduction of computers, on balance, has obsoleted manual methods to a considerable degree. In the long run, those who do not move into computer technology will be unable to compete except in small, narrow fields.

Companies are encountering growing pains in this expansive era of computers, however. Massive amounts of computer printouts, for example, are not only being generated, but like so much other correspondence, they too are being reproduced and becoming information storage, or are lost in the maze of informational paperwork. One CEO was so concerned about this burgeoning problem that he had a memorandum placed on the copy machine in which he raised the question "Have you read yesterday's 26 copies yet?" While an advantage of computers is their ability to quickly generate a large amount of information, computers tend to carry the corollary presupposition that more and more information is needed, and in many instances, they have become the basis of unnecessary information regeneration.

There are also growing pains associated with adapting such technology to existing company systems. Some firms have introduced computers into various organizations, which now have *dual* paperwork systems. Lack of confidence in the use of computers has kept old methods from being discarded, and as a result, considerable redundancy can be found. The issue confronting managers today is not *if* they should invest in computers; it is how much, when, where, and what kind of units or systems will best serve the company's needs. Old ways also need to be unlearned. In many instances, education will need to play a major role in the conversion process. Computers as "toys" are helping individuals to overcome the "intimidation syndrome."

With or without the use of computers, planning and forethought will determine whether the paperwork system will add or detract from the occurrence of error. An information system can be the source of significant cost avoidance. It will prevent open loops in communications, but like other unmanaged activities, it can be destructive if allowed to run out of control.

Convert Commitment Into Improvement

A word which is perhaps becoming over used is *commitment*. The real challenge facing most executives is not so much making the commitment, but converting such commitment into improvement. Plant managers have exclaimed, "I am committed to productivity improvement; we are measuring output; I have organized a staff to look into these matters, but still no apparent improvement is taking place." Unless commitment results in improvement, it actually has very little meaning.

Executing Improvement. Hundreds of books have been written about management in which the major functions are described as planning, organizing, leading, and controlling. Historically, these have provided an adequate basis for describing management functions and responsibilities. However, another aspect of management which has grown in manifold proportions and causing considerable concern is *execution.* Some argue that the traditional list of management functions is sufficient to house any activity that relates to implementation. But based on the difficulties encountered in carrying out solutions, execution should be given equal billing.

There is a growing tendency to identify what is thought to be a problem, arrive at an answer and propose a solution, but for whatever the reason, further action tends to stop at this point. Were there parallel efforts being undertaken simultaneously? Did other priorities interfere with the execution of this solution? Did support for the concept fade with organizational change? Or, did it simply get lost in the maze of other projects and issues? Unfortunately, the originator may never know why no further action was taken on his or her proposal.

Real improvement may take longer than some seem to be willing to wait. Execution needs to be planned, deliberate and systematic, and be given the necessary time for all elements to be in place and functioning. Anxiety and impatience to show improvement without building a good foundation are manifested by the constant changing or cancellation of plans before their feasibility can be adequately tested. This is not to imply that plans do not need to change; rather it means that if plans or solutions are in a constant state of turmoil, implementation is sacrificed or left wanting in action. If this happens, efforts toward improvement ironically are themselves either wasteful, or contribute to wastefulness.

Numerous examples can be given which might provide some insight into why good ideas do not progress from the solution phase to the implementation phase. Several are offered.

Over several weeks of reporting, inspection data indicated an unusually high percent of defectives produced at a given work center. Quality engineers, through equipment capability studies, etc., concluded that certain machine adjustments needed to be made, which involved changes in tools and ancillary equipment used in the process. The quality department has been under pressure to solve this problem because of nonconformance costs. Now, based on their findings, after several weeks of investigation, the quality department expects to make the desired changes immediately to eliminate this high cost situation.

There are layers of barriers that can be encountered in such circumstances. A response from the production department might be: "This machine is critical to the entire production process. We cannot shut down operations while you 'experiment' and cause us to get even further behind schedule." A credibility gap obviously exists in this case. However, the issue is not only to correct this immediate problem, but to solve a broader cultural problem.

A similar example can be given for the industrial engineering department. IE's may know that a rearrangement of a department is very important; parts are getting lost, safety hazards exist, large waiting times are witnessed, and bottlenecks disrupt flow, all of which could be significantly reduced by rearranging the department. The solution to the skillful IE is obvious; on paper it can be shown that throughput and productivity could be markedly improved by the change. Like the quality issue however, the *execution* phase will likely meet with resistance unless the proper groundwork has been laid during the development of the plan. If there is a history of conflict between such problem solving functions and other departments, execution difficulties are inevitable.

These examples raise the question about how successful quality and industrial engineering departments have been in the past in solving such problems. Also, what degree of esteem do these departments hold with senior managements? If the departments have successful track records and if upper managements are serious about productivity improvement, plans will probably be executed more readily.

If the departments have been successful in the past, such successes have probably been based on gaining cooperation by those affected by the changes and winning the respect of upper management. If the people who will be directly affected by the change fully understand its reasons and implications, and were allowed to participate in the analysis and planning stages, enthusiastic cooperation has a better chance of being gained. Resistance or outright refusal to cooperate may be experienced unless there is early buy-in from those who must directly work with the change.

The execution of solutions can also be hampered by broader management related situations. Four kinds are discussed.

Example I

A quality engineer was assigned to study the feasibility of instituting statistical process controls. This was considered a top priority by upper management. The engineer selected several appropriate areas and began his study. The scope of the analysis tended to grow; as it progressed, machine *incapability* became more apparent than had been anticipated. But, pressure from the top to institute control charts mandated action.

Meanwhile, a consultant had been meeting with the plant manager and sold him on the idea that his consultant firm could get the job done quickly because they had a successful record and knew what was needed. Three months and one hundred thousand dollars later the company had control charts that for the most part were never used. The consultant was hired to institute control charts and that he did, but the subjects of behavioral change and process incapability had not been adequately addressed. During this period the quality engineer had become convinced that most of the processes in question were no longer capable of holding the required tolerances, causing considerable inspection and matched assembly work, but he and his immediate superiors were unable to convince senior management. The end result was that all parties lost credibility.

Example II

A company was growing rapidly and changes seemed to be occurring more quickly than accurate analyses could be made to verify that all the elements were in place. The fiscal budgeting process was inadequate to deal with the rapid expansion, and capital forecasting seemed to be constantly out of phase with need.

A critical organizational and relocation change was pending. Many hours had been devoted to planning the project before the decision was made to go ahead. Shortly before the change was to begin, it was realized that two critical capital items had been red lined from the next year's fiscal budget in favor of other items not related to this project.

Reasons for the budget change were lost in organizational networking. The net result was a substantial rework and compromise, which negated important benefits of the change.

Example III

A director in a large electronics firm once maintained that he would not support his managers in their plan to make a certain change in the fabrication department. Not to do so defied all logic and the advocacy of *all* his immediate subordinates. He persisted in his admonishment that the idea was not good, based on an allied experience he had encountered on a previous job. A consultant was brought in who quickly recognized the advantages of the change. After several discussions, which included the senior managements, the director was "convinced" that the change should be made. Layouts were drawn up and the concept quickly turned into a more detailed proposal. This showed precisely what equipments were needed, which items were involved and costs of the change.

The proposal, however, left several areas open which could be cited as obstacles by the unwilling, namely still the director. Although he was in the position to effect trade-offs of capital money, etc., and easily make the change, he chose to exploit several minor loop-holes and exclaim, "I told you so; this whole idea won't work." Hundreds of hours had been spent by subordinate managers and others in the investigation and solution of the problem and major benefits were unquestionably at stake. The proposal finally died, but the pain lingered on. Subordinates still huddle to try to figure out ways to be creative and implement changes in spite of conditions. There are several points that can be made from this scenario.

1. It is possible that the director was actually right in this instance, although no one else believed it. The climate was such that rational thought and reason were replaced by bias and a win/lose attitude.

2. The director was left no way out; no option was available to save face. He had to prove he was right.

3. Proposals should not contain loop-holes. Even though they may appear to be of little real consequence, the prophets of gloom will use these (sometimes very effectively) to divert attention away from the real values of the proposal and ultimately cause its rejection. If there is an

area of doubt, regardless how small it appears to be, it can be the object that will thwart implementation of a significant improvement.

Example IV

Quality audits were being conducted and results reported, but a growing number of violations were not getting corrected. The audit procedure in place was based on the notion that the audit group should *find* infractons to quality policy and make certain these were reported. This procedure involved a check list of items that the quality assurance department deemed important, then the periodic review of conditions against these criteria. Audits were conducted unannounced in an attempt to assess conditions as they really existed. However, as it turned out, this provided the quality assurance department with a mechanism to occasionally "nail" certain functions when they were found in violation of policy, etc. This practice resulted in growing animosity between the quality assurance department and those being audited. Over a period of years the culture had developed a clear "us and them" identity.

Gradually, in the absence of camaraderie, excuses, charges and countercharges were increasingly levied, with less and less improvement. Reports by the group were submitted, but very little action was taken. There was sufficient confusion that upper managements would not force an issue. The audit group had become almost entirely perfunctory, but it continued to conduct its regular audits and *report* findings.

Several points can be made from this scenario:

(1) All parties being audited should be privy to the same information as the quality assurance department. If certain criteria for review are important enough to have an audit group, the departments being audited should be at least equally informed about the severity of the situations listed on the check sheet. A good place to begin is a *coordinated* list of criteria which is known by the activity being audited. This will place the emphasis of the true value of the audit group by demonstrating a helpful attitude. The importance of certain items may necessitate some education, but principal parties should be the first to know about what and why certain procedures, etc. should or should not be followed.

(2) Upper management should take whatever action is necessary to keep an audit group from becoming perfunctory. To dandify the

organization by having all the traditional units covered on the chart may be far more costly than having a simple system in which people cooperate to do the job right the first time through a better understanding of the importance of quality factors.

Means Can Become The End. While a principal purpose of such departments as quality and industrial engineering is problem solving, oft times they find themselves out of phase with this purpose. It is questionable if such departments generate as much improvement as they should because of such circumstances as described in the previous examples. Much of the work accomplished by problem solving groups deals with data collection, measurement and analysis, and a visible line connecting cause and effect relationships to improvement sometimes turns out to be nonexistent. Ultimately, these departments can become so involved in the *means* to an end that the means become the end. Analyses beget further data collection, study, and measurement; these, in turn, lead to further investigation and so the vicious cycle continues.

This process is shown in the closed loop system illustrated in Figure III-7. Without the management fully realizing the implications, these problem solving people find themselves on a closed loop treadmill which excludes the most important elements—namely, decision, action and improvement.

This outcome partly develops from repeated attempts by problem solvers to see their solutions implemented, but with less than satisfactory success. In the long run because this is their job, they find themselves cycling and recycling solutions with no further action taken. A goodly number of recommendations become scattered in bureaucratic networking or clouded by biases of a high authority. As a result, problem solving functions find themselves devoting much of their time to activities which have little positive influence on improvement. While senior managements must shoulder the primary responsibility for allowing this to happen, problem solving functions need to guard against becoming conditioned or comfortable in such roles.

A complete treatment of this subject will include the management's prerogatives, however. Not all solutions presented by problem solving functions are in line with current management wisdom or prevailing notions at the time. Neither are some solutions worthy of adoption, of course. The management exercises its option to weigh alternatives and some proposals will succumb under close crutiny. Oblique actions are sometimes also taken by the management which appear to problem

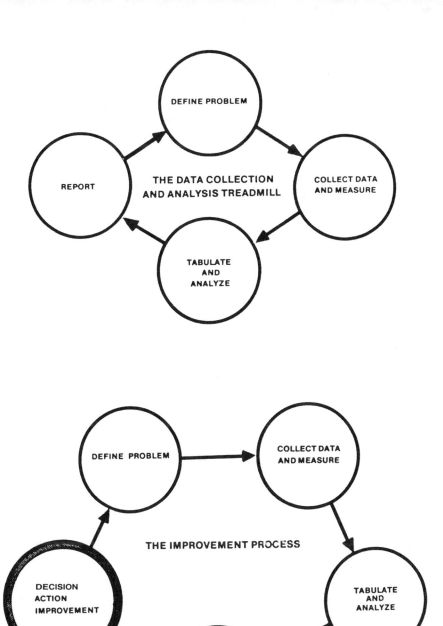

FIGURE III-7. PROBLEM SOLVING WITH AND WITHOUT IMPROVEMENT

solvers that *no* action was taken. While an originator may feel less than enthusiastic about his or her proposal not being accepted and implemented, its contents may have provided critical information for a lateral decision. Unfortunately, authors of proposals may never learn of this benefit. Irrespective of kind, feedback to originators of plans, proposals, projects or any other completed work is always a requisite for efficiency.

Requisites for Improvement. Part II of this book broadly covers the processes of achieving improvement, so let it suffice here to identify some principal areas where attention can be focused.

1. *Assure effective two-way communications.* Make certain that communication channels are open and working. Unfiltered feedback is critical to decision making and to the improvement process. If a strong top-down communication style exists, management efficiency can be improved with a shift toward more bottom-up involvement.

2. *Educate and train.* The relationship of quality to productivity must be generically known among the employees, and especially throughout the management hierarchy. Having a good appreciation of each other's missions at the department level is very important.

3. *Generate coadjutant interests.* Helpful attitudes lead to teamwork, and teamwork generates efficiency.

4. *Select targets for improvement.* Such targets can be reduction of scrap and rework, or improvements in preventive actions. They can be the implementation of statistical process control or simply improvements in paperwork. An important point is not to allow affinity toward "measurement and sensors" (albeit they are necessary) to overshadow the principal purpose, namely, *improvement.*

As previously mentioned, in American industrial culture there is the ever present hazard of becoming so entangled with methodology itself that purposes (in this instance improvement) are either forgotten or receive secondary attention. Faith in the wisdom of established truths, together with tenacious pursuit of productivity improvement goals which best fit company characteristics and products, will be necessary.

5. *Establish improvement objectives.* Yearly, quarterly and monthly objectives, specifically for improvement, should be established so that improvement targets can be incorporated into goals and schedules. Improvement begets further improvement, and success builds enthusiasm and intrinsic confidence.

6. *Organize and assign responsibilities.* Productivity improvement objectives need to be manifested by the organization itself. Organizational visibility for the improvement process needs to be established, as previously discussed. Assigning responsibilities for productivity improvement and establishing organizational units to carry out the mission are good management practices. Unless someone is assigned this responsibility, measurable improvement and even an accurate status will remain elusive.

7. *Execute.* The success of this entire venture will be dependent first on upper managements ongoing participation, then on establishing an organization through which productivity improvement can be assessed and executed. In any case, executed commitments must begin with the top officials. Persistent and perhaps even strong actions may need to be employed by senior managements to overcome inertia and set a new pace at the lower levels in an organization. In an interview with the authors of their book, *In Search of Excellence,* Peters addressed this subject in his answer to the question, "Can a mediocre, underachieving company turn itself around without a forceful personality at the top? Peters reply was, "Flat out *no . . .*"[8]

CHAPTER IV

Historical and Societal Factors

In addition to the challenges discussed in Chapter III, other issues continue to evolve which further complicate efforts to increase productivity rates.

Developing historically and socially, these factors are associated with the influences of scientific management and current efforts to expand humanistic approaches to leadership, social and logistical changes in society, increasing non-work interests, labor union interfaces and education mismatches. When one studies the causes of slowing productivity in the U.S., these and related factors need to be included in the assessment.

Influences of Frederick Taylor's Scientific Management

Dating back to the time of the industrial revolution, getting people to work "harder" to increase output in factory environments has been an issue. Most efforts dealt with ways that excluded human interaction and behavior. The first decade of this century saw the advent of a new approach to increasing productivity called scientific management. This concept was first advocated and articulated by Frederick W. Taylor, and it spawned a new industrial discipline called motion and time study. Taylor's attempts to make workers more efficient involved the use of scientific methods to eliminate unnecessary steps and motions, and organizing work areas in such a way that workers' efforts had a positive effect on productivity. Some believe that Taylor, in effect, attempted to by-pass human interaction and thought processes with the use of scientific methods to deliver higher output.

Whatever his logic was, Taylor's work has left an indelible mark on modern-day industry. Although his critics now believe that his scientific management concepts have had an overall negative impact on American industry, many of his theories set forth early in this century are being practiced with success, and are widely credited with having transformed a young agricultural nation into the most successful industrial giant in the world.

In 1911, Frederick Taylor, in his book, *Principles of Scientific Management,* discussed the issue of motivation and his words could easily apply now in many instances.

> " 'The elimination of soldiering,' (pretense of working; shirking), and of the several causes of slow working would so lower the cost of production that both our home and foreign markets would be greatly enlarged, and we could compete on more than even terms with our rivals. It would remove one of the fundamental causes for dull times, for lack of employment, and for poverty, and, therefore, would have a more permanent and far-reaching effect upon these misfortunes than any of the curative remedies that are now being used to soften their consequences. It would insure higher wages and make shorter working hours and better working and home conditions possible.
>
> Why is it, then, in the face of the self-evident fact that maximum prosperity can exist only as the result of the determined effort of each workman to turn out each day his largest possible day's work, that a great number do just the opposite, and that even when they have the best of intentions, their work is in most cases far from efficient?"[1]

Taylor's analysis of the above situation is strikingly congruent with comments one sometimes hears today.

1. That a material increase in output of people and machines would result in throwing a large number of people out of work is a fallacy, which has from time immemorial been universal among workmen.

2. Defective systems of management make it necessary for people to work slowly, in order to protect their own best interests.

3. The use of inefficient rule-of-thumb methods, waste a large part of an employee's effort.

An evolution of scientific management—dividing work into discrete elements with the expectant outcome of reduced effort and higher performance—has left questionable results especially in terms of human coefficacy. So far as the inanimate inputs of systems and technologies

1. Copyright, Harper and Row Publishers, Inc., reprinted by permission.

are concerned, there have been remarkable achievements. But, while high technology has changed the *forms* of work, beharioral scientists claim that technocracy has also lead to more and more dissatisfaction with the job. Taylor's early work emphasized the "mechanical" aspects of achieving output which had the effect of de-emphasizing the human side of work. As a result, scientific management produced resentments, because workers could observe improved productivity with no advancement in pay and they felt exploited as a result.

In spite of negative reactions, Taylor's emphasis on improving methods has proved to be a very important approach toward increasing productivity, and it continues to find advocates and strong support. Perhaps Taylor's worst shortcoming was his limited knowledge of human behavior. While his premise that good methods predetermined efficiency was quite sound, the human factor of *motivation* was an element that people at that time sorely underestimated and misunderstood. Most of the problems that developed out of scientific methods did not come from the principles; they grew out of abuse and short-sighted approaches taken by the managements who implemented them. Now, more attention is being focused on people and *their* roles in productivity improvement.

During the last several decades, beharioral scientists have conducted considerable research on the human side of productivity and performed enumerable experiments involving motivational factors. Mayo's studies at Western Electric; Maslow's hierarchy of needs; McGregor's theory X and theory Y premises; Herzberg's hygienic and job enrichment theories, to name a few, span over 50 years of study all of which focused on motivation and the human side of job performance. While beharioral researchers have made progress on what motivates people in job environments, much still remains to be done. It is interesting to note that in spite of all the study that has been completed on motivation, the same kind of issues to which historical and contemporary authorities have devoted a lifetime of work, continue to plague U.S. industry.

There is both the need and room for scientific and people-oriented approaches to function smoothly. Figure IV-1 illustrates the gap and the need for movement of these approaches to an integrated operating network. Co-existence is insufficient to maximize benefits of either. For example, methods improvements should result in job satisfaction and improved quality of work life; performance standards and management by objective should result in increased creativity and problem solving; systems analysis should encompass methods of reducing boredom, employee frustrations and so forth.

The gap between the humanistic and scientific approaches can be

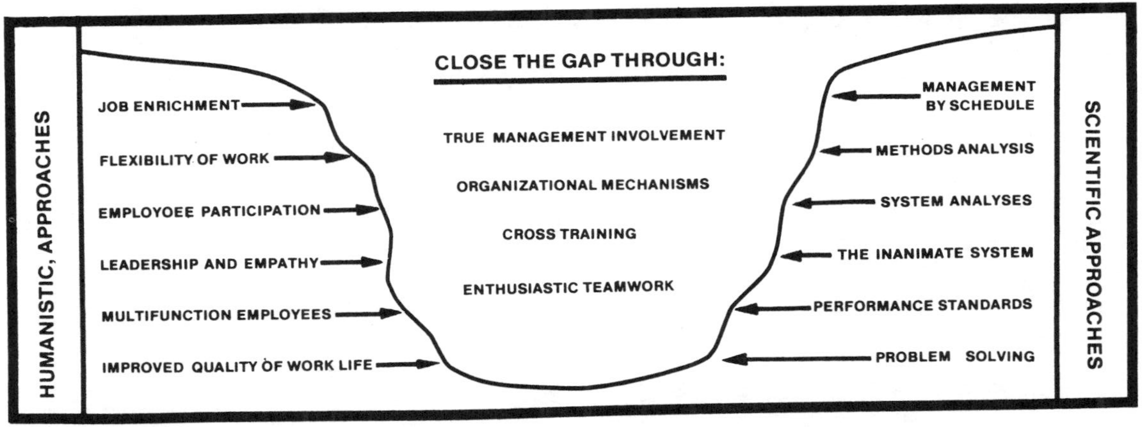

SCIENTIFIC APPROACHES

MANAGEMENT BY SCHEDULE
METHODS ANALYSIS
SYSTEM ANALYSES
THE INANIMATE SYSTEM
PERFORMANCE STANDARDS
PROBLEM SOLVING

CLOSE THE GAP THROUGH:

TRUE MANAGEMENT INVOLVEMENT
ORGANIZATIONAL MECHANISMS
CROSS TRAINING
ENTHUSIASTIC TEAMWORK

JOB ENRICHMENT
FLEXIBILITY OF WORK
EMPLOYOEE PARTICIPATION
LEADERSHIP AND EMPATHY
MULTIFUNCTION EMPLOYEES
IMPROVED QUALITY OF WORK LIFE

HUMANISTIC, APPROACHES

FIGURE IV-1. CLOSING THE GAP BETWEEN HUMANISTIC AND SCIENTIFIC APPROACHES TO MANAGEMENT

97

continually narrowed by the management (1) manifesting real interest, (2) making participation and teamwork come alive in the organizations, (3) creating organization vehicles that will build teamwork and bond disciplines, and (4) ensuring the kind and degree of training and education that will break the barriers built into organization structure.

The Work Ethic

It has been said that one should be thankful for the opportunity to get up every morning and have something to accomplish that needs attention. Working on a project and doing ones best will breed temperance, self-control, diligence, strength of will and a host of other virtues which the idle can never experience. Another writer pointed out that a good test of a person's qualities is the way he or she works. "Work is the test—not the importance of the work from a prestige point of view—but the fidelity with which it is done."[2] A company does not so much need people to do extraordinary things; it needs those who can do ordinary things extraordinarily well.

Such statements express a fundamental truth, but they overlook the reality of certain human needs. While employers complain that it is difficult to find people who really want to work and give a fair day's work for a day's pay, employees are asking for a better quality of work life. Company officials point out that employees want increases in benefits and base pay, but lack loyalty and are passive about matters affecting productivity. Further, it is said that employees have become increasingly less willing to begin at a point commensurable with their abilities, then progress as they develop. Are these outcomes indictments on employees, the management or society? There is probably no need to decide. Cultural circumstances in which such conflicting values are manifested simply deserve attention. Some researchers claim that a major cause of slowing productivity is that society has not been providing a rewarding environment outside the company for motivation within the company. "Motivating employees by building better job environments and improving the quality of work life is important; but, by focusing only on the job, only half of the motivational problem is being addressed. The other half, the social environment outside the company, is being overlooked."[3]

Many of the conditions which work against productivity gains are the same as those which prevent people from capitalizing on rewards that can be found in work itself (e.g., monotony, boredom and idleness). Pascarella reminds us that when employees have something meaningful to commit to, they can help make their organizations more effective economically, technologically, and in human terms.[4] While methods of research differ, there is general consensus that achievement and earned recognition for such achievement are strong work motivators. There are extrinsic factors which include money, status, and power. For some, these are the spur to fame and fortune. Most agree however, that feelings of inspiration, self worth and pride which come from effort and achievement, not only have complementary and integral meaning, they have deep and lasting value to the soul as well. Both society and industry need to find ways to put people to work in environments in which work is satisfying and where pride of workmanship and high performance have virtuous connotations.

A growing number of incentives and circumstances have developed which tend to replace the opportunity for employees to experience intrinsic rewards. Over a period of time, work factors which slow productivity have matured to the point that they now are either tolerated or accepted as a normal part of the industrial work ethic. Rooted deeply in cultural and organizational development, management-employee disagreements in philosophy, objectives and means to these objectives prevent both the managements and employees from realizing their output potentials. On one hand, managements are faced with creeping system anomalies, accompanied by a need to devote an increasing amount of attention to ways to motivate employees and increase output. On the other hand, a "that's not my job" attitude, which is manifested in many forms, is commonplace among the work force. For example, someone has joked that in some plants narrow definition of jobs has progressed to the point that it takes three people to change light bulbs— one for carrying the lights, one for holding the ladder, and one for screwing them in. In another instance, the job definition for machine maintenance calls for a mechanic to make the necessary adjustments, and a second employee to carry the tools. Unproductive waiting and attendant idleness factors have grown to enormous proportion in some plants.

The "not supposed to" comportment is also well enlaced among white collar workers. For example, during slow periods, some supervisors feel that they must "make work" for their secretaries, rather than making them available to help others who have work backlogs. Narrow job descriptions and restrictive notions about jobs not only contribute to boredom, but restrict output as well. A language of lethargy and limits has crept into use at all levels of the work force. Without fully realizing the significance, expressions such as these are excuses for inaction.

1. It's not in our budget.
2. We tried that before and it will not work.
3. The company is simply not ready for that.
4. It's too difficult to administer.

5. It doesn't conform to our policy.
6. It's a good idea, but the time isn't right.
7. It's too risky—they'll never buy it.
8. That's not our problem here.
9. We're doing alright, don't muddy the water.
10. It will take further investigation.
11. That sounds too good, there must be something wrong—research it further.
12. We can't take the chance.
13. You 'wanta' what?!!; don't be ridiculous!!
14. I don't have time to discuss that now.
15. Our schedule won't permit it.
16. You're obsoleting half our inventory!

The Service Ethic

Another aspect of the work ethic is *service.* Among the attributes suggested in their book, *In Search of Excellence,* Peters and Waterman suggested that staying close to the customer is an important virtue. This idea applies as much to service organizations and businesses which deal directly with the public as it does to large industry. There is substantial evidence that those service companies, agencies and businesses that have prompt, courteous and patient service will enjoy more long-term business success than those which manifest nonchalant attitudes about customer feelings. That these principles are understood by the managements is not widely evidenced. On the contrary, from department stores to service stations, and from restaurants to utility companies, customers face indifference instead of genuine customer orientation and commitment to service excellence.

It is not unusual to shop in a major department store and be unable to find assistance; neither is it rare to have difficulty in getting an error in a bank statement removed from the computer; it is also not uncommon to be placed on hold by a company employee while he or she investigates an overcharge, but either does not return to the phone or delays until the line has been disconnected.

While general societal values probably play an important role in this matter, some of the problem must be attributed to priorities established by the management which govern the orientation, attitudes and skill levels of the employees.

The U.S. is becoming even more a service oriented economy. Data from the Department of Labor and other sources indicate an expansive

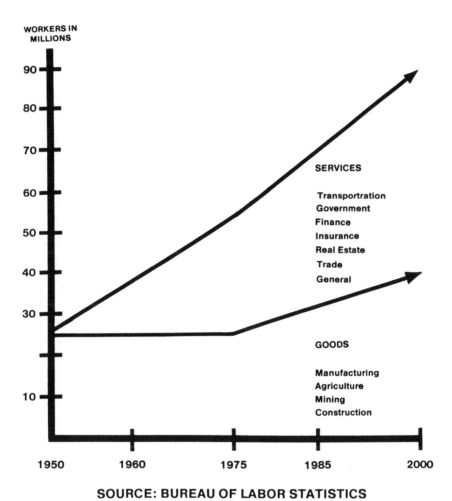

WORKERS IN
MILLIONS

SERVICES

Transportration
Government
Finance
Insurance
Real Estate
Trade
General

GOODS

Manufacturing
Agriculture
Mining
Construction

1950   1960   1975   1985   2000

SOURCE: BUREAU OF LABOR STATISTICS

FIGURE IV-2.   CURRENT AND PREDICTED TYPES OF EMPLOYMENT

trend of service type organizations and businesses in relation to goods producing industries. This pattern is illustrated in Figure IV-2. With the expected growth of service oriented businesses, fair and genial treatment of customers and timely responses to their needs will undoubtedly become increasingly important factors in demonstrating productivity improvement in the service sector. Allegiance to the old adage "the customer is always right" is still found to have merit by those who strive hard to practice it.

Employee Needs and Interests

It is through work that talents and abilities are applied. It is no coincidence that people who get the greatest satisfaction from their work are also the best producers, the most service-oriented, the best adjusted workers, and the most cooperative. However, employees who do adequate work may have the potential to do exceptional work, but are motivated to perform at the lower level.

In a world of rapidly changing social values, many workers today are putting job satisfaction ahead of job performance. They want to work at something they believe in. They respond more to their own inner feelings than to the requirements of the job. Employees tend to think in terms of themselves and their families, while employers are more concerned with the problems of the business—more productivity, greater efficiency and increased profits. Managements set the tone, establish policies and make the decisions in terms of *company* values. Employees make decisions in terms of *personal* values. In this era when people are more self indulging and assertive, this contradiction creates a conflict in which only the wisest of managers can redirect energies to meet productivity improvement goals. When singled out for earned recognition, and invited to increase their contributions, workers frequently will respond with renewed interest and cooperativeness. Employees want to feel that what they do is worthwhile and appreciated—this principle applies from the CEO to the custodian.

No one is immune to a sincerely kind word, a simple expression of warm recognition and genuine appreciation. The manager and supervisor who understands this principle is on his road to keeping high performers, developing new ones, and maintaining increasingly higher employee loyalty and productivity.

Industry and Society Must Share the Responsibility

An often heard modern day cliché is, "workers should work smarter not harder." There may be good reason to question the validity of this statement. Reports from the Department of Labor indicate a shorter work week and increasing absenteeism in the midst of productivity difficulties. Studies also indicate that white-collar employees (which includes the management) waste more time than blue-collar workers. All this leads to the question of who should be working both smarter *and* harder. Conventional wisdom says that the boss' efforts and performance largely predetermine those of subordinate employees. Also, authorities agree that 80 to 85% of quality related problems are controllable by the management.

An unanswered question, central to the productivity improvement issue, is: Can managements by means of internal policies, improvements in the quality of work life and styles of leadership, etc., provide sufficient stimuli, motivation and direction to supercede or cancel the effects of those external societal values and governmental constraints which oppose productivity and quality improvement? If the answer is yes, then the job of transforming a company which has not modernized and has fallen behind competition should be easier than one in which externally formed predilections of employees must also be reshaped or fused with new internal company changes. If the answer to the question is no, the job of molding company culture to one most favorable to quality and productivity improvement, will be both complex and time-consuming under the shackles of exterior forces.

Employees and managers are constituents of the community where they work, and bring personal traits to the job which have been learned from other "institutions." Many of these values are not only well established, but play a pivotal role in whether or not and how much retraining and behavioral change are necessary before effectiveness can be maximized. Perhaps a more descriptive distribution of the responsibility for productivity improvement should be as shown in Figure IV-3.

Society and Culturally Based Value Systems	Worker Controllable on the job	Management Controllable on the job
15%	15%	70%

FIGURE IV-3. ACCOUNTABILITY FOR QUALITY AND PRODUCTIVITY

The four major institutions which should carry some of the responsibility for productivity improvement are education, family, religious and political. Efforts to improve productivity and quality should be undergirded by a broad based sense of integrity, trust, appreciation of quality, and pride in ability and achievement. Trust between individuals and groups needs to be restored; educators need to exemplify "noble" values and teach subjects that will make high standards and productivity viable concerns and goals of students; families need to reward honesty, high standards, cooperation and trust. The church should work harder to characterize, dignify and set examples of integrity, charity and high moral conduct; and finally the time has come for politicians to find ways to shed the stereotypes and images of distrust that exist about their roles, and to demonstrate honesty, efficiency and competence in public service. These factors affect the community quality and productivity ethic and are longevous foundation blocks for company progress. Values learned from these sources have a profound effect on the ease with which a management can manage and control resources within the boundaries of a plant. While many "islands of excellence" can be found among industries across the land, this challenge could be made less formidable with a higher national productivity and quality ethic.

Employee Absenteeism: A Growing Concern

Absenteeism in the U.S. is also a growing concern of industrial managers and supervisors. Department of Labor Statistics indicate that approximately 80 million hours are lost per week due to worker absenteeism, many of which are classified as unwarranted. During a typical work week about 5 million workers are absent for an entire week, of which more than 2 million receive pay.

While the major cause of absenteeism is illness, a large percent is attributed to other causes. Uninteresting and unrewarding work, conflicts among peers and with supervisors, liberal absentee policies, or lenient compliances with policies, increased stress, alcoholism and drug abuse, problems of transportation and child care, personal business, weather conditions and low quality of work life are also influential factors. Employers report that non-attendance is most common among young workers, and those with less than one year with the firm. Results of surveys also indicate that young people are generally less satisfied with their jobs and change places of employment more frequently than middle aged employees.

In comparing absenteeism of blue-collar employees (essentially direct personnel) with those in white-collar jobs (largely indirect personnel), a higher incidence is reported among blue-collar employees, although the gap is reportedly closing. This does not mean that blue-collar absenteeism is decreasing; absenteeism among white-collar employees is on the increase. Effects of absenteeism among the ranks of indirect personnel are usually less visible than those in direct activities.

Unfinished work left by an absent indirect employee is either "absorbed" by coworkers, or projects are postponed until the employee returns to work. In fact, the impact of an absent white-collar employee in terms of specific lack of accomplishment is often undetectable (secretaries are usually among the exceptions).

More attention historically has been focused on the attendance of front line workers. In some plants, part-time employees have to be brought in to keep production going because so many workers are absent on Fridays and Mondays. Blue-collar absenteeism is reportedly as much as 15 to 20 percent on these days. The slogan "Thank God it's Friday" and the calendar illustrated in Figure IV-4, even though they are conveyed in a joking manner, seem to reflect some truth about cultural attitudes about work.

Can Absenteeism Be Reduced?

A variety of techniques ranging from the more indirect means of making the job more enjoyable to outright threats and punitive measures are being tried in efforts to reduce unwarranted employee absenteeism. In order for an organization to effectively deal with this issue, it should be viewed as a condition which *can* be improved. In fact, there is mounting evidence that it can. Some companies have tended to accept absenteeism as merely a period through which general industry is moving, and have made no concerted effort to reduce it. Meanwhile, it has steadily increased in many cases. Some people stay away from the job because they feel that their work is not important to the company. Others have pressing personal needs. Others have moonlighting activities that interfere with their principal jobs. Still others wish to use up unused sick leave. Also, more than ever before, Americans are placing a higher value on their free time and recreational activities.

Recognizing the high cost of absenteeism, some companies are attempting to improve the quality of work life as a hedge. Direct efforts include financial incentives, improved working conditions, counseling aids to employees who have personal problems and a more employee oriented style of leadership. Most find that improvement in these areas also manifests improvement in the related areas of workmanship, personal responsibility and productivity. Other methods used for various purposes, but which have a salutary effect on absenteeism include job enrichment, flexible working hours and participative decision making.

Indications are that the customary legalistic and punitive methods of controlling absenteeism are not as effective in the long run as the positive incentives previously mentioned. Employees who are dissatisfied

FIGURE IV-4.   A DAILY CALENDAR

MONDAY	TUESDAY	WEDNESDAY	THURSDAY	FRIDAY
DON'T SPEAK TO ME!	GOD, GET ME THROUGH THIS DAY!	PLEASE, LET ME DIE!	LIFE SLOWLY SEEPS BACK INTO MY BOD...	ANTICIPATION
8-4214	SR706	5-3946-A	8-4214	42X-50
SR706	1-4631	8X-306	1-4631	SR-706
SR706	SR-700	7R-105	42X-23-A	3-3009
42X-23	5-3946	42X-50	6-4081	7-6079
6-4081				

106

with their jobs will find ways of using accrued time for sick leave if policies controlling this benefit are loosely administered, and if incentives for non-work are greater than those at the job. Several formal ways in which companies are able to reduce absenteeism are described as follows.

Counselling is used by the employer to let employees know how important attendance is to the company and make sure they understand that attendance is seriously considered in raises and performance reviews. *Recognition* should be given to employees who report to work everyday. One supervisor reduced absenteeism in his division by 40 percent by making notes of perfect attendance records every six months for personnel files and then sending copies to the employees in question.

Giving rewards for good attendance is another method used to reduce absenteeism. Rewards can be in the form of a bonus or an honorary banquet, etc., at the end of a period. Companies have experienced substantial decreases in total sick leave expenses over the previous year by using various reward techniques. Some companies are employing both positive (prevention) and negative (corrective action) techniques to check absenteeism. For example, a California firm reduced absenteeism by 20% by giving bonuses for perfect attendance and taking standard corrective action with employees who are frequently absent. The key to the program is pay for attendance and not for absences. Employees are credited, depending on the length of service for each month of perfect attendance. Corrective action of the serious offenders is a progressive technique with an arrangement for an employee to take a leave of absence to work out personal problems. Dismissal is the final resort.

Another approach is the no-fault policy which also can be effective in reducing absenteeism. Under this procedure, management recognizes the inevitability of an occasional absence, and, avoids the tendency to blame the employee for not coming to work. This approach does not recognize any difference between excused or unexcused absences, which removes the burden of having to prove the legitimacy of an absence. With this approach, each absence is recorded as one occurrence. One absence is recorded for an employee regardless of whether he or she is absent for one day or continuously for more than one day. If a person is absent on Wednesday and Friday, for example, he or she is charged with two absences. Also, by recording absences this way, the chronic offender who has a larger number of single day absences is penalized more heavily. Some no-fault approaches also take into account absences that are less than one day where employees do not call in.

Another method that some organizations use to reduce the absenteeism rate is the sick leave bank policy approach. This procedure establishes a leave bank against which employees can draw, in the event that they need time off.

Perhaps the most effective long–term deterrent to unwarranted absenteeism, which is controllable on the premises of the company, is to establish and maintain strong incentives in the company for people to go to work. Among other considerations, these relate to teamwork, good leadership and employee involvement in creative roles. (This subject is further discussed in Chapter 7). Absenteeism is an ongoing and sizeable undertaking when there are so many incentives or influences outside the job that are uncontrollable by the management. Absenteeism due to alcohol and drug use, alone, result in annual losses of productivity of approximately 4.9 billion dollars.[5]

Union Influences

Unions historically have played very influential roles in American industry. The union movement thrived amidst growth of scientific management early in the 20th century, and has since gained strength where leadership styles embraced scientific approaches at the expense of employee interests and needs. Historically, unions derived their strength from a polarized industrial culture. Unions originated out of controversy and became self-perpetuating under adverse conditions. The more aloof and remote that managements have become, the more it seems necessary for workers to band together to protect themselves against the "strategies" of management. As a result, unions have been both blessed and damned by various segments of society.

Although unions have grown to mean other things, one fundamental purpose is employee protection against unfair practices. These are usually associated with seniority rights, salary increases and promotions, performance expectations, safety, and so forth. In today's complex business environment, definition of what is fair or unfair, however, is often not a simple matter, and may be perceived differently by management and employees.

In some companies where unions have been strong and played an important part in the operation of the company, it is difficult for union officials to develop a trust for managements. If any degree of harmony is achieved, it is often viewed with suspicion by union leaders. Where mature unions exist, cooperation tends to be regarded as a sign of weakness. In companies where a history of management/union problems exist, they are usually accompanied by a covert, if not overt, "defensive" attitude in both labor and management. Conflict seems to be both a strategy and a result which directs energies toward non-productive activities instead of teamwork and efficiency. Even with a turnabout in management practices, union influences are difficult if not impossible to dismiss. A management may make a sincere effort to enrich employees jobs and enhance conditions that lead to long-term security of employees, but be shackled by union resistance. Ironically, long-term job security is a principal goal of unions.

Once a union has become well entrenched in a company, several situations generally emerge. In companies, where strong unions exist (where there is a distinct adversary relationship between the management and employees), a sort of paralysis exists which stifles *improvement* creativity. Employees can be very creative, but in activities that oppose improvement. Teamwork means that all players are pulling together for a common purpose in the same direction. Anything short of this restrains progress of the team.

Efforts by managements to devise ways to improve teamwork with employees is viewed by some unions as another way of "conning" employees. There is much hesitation in some union plants to condone participation, or for that matter, any other management improvised method of achieving teamwork. Unions tend to be more comfortable in their roles as adversaries because they are not "supposed" to cooperate with management. Anything that threatens the "us and them" dichotomy becomes suspect.

As a management/union relationship reaches full maturity, management becomes conditioned to working with unions. This is an obvious conclusion if a company is to survive. However, some companies are so geared to this dual system (people and paperwork needed solely for union activities together with long standing provincial attitudes by both sides) that there is some doubt that companies could survive long without a union. This process is not without unproductive costs; time and energy are directed toward handling grievances, grievance avoidances, arbitration, strikes, threats of strikes, and destructive rivalry. Long-term effects are amplified by growing interdependence in the decision making process. Managements are often forced to use their creative skills in working with unions rather than setting up ways to achieve higher productivity levels.

Quality attitudes and workmanship equal to those found in Japan are proclaimed by union members. Likewise, managements are heard making statements about their company's ability to produce products of unmatched value. Yet, in an adversarial setting there is proclivity to act in ways that are known to be contrary to improvement, efficiency and quality effectiveness. Where suspicion, fear and combative attitudes are normal parts of the work environment, neither high productivity, nor efficient quality will likely be found. Well-developed negative attitudes between management and worker will not only take their toll on productivity, but will perpetuate an environment which opposes cooperation.

In companies where management and labor have become adversaries, considerably more work needs to be accomplished to untie managements hands so that they can be more flexible in making worker assignments, and providing employees greater opportunity to become involved in the more thinking roles of the work place. Cross training and job enrichment are effective hedges against boredom. Ironically, restrictive job classifications which have high priority in most union contracts, reduce flexibility and increase boredom. In most cases, union wage scales are sufficiently high that one's job classification should not preclude reasonable job enlargement or flexibility in assigning work. Employee apathy, low quality and concomitant boredom are high prices to pay for rigid doctrine.

Local union leaders usually prefer that management initiate ideas for change, etc. One union leader pointed out that unions are so accustomed to the company acting and unions reacting that it helps tremendously if management launches the first cooperative steps. Union leaders point out that they do not want to block cooperation; rather, they have been trained as counterpunchers.

Unions are experiencing change, however, that will influence their approaches. In many companies today unions are seen as the bad guy fighting against the company. Union leaders are beginning to understand that they must work together with a company for the good of both, and will probably be closer to companies than they have been in the past. Douglas Fraser, former President of the UAW, asserted that, "We are realists. We understand that bargaining doesn't go on in a vacuum. You have to face the economic realities."[6] Lane Kirkland, president of the AFL-CIO exclaimed, "We can survive adverse public opinion. But we cannot long survive the erosion of support for programs and policies on the part of the membership."[7]

The character of management-union roles is also undergoing change. The Japanese have showed both managements and employees it *is* possible to cooperatively unite efforts to make business successful, and changes taking place in U.S. society are fueling change in unions. A growing spirit of cooperation between management and labor is developing, because both sides have begun to understand their own vulnerabilities, and appreciate each others strengths. Both have been hurt by foreign penetration in markets that have been traditionally American. Unions have won short-range battles, but have lost wars;

corporate executives have seen "scientific management" fail in its attempts to improve productivity; and many employees have become wary of both their employers and their unions.

A cooperative union-management relationship fulfills two criteria. It allows employees to enrich their work life experiences, and it requires that the company and union representatives spend as much time nurturing a new way of relating to one another as they do resolving conflicts—the objective is to build a new cooperative freeway, not merely to repave an old adversarial road.

Unions May Not Be Necessary

The majority of companies which now have unions, at some previous time practiced policies and leadership styles which failed to recognize human interests and needs. An often heard cliché is "if employees develop a serious interest in unions the company probably deserves one." This message implies that if employees are treated properly, they will not have the need or desire for a union.

Managers/supervisors in a non-union company who practice unfair tactics and develop coercive or indifferent attitudes will eventually become ineffectual; and the company may lose its ability to pacify employees and arrest grievances. The managements must be able to adequately answer employee questions with something beyond solace; otherwise, employees will seek grith in a union. People who otherwise would not consider a union, can be converted in a climate characterized by unfairness, inconsistency and distrust.

Non-union companies are working harder than they once did to ensure that employees are treated fairly. Big business in general, is taking this subject much more seriously than it has in the past. Personnel departments are increasingly responding to employee questions about human relations and how *they* are being managed. Approximately 30% of all non-union companies employ some kind of formal grievance procedure.

On balance, employees in *well managed* non-union companies have little desire to have a union speak in their behalf. Only the uninformed or those with ulterior motives could honestly say otherwise. In a well managed non-union company, when disputes arise, the managements busy themselves at finding solutions to the problems. A worker who believes his problems are being properly handled does not need a second or third party intervention.

Companies which are dedicated to union avoidance recognize that management practices that are conducive to union organization also are counter productive in meeting company goals. Factors that build teamwork among workers and respect for the management tend to obviate sentiments toward forming a union. Some managements have learned that efforts to maintain an atmosphere of cooperation and creative expression pays back manifold dividends in performance and a better business posture. Can one legitimately infer from this that non-union companies do not have management/employee problems?—hardly. In American industrial culture, the question is not how to eliminate management/worker conflict. Conflict is an inherent feature of the free enterprise philosophy. The question is how best to deal with disagreement to produce the best results.

There is a growing army of attorneys and labor-relations consultants who make no secret of their goal to keep unions out of non-union companies. Employers invest heavily in educating their executives on modern anti-union techniques. American Bar Association officials estimate that about 500 of the 12,000 lawyers in their labor-relations section 9, represent employers. Many of these management lawyers, joined by employer associations, sponsor regular anti-union seminars all over the country.

Irrespective of an individual company's stand on unions, there does appear to be a positive correlation between the avoidance of unions and effective competition for a good market share. The reason is not so much that a company has or does not have a union; it is because the management policies and practices that make unions unnecessary produce the best results. Managements of successful companies with unions have rallied their unions around company missions and have promulgated a cooperative environment.

Grievances and their processes in both union and non-union companies take their toll on the effectiveness with which output goals are reached. The time directly spent on grievance handling as well as the indirect diversion of thought away from productive work during the build-up and disposition of grievances can incur great amounts of time and energy, much of which otherwise could be devoted to improving productivity. A strong commitment should be made by a company— both union and non-union—to promote and exercise those leadership and management strategies that will minimize grievances and hold down destructive conflict. Formal mechanisms for handling grievances are necessary in both union and non-union companies. Lack of policies and procedures in this area will add to the confusion and cause employee/ management disagreements to escalate into covert situations that become even more troublesome.

There are several principal reasons given as to why employees desire to form or keep a union, but pay hikes, which many believe to be the prime reason does not hold a high place on the priority list. The real reasons that employees most often cite are as follows:

1. Inconsistent policies and management practices.
2. Arbitrary and abusive supervision.
3. Poorly designed benefit packages.
4. Biased promotion policies.
5. Unfair discipline.
6. Failure of management to listen, or pay attention to employees opinions and sentiments.
7. Poor working conditions.
8. Poor general communications between management and employees.

It follows that companies without unions which reportedly do well utilize practices that deal effectively with the aforementioned subjects. Major thrusts of these efforts are in the following areas.

1. *Promotion from Within.* Only when the company is in a rapid growth pattern or has unique requirements for people will the company pass up the opportunity to promote from within.

2. *Merit Increases.* These companies are dedicated to having well planned and executed salary review procedures and reward high performance, work completed on schedule, and high quality with increased scope of work and attendant salary increase.

3. *Management Empathy.* Another attribute for which employees seem to hold high esteem is the assurance that management cares about them. This feeling can be conveyed in a number of ways. One technique used is for top management to meet directly and regularly with employees. Quality circles is another technique used with widespread acceptance to demonstrate management sensitivity to employees' abilities and desires. Any method to achieve management involvement at all levels in the hierarchy as well as worker participation is fundamental to building teamwork. When employees feel that their efforts are appreciated through overt recognition, they do not think about organizing a union; they devote their energies to making the company a better place to work and to making it more profitable.

4. *A Listening Environment.* Someone has said that the traditional

manager/supervisor can be characterized as having a mouth but no ears. One of the first principles of leadership is to learn the art of listening. Many a wrong decision has been made by not *hearing* what has been said. Management empathy, described previously, will have little meaning in a non-listening atmosphere. Open door policies, quality circles and rap sessions are techniques used to create and develop listening environments. These have been met with varied successes as discussed in other sections.

5. *Flexibility.* Some companies have moved more and more to an honor system in which workers can come and go according to the work schedule as *they* desire. Some have allowed both flexible working hours and shifts, with removal of time clocks, believing that the company will reap greater returns through employee loyalty generated from these features, than the inconveniences occasioned by having to manage these fluid situations.

6. *Job Security.* One of the most difficult tasks which confronts managements today is maintaining a stable and well balanced work force through business cycles of peaks and valleys. Cycles of prosperity and recession are much sharper and are felt much more by some industries than others. Some business cycles are highly correlated with national and international economics. Still, business strategies and the way companies are managed can markedly influence both the frequency and amplitude of a company's down cycle.

A downward trend is usually accompanied by past short-term thinking on the part of company strategists. The compulsion is to sell as much as possible while business is good; however, there is usually a secondary effect. When business is good, there is danger of creeping disregard for internal factors of efficiency and the efficacy with which assignments are being carried out. Dependency on sales subtly dominates management's thinking. Meanwhile, new competitors enter the market, or former competitors suddenly become very effective at meeting customers' demand of quality, price and schedule.

Companies that have been successful at avoiding layoff situations are found to have good management-employee relations. Steady employment, good business posture, quality prone culture, and effective employee relations are positively correlated. In companies which possess these characteristics, employees are more willing to take a leave of absence without pay, or work a shorter week to avoid a layoff during slow market conditions.

Companies which must resort to layoff usually have exhausted all other immediate options because layoffs have serious cost and other penalties. The company is encumbered with unemployment compensation, severance pay, health and other benefit costs, administrative and legal costs, and new worker orientation and training. Even more serious, a layoff often results in severe operational disadvantages. Good people relocate to more "stable" companies, leaving the "others" to run the business. Morale always suffers in one form or another. Companies develop a reputation for poor employee relations; if the company is non-union, a layoff can set the tone for union organization.

Most employees will reward a company with their loyalty and good performance if they believe the company is founded on solid principles and led by an effective management, especially if this belief can be translated into lasting employment.

CHAPTER V

A Question of Competence

Virtually every factor that is associated with productivity improvement is correlated with education and training. At the very heart of the productivity issue is the need for employees and management alike to stay informed about quality and other matters affecting productivity. From making the best choices when hiring people, to broadening the general skills of personnel, achieving adequate competency in employees is a critical objective. Further, creating a sense of awareness in top executives about the importance of quality, and instilling quality values in first line supervision, should rank high on a company's priority list, especially if productivity improvement is the objective.

This subject as it relates to the complete picture of productivity has not been addressed well in the United States. This chapter is a macro treatment of education and training, and how these factors influence productivity. It is hoped that a discussion of some of the issues that relate to this subject will trigger a greater commitment toward improvement, and an introspection into areas that need change, with the outcome that new ideas for improvement will be generated.

Education Paradoxes and Mismatches

No greater a foundation for the economic health of a country can be found than in the education of its people. Knowledge is a precious resource and a better educated work force—at every level of the productive process—is a prerequisite for future economic vitality. Education carries *long-term* as well as short-term implications to productivity improvement. Quality values (attitudes about workmanship and performing work with diligence and accuracy) are learned early. While no research has been conducted to prove this statement, a high correlation is believed to exist between the quality of education and long-term productivity gain.

Concern continues to be expressed that the United States is falling behind other countries in providing the necessary quality and the proper kind of eduction for its citizenry. For example, the U.S. is faced with a growing shortage of scientific and vocational skills that are in high demand and essential to improving the overall effectiveness with which products are produced and marketed. One of Westinghouse's presidents, Thomas J. Murrin, pointed out that: "While Americans are among the most educated people in the world, they are not as well trained, in many cases, as the workers of our foreign competitors."[1] More and more college graduates are taking jobs for which they had insufficient training. Moreover, attention has been directed toward the need for qualified people in high technology while the need for skills in "low" technology jobs is equally great. Estimates from the U.S. Bureau of Labor Statistics indicate that job growth over the next decade will include and perhaps even favor low-skilled, service and clerical jobs. The number of new jobs for custodians, cashiers and secretaries, for example, will be as great if not greater than the number of new jobs for computer operators, computer system analysts and electrical engineers.

Engineers Shortage A 1983 study conducted by the American Electronics Association indicated a severe shortage of electrical and computer science engineers. It concluded further that there will be a 113,406 shortage generated over the next five years.[2] If the U.S. is to aspire to world technological leadership, it must be willing to assign the financial and other resources necessary to close the gap between anticipated jobs and the available kind of expertise needed for these jobs. This will take a longer range look at the educational process. During the past decade, and until only recently, there has been a move away from technical fields by many students in U.S. schools. Compared to other countries which are competing for high technology dominance, the U.S. finds itself lagging in the number of graduates in technical fields such as engineering.

In the U.S., choices of professional fields are largely influenced by political, social, and economic forces and there is usually a lag between the need for certain degrees and enrollments to meet this need. While the Government essentially plays a nondirective role in educational policies in the U.S., it is more actively involved in this matter in countries like Russia and Japan. Russia graduates approximately 250,000 engineers per year, a five to one ratio with the U.S. Japan graduates about twice the number of engineers as the U.S. does—even though Japan has only half its population. While Soviet engineers are engaged in weaponry, Japanese engineers concentrate on industrial initiatives.[3]

The Japanese are educating their population for competition in the economic arena for the 1990s and beyond. Studies continue to indicate that approximately 95% of all Japanese teenagers graduate from high school, compared to only about 75% in the U.S. Surveys show, also, that particularly in math and science, the mean achievement levels of Japanese school children are the highest in the world and considerably above those in the U.S.

National Status and Standards The aforementioned educational orientation is coupled with a broader education problem in the U.S. In a nationwide study on the excellence of education, a team commissioned by the Department of Education concluded that educational standards are far below what they should be. The commission recommended the following:

• Restoring the value of grades, ending social promotion, and using standardized tests to measure achievement.

• Requiring high school graduates to complete four years of english, three each of social studies, mathematics, and science, and one-half year of computer science.

• Raising college admission standards and including two years of foreign language.

• Imposing tougher standards for teachers colleges, study of academic subjects instead of educational methodology.

• Making basic changes in teacher salary and recognition practices.

• Reducing the number of high school electives and assigning more homework.[4]

Some believe the decline in educational standards is correlated with ineffective teaching and insufficient funding. Others believe that low teachers' salaries is a key factor. According to the American Federation of Teachers, the national average is $15,000 per year compared to an $18,000 to $22,000 per year starting salary of graduates with comparable education.[5] An employee with a new bachelor of science degree in most fields of engineering can choose from multiple offers starting at over $20,000 and sometimes as high as $32,000. Universities can afford to pay an assistant professor with a new Ph.D. about $24,000, on an average, for a nine-month year. Since it takes up to six more years in school and in penury to earn the Ph.D., the question is being asked, why bother?

The challenge to Americans is to strive for excellence—a focus on basic courses of study, quality teaching and meaningful standards of achievement. Although the cost could be high, it is more significant that such a change will require deep personal commitment and involvement by parents, and public officials. It will mean tough decision making by some who have become satisfied, and a deeper dedication to improvement by others.

Education is on the move to the front burner in the U.S., but a real turnaround will be seen only through an alliance between educators, business and industry, and community leadership.

Curricula Orientation Vs. Need

Engineering schools began to accentuate theoretical disciplines at the expense of applied content in undergraduate curricula after World War II. During the war, top-notch scientists turned their attention to technology with such success that engineers became infatuated with innovation and research. Engineering schools began to emphasize abstract concepts and dropped or de-emphasized practical subjects that dealt with how to improve the value of products and services. Some engineering programs moved almost entirely away from hands-on activities. In addition to ignoring applied technology, J. Juran pointed out that "academia has remained mostly aloof from quality and productivity education, except in the areas of statistical methodology."[6] Statistics has been decidedly helpful but minor in importance compared to the full spectrum of need. While there are exceptions, academia has essentially ignored subjects which are now recognized as fundamental to industrial health.

Baccalaureate degrees in engineering typically require from 140 to 148 semester units for graduation. Rapid growth in all areas of technology has increased the complexity of controlling the balance of subjects within this parameter. Some universities have increased the number of units required for engineering degrees in order to better address the expansive needs. Still, more and more people who hire young engineers believe a better balance of subjects is needed to properly deal with the complex technological issues facing modern industry.

Curricula for business as well as engineering graduates lack courses in applied fields, human relations, quality, and productivity disciplines. Cartin concluded, for example, "In interviews of recent college graduates, it is clear that business and engineering graduates have no understanding of product quality concepts and only a vague notion of the role of the employee in either quality or productivity improvement."[7]

119

These educational issues have a number of implications, and have given rise to other situations which have evolved over the past several decades.

Engineering and business graduates find themselves in jobs outside the specialized disciplines for which they have been educated. Some reports set this level as high as 50%. Graduates with liberal arts degrees should expect to need additional training, since general education is the objective, not employment per se; however, programs such as business and engineering which are intended to put people to work, should be more successful at addressing community needs. The disparity between curriculum content and industry's needs for certain disciplines has caused an increasing number of companies to assume responsibility for the education or re-education of their employees. The slogan "do it right the first time," though usually associated with corporate environments, apparently also has relevance in the context of higher education.

In-house industrial training and outside seminars on the subjects of quality, productivity, sales, leadership and even technical matters are a multi-billion dollar business in the U.S. The need for re-education, or extended education is manifested in a number of forms.

1. Quality engineers with theoretical bents or statistical backgrounds, who have engineering or business degrees attempt to "sell" process control concepts to production line supervisors and operators, many of whom have already been intimidated by the bell curve, and standard deviation, etc.

2. Industrial engineers, having been educated in operations research, queuing theory etc., attempt to set standards, and implement changes in production departments where the cultural climate is not receptive to such actions.

3. Comptrollers with financial backgrounds structure cost accounting systems and report costs in conventional ways, while quality managements attempt to draw their attention and enlist their cooperation to more effectively report *quality* costs (A gnawing communication gap tends to exist between finance and quality organizations).

4. Sales and marketing engineers find themselves comforting disgruntled customers, without the technical know-how to help a customer out of his predicament.

5. Employees, (even college graduates) frequently have difficulty in writing good proposals, specifications, or even effective business letters,

but find themselves in positions where these are critical to success.

6. Purchasing agents usually know where to find the lowest price for goods and services, but are less knowledgeable about quality and the need to balance it with other priorities.

7. Plant managers and other top officials tend to be polished in human relations, have MBA's, or similar advanced degrees, but indirectly resist involvement with their people. They tend to press on for higher output, at the expense of long-term quality factors, and downplay the lasting importance of their interaction with employees.

Curricula Revision in the Traditional University

People who "manage" curricula in all sectors of education need to be more aligned with real needs of the country. Donald N. Frey, C.E.O. for the Bell and Howell Company, urged that our curriculum planners must recognize that neither traditional vocational education nor liberal arts programs are providing the kind of career preparation students need for the jobs of the future. Similarly, the typical liberal education must go beyond arts and letters. If students are to develop job-related skills, courses in computer science, productivity, electronics, and so forth, will have to be required.[8] Albeit technology has become an important part of general education, this has not been appreciably manifested in college curricula.

In university systems, curricula revision, and the ratio of liberal arts courses to technical courses, etc. are largely accomplished via the democratic process; changes are drawn up and approved by committees at various levels of academia. While this practice is ideal in principal, it has certain drawbacks. In most institutions, the preponderance of voting faculty are found in liberal arts disciplines, with the result that the technical content of programs is often forced onto the back burner even in technical programs. Administrators of many engineering and technology programs continuously struggle to hold on to sufficient technical content in their curricula.

Another factor which can be a great boon to curriculum improvement, or place restrictions on progress is *accreditation.* Curriculum parameters which are imposed on university programs by accrediting agencies, together with the judgment of those assessing a program against accreditation criteria, represent a target for improvement for weak programs. On the other hand, being accredited without questioning the balance of subjects which led to the accreditation, may not be in the best interest of a program. Accrediting teams can usually give very important advice, but be so bound by custom that important changes are not recommended. For example, courses in reliability, quality engineering and nondestructive testing should be encouraged, but few can be found in engineering curricula. *Having* an accredited program should never take precedence over *what* is being accredited. Professional accreditation standards are indeed important, but they need to change with the need for change. That the standards applied by regional accrediting agencies are applied uniformly, and keep educational standards high, also need greater assurance.

On the other hand, professional accreditation boards, such as the Accreditation Board for Engineering and Technology programs (ABET), are vitally important to the long-term health and stability of the professions. Such agencies are needed to slow the momentum and offset the proclivity of liberal arts academia to legislate outcomes of curricular content of professional programs.

Higher Education and Industry: Some Common Characteristics

College and university systems are not unlike corporations, in dealing with controversy and progress. In both instances, effort is directed toward winning over some controversy, or cavilling about something unorthodox or novel. In industry, this has the effect of siphoning energies that should be directed toward effectively meeting customer requirements. In higher education, a large amount of time is devoted to adversative discussions of policies and administrative issues which have no bearing on improving the quality of education and meeting genuine needs of the community.

Another analogy can be made with regard to *layers* of management. Experts who have studied modern enterprise agree that the most effective firms have been able to prevent excessive growth of management hierarchy. While exceptions can be found, organizational bureaucracy has crept into both industry and public supported institutions. In many instances, organizational units have been created for viable purposes, but have shifted to directly support top officials with questionable results. If an authoritarian style of leadership prevails, individuals and functional units in these positions tend to become lackeys and much of the creativity and productivity that could be otherwise gained is lost in protectionism, blind redundancy, and servitude.

Budgetary control is another example: In both industry and public supported institutions, as organizational or political distance increases between where funds are budgeted and where they are disbursed, two results are likely: (1) unabated bureaucracy will exist and (2) the allocation of pecuniary resources will receive less than evenhanded treatment. These situations tend to be more pronounced in public supported institutions where the profit motif is obscure or nonexistent.

In order for degree programs to be strong, both professors and university administrators need to take more leadership. Many universities appear to have chosen followership over being the kinds of agents for change that will generate productivity. While it is sometimes heard that university professors and equipments they use are behind the state-of-the-art by five years or more, like employees in industry, faculty creativity is frequently hampered by regulations, low budgets, inconsistent application of policies, and awkward and cumbersome paperwork systems.

Professors are viewed with favor by university administrators if they demonstrate excellence in scholarly and creative activities, teaching and community service, and many bring great credit to their universities. Ironically, the systems in which they function also need their expertise, but, the "management/employee" barriers—similar to those found in industry—preclude using faculty talents in this important way. The need for teamwork is as great in public supported institutions as it is in private industry.

A department faculty which knows what is best for its graduates may be shackled by a hierarchy of committees whose members have perspectives and interests which lie in totally different areas. As a result, even proposals which survive the process, have sometimes lost key elements. Where industry exercises its power structure to direct decisions and change, decisions in higher education (at least as they pertain to curriculum matters) are less decisive and inherently longer.

Traditional Vs. Progressive Education

While better methods of dealing with such campus-oriented curriculum matters are being sought, a broader curriculum issue is unfolding. A philosophical rift between traditional educators and those who are more liberally oriented has been developing for several years. Traditionalist educators have held fast to their interpretation of "standards," and wish to apply them across the board, while "progressive" educators have taken the view that experiential learning should count for more than token acknowledgement, and believe that those who desire to extend their education at a later stage of life should be entitled to have "wisdom" count for credit. The implication is that these people should not be subjected to the same classroom rigors as the young (18-24). (The average age of college students is reportedly approximately 27-28 years, with an increasing number of older people desiring to take certain courses, or electing to complete baccaleaurate and even advanced degrees.)

Traditional educators have been so unbending in their ideals and mechanics of teaching, that people in business communities have sought other ways to achieve their degrees. As a result, countless programs (e.g., various external degrees and even new colleges) have sprung up which are attempts to better address the needs of communities. Proponents of these programs argue that conventional curricula are at variance with many educational needs, and that state controlled systems are sluggish in responding to the burgeoning and changing educational needs of the public. Private universities tend to be responsive because their livelihood is based on offerings where student appeal exists, and where high tuitions will be supported.

This entire movement, however, leads one to the fundamental issue of *standards*. Regional accrediting boards now accredit programs that once were considered marginal or even unaccreditable. Questions are being raised. Are concentrated weekend type degree programs, or those which shorten the number of student contact hours compromises of academic standards, or is this simply progress? While pros and cons are being argued, this dilemma has reached industry, as evidenced by different practices being followed on reimbursements of costs for education. Some administrators of reimbursement programs set very tight controls, and will reimburse for tuition and books for certain well-established and recognized programs, while others tend to follow the lead of accrediting bodies; still others seem to be uncertain about the direction they should take.

Many of these concerns can be alleviated by more *bi-directional* involvement between educators and community leaders to break down communication barriers. Past difficulties have probably been caused more by an incongruent communicative *wavelength* problem, than a lack of interest or cooperation. Academia and industrial leaders tend to communicate in different channels, with each giving answers to questions the other did not ask. As a result of educational mismatches, communication breaches, and lack of knowledge about each others strengths, weaknesses and potentials, companies and institutions of higher learning have apparently opted to take independent paths in many cases; companies continue to increase their budgets for sundry educational programs of their own, while educators pursue courses that they believe are best.

Separate Efforts by Industry and Consultants

During the past two decades, for whatever the reasons, many firms drifted away from relying on educational institutions to meet these needs. More and more companies began to assume certain educational responsibilities that historically were left to school systems. This included a considerable amount of advanced research funded by the Government.

Born out of this educational turmoil is a new breed of consultant. Educationally oriented consultants have found this field to be very fertile and lucrative. With the growth in the variety of inputs from this "third party" (which is essentially an attempt to bridge the educational gap that exists between education and industry) the question of efficacy must be raised. How effective is this tripartite attempt to make education and training an effective process? Consultants tend to come and go. While some have been minimally successful at best, others continue to render invaluable services to the industry. But, this is usually at a high price, irrespective of the degree of success. Meanwhile, educational institutions and company initiated educational programs continue to follow separate paths, leading to different outcomes, with both believing they are effective.

This mismatch is further complicated by industry's quest for highly qualified technical personnel. The carrot of higher salaries has made "technically oriented" professors much more vulnerable to the lures of industrial recruiters than they once were. Also, graduates with technical degrees are quickly picked up by industry, given top salaries, leaving only a few potentially good candidates who would opt for the Ph.D. with professorship in mind. For a number of years engineering deans have been admonishing businessmen with the warning: "You are eating your seed corn." Industry seems to work at cross purposes with its *long-term* interests, hiring the best students, the bulk of the graduate students, and sometimes the professors too.[9]

A turnaround is being witnessed, however. There appears to be an increase in the number of companies and universities that are attempting to combine independent resources for the betterment of both. Recently, industry has begun to respond to schools' needs on a scale beyond its usual philanthropy. Corporations are entering into a variety of deals to help the schools: forming consortia to set up and help run advanced research facilities, commissioning research at universities, supporting graduate students and young professors with pay supplements, and providing tenured professors more opportunities to earn money as consultants.

Industrial Training Programs

Education dilemmas will probably be in existence for quite some time. In the meantime, in firms which are committed to having *training* departments, upper managements should sharpen their focus on factors that will improve them.

Senior managements need to make evident their belief that an effective employee development and training program has a cost avoidance significance—not a cost burden. Also, as part of this educational strategy, senior managements need to *organize* so that hidden talents and ideas of employees can be exposed and utilized with effectiveness in the improvement process.

A wave of need for training which has swept across American industry has begun to offset some of the image problems that training departments once encountered, and training departments in some companies are receiving more attention than they once did. If they continue to be supported by the top management and operations managers, at least half of the battle encountered by industrial training directors will have been won. Where this support does not exist, an extraordinary kind of leadership that only a few training directors possess will be needed in order to make training truly effective.

Traditional company training objectives have focused on specific job areas—certifying employees in specific operations or functions, and providing them with job skills to help them be proficient and promotable. However, more training emphasis is needed in company-wide or interdepartmental areas than most companies are devoting. American organizations are characterized as conglomerates of different departments, each having a mission independent of others in the total organization. Knowledge of how departments' activities dovetail with each other in meeting company objectives will reduce the proclivity to unknowingly produce or perpetuate system problems. The additional benefit of providing employees with the job enrichment which originates from this broader understanding is too easily gained and worth too much to ignore. Rivalry and dissension which originate from interdepartmental naivety can be readily converted into constructive creativity and cooperation, through greater understanding of interorganizational aims and concerns.

Building Confidence in Training Functions. Sometimes training departments, like other indirect functions, experience low budgets, frustrations of being understaffed and may even lack credibility with other departments. The continued support that must come from other departments needs to be *earned* by training departments by meeting others' needs for training. Some training managers are unbending about the kind and selection of courses and training they will offer and are reluctant to listen to the department heads they serve. If the training department is organized under the human resources directorate, it owes much of its success to its ability to support and accommodate the needs of other departments. If it has organizational stature, (for example, reporting directly to the vice president of operations) its objectives of service responsibility and active support to manufacturing organizations will more likely be met.

Training departments should take the leadership in areas that involve education and training. Unless an educational value already exists in the company, a certain amount of assertiveness by the training director will be necessary to overcome complacency about education and training. Periodic surveys, are frequently used to expose needs and obtain information about training priorities. This expression of overt interest in other organizations, not only builds confidence and demonstrates real interest in other functions, it also serves as a reminder that other organizations may need certain forms of training.

Training departments often do not enjoy as much professional imagery as do other departments. Training activities are subtly played down and sometimes outright opposed by managers and employees. The value placed on training in such instances ranges from passive acceptance, to being "forced" to attend training sessions. In such a culture, overcoming this condition and making education a viable and important interest to everyone concerned is important, but difficult. In order to redress the situation, involvement and nudging by the top management will be needed. The utilization of people who are proficient at training is always a prerequisite.

Understanding the Importance of Training. Benefits of training are usually not easy to measure. Since part of this subject is covered under prevention in the next chapter, let it suffice here to present three major reasons why training benefits are frequently not understood.

1. The time span between when a person receives initial training, and when better or higher output resulting from such training takes place, may be longer than expected. This makes it more difficult to attribute better performance to earlier training.

2. If training is done well, segments of that knowledge are "absorbed" into the jobs. While there may not be startling or immediate changes in behavior or performance, small changes are inevitable. Such intangible factors are sometimes more important than those which can be readily observed or measured.

3. Training departments need to do a better job of communicating and selling the importance and scope of training to operations managers

and senior managements.

To achieve the status and recognition that training departments deserve, they need to (1) demonstrate quantitatively their results in terms of economic payback of return on investment; (2) overcome the image that they are an adjunct personnel function; and (3) strengthen their position as a management function with both short-term and long-term payback.

If managed effectively, training can contribute greatly to increased productivity and organizational effectiveness. The long-term efficacy of the training department hinges on its ability to earn the respect of the departments which need this service, and on senior managements' comprehending the benefits of training and giving their active support.

Training departments may have to recommend and sell the kind of training that will produce the desired results in both the management and workers, while at the same time, generate confidence among operations managers. This can be a formidable task. In any case, such efforts, whether they are accomplished by internal specialists or outside consultants, should focus on the real needs of the company.

Training Should Address Relevant Issues

Achieving quality mindedness in every employee and an understanding of how best to meet customers' requirements will be the challenge of every company throughout the 1980s and 90s. Employees need to understand their roles and responsibility for quality, the cost implications of quality, and the relationship between quality and profit. Essential to building a good quality culture is the genuine belief by the employees in the importance of (1) doing their jobs correctly, (2) doing their jobs on time, and (3) and developing a low tolerance for conditions which prevent (1) and (2).

Management and employee seminars for these purposes have become commonplace. While some address important needs, many tend to focus on special or unique theories that have less application. Also, some are attended by people who do not have the influence or opportunity to put the information learned into use.

Some seminars have philosophical overtones, making it more difficult to glean specific information which can be readily put to use. Managers who are seeking viable and executable ideas for improvement must be able to adapt theory, principles and other information learned to their situations. This involves progressing from the idea stage to actual improvement—a task which will require perseverance even by the committed.

Executives who can authorize and effect change have a special challenge in this process. A knowledge gap frequently exists between those who can authorize needed change, but do not, and those who would like to make certain changes, but cannot. Bridging this comprehension gap will result in disbanding poor ideas and implementing good ones.

In structuring an effective quality and productivity training program, emphasis should focus first on the meaning and value of quality, then on the rudimentary and practical aspects, with less emphasis on theoretical concepts. Unless employees comprehend the importance and the meaning of quality, training in the use of controls, procedures and tools will only be partially effective. Quality and productivity training at any level, while based on theory, should address the needs of trainees, and excite them about having new tools with which to do a better job. In order to be fully successful, training must generate and maintain employee interest by providing information that can be applied to current situations, or issues anticipated in the near future.

Anything short of relevant material made interesting will likely result in an apathetic attitude about training. Especially in operations departments, theory that is not expressed in fundamental and applied forms will produce "ho-hum" responses of trainees. When passive or negative attitudes develop, people attending important sessions will be predisposed not to take the information seriously with consequent ineffective outcomes. Thus, an important step in the education and training process is structuring courses that meet the *real* needs of those who are asked to attend, whether it be management or worker.

In the proper setting, employees can expect to gain greater comprehension of their roles and responsibilities through the knowledge conveyed to them. Real learning means that a person has comprehended and mastered the material well enough to express and apply it with excellence. Although there are undesirable differences in peoples' attitudes and physical capabilities, effective training will maximize overall skill potential and reveal employee talents heretofore unknown. The opportunity for employees to apply or demonstrate their understanding of the new material is necessary in order to achieve behavior change. Without concrete examples and an opportunity to practice what has been learned, much of the material will soon be forgotten.

Following are some training principles which should apply to a quality or productivity training program for employees and first line supervision.

129

1. Training should focus on issues which are relevant to the trainee.

2. Quality responsibility rests with the management and those who influence or create it, and training efforts must place this truth in the proper perspective.

3. Quality and productivity training needs to address preventive concepts, the compounding and consequent costs of corrective action, and the quality-productivity connection.

4. The value of teamwork should also be demonstrated. For example, it would be healthy to group production and inspection people, and perhaps other functions when classes are formed.

5. Concrete concepts and methodology need to be provided to the students. These include statistics, problem solving techniques, work simplification principles, pareto and data gathering techniques, etc.

6. This kind of training takes a real investment of time. In planning for quality/productivity training, for example it should be noted that some companies have determined the optimum to be close to 60 or 80 hours of classroom and practice exercises. In any case, at least one-third of the time should be devoted to on-line experiential learning in order to maximize effectiveness. Instructor cleverness can never replace actual work examples. Upper management training should concentrate on teamwork, organizational strategies for productivity improvement, productivity measurement and how to reduce quality associated costs. These sessions may vary from 6-24 hours. Some companies do not have training specialists who can adequately deal with these subjects, and are using outside sources to provide this service.

Companies which are late in realizing the need for such training can find themselves in the position where nearly all of their attention must be focused on making deliveries so that payrolls can be met. While training frequently carries the latent perception that time devoted to this activity could be better used in driving for more production, in reality, good training is a necessary step in preparing the company for long-term progress. The constant, anxious drive to increase production without clearing the way for solid progress through training, is a good example of working harder, not smarter. In many instances, working smarter is simply stopping to take a calm, realistic, and systematic look at the situation, and undertaking the necessary preventive measures of planning and training, then strategically moving ahead.

Another very important aspect of training not given enough attention is the need to reorient or *unlearn* old ways that are no longer productive. Whether this is accomplished on the production floor by the supervisor or in formal training sessions, many old habits and attendant attitudes need to be redirected. Attitudes are changed by first reaching the knowledge level of understanding, then the emotional level. The emotional level involves greater comprehension and comes from involvement, practice, and finally total belief in the new way. Addressing the knowledge level only, seldom will change attitudes more than superficially. Education which reaches one's *belief* system will produce more lasting results. This is the experiential level that is also needed to produce cultural change.

Unlearning unproductive past practices and relearning new ways is usually difficult, but these are vital steps that may need to be taken if the company is to win the battle of productivity improvement. Efforts to develop and educate the work force need to be respected and usually expanded, if a breakthrough in attitudes and knowledge is the goal. This will be accomplished by a *forward thinking* top management which gives credence to the educational process.

Extended Education of White-Collar Workers

Graduates of the typical college or university begin their jobs with certain specified knowledge of theory and tools for the job. While "commencement" exercises take place at the end of a degree program, they mark the beginning of a career for the graduate. While some graduates may consider the commencement exercise as the grand finale of their college association, others find this only the beginning. As jobs unfold and as technology advances, it becomes necessary to extend one's education beyond the initial four or five years of college work.

Engineers generally need to extend their education in quality disciplines and the "practical" aspects of design. Because such knowledge is very important, and since most graduate engineers have taken no reliability or shop oriented courses in the regular college program, more and more are acquiring this knowledge and experience through other means while on the job. Additional courses in business and writing also have been shown to be very helpful.

Like engineering graduates, graduates with business degrees in manufacturing companies typically need to expand their knowledge into manufacturing and technical fields such as blueprint reading, machine technology, and quality assurance. In general, people working in the eight key functions presented on page 39 should achieve a better working understanding of each other's jobs.

Attending regular meetings of professional societies is a valuable source of such information. For example, both the American Society for Quality Control (ASQC) and the Institute of Industrial Engineers (IIE) not only focus on the subjects covered throughout this book, but offer special courses and seminars as well.

The Hiring Gap

Most hiring policies state that the initial contact with a company by a prospective employee must be made with the personnel department. Concern is sometimes expressed by operations people, however, that interviewers in personnel offices do not properly assess the qualifications of prospective employees, pointing out that some potentially good candidates are turned away before they (operations supervision) have a chance to interview them. Persistent applicants who have had past difficulties with interviewers find that they can sell themselves to operations people more readily because they can speak their language. As a result, candidates learn ways to by-pass personnel offices. A not uncommon perception by operations people is that interviewers in personnel departments have insufficient technical education to adequately evaluate some candidates' qualifications. This is often complicated by interviewers having only a very brief description of the job. While the secondary interview with principal departments is the procedure established to deal with this gap, some good candidates can be unwittingly overlooked with less qualified applicants being scheduled for secondary interviews. Some personnel departments have overcome this problem by hiring or training personnel people with relevant technical knowledge.

Orienting New Employees

During the first couple of weeks on the job, both new employees and the employer have needs that should be addressed. The initial hours and days on the job can make the difference between having an employee who will ultimately form a good impression of the company—seeing his or her job as a vital productive element in the future of the company, or developing the opinion that the job is just a place to spend eight hours each day on a job that lacks meaning.

In addition to general indoctrination on such matters as safety, personnel policies, fringe benefits, etc., new employees have other needs as well. They need to be able to see the big picture; introductions to associates and key people with whom the person will have contact are important; an initial plant tour designed to provide the opportunity for them to observe related activities as well as the direct functions in which they will be working, are also important; an overview of the product lines and how the person's job relates to these functions deserves much more attention than is often devoted, and finally, the supervisor, or a qualified designee, should initially familiarize the new person with the operations of the department.

The supervisors should observe areas of potential strengths and indications of employee difficulties during the first few weeks he or she is on the job. During this period, undesirable traits or habits, which were originally not observed, may surface. By working closely with new employees, the supervisor can take early corrective measures such as training, or counseling.

New employees often experience considerable stress during the first few days or weeks on the job because of estrangement or fear of the unknown. This sometimes is not recognized and properly dealt with by supervisors because daily pressures of the job direct attention to other matters. New employees are sometimes left to fend for themselves. "Warm-up" activities are needed for both exempt and non-exempt employees. Attention should be given to both the specifics of the job and interdepartmental matters.

If a blue-collar employee is brought in and immediately assigned to a machine and essentially ignored without giving the person a sense of purpose in the organization, negative opinions about the department and company are already developing. Similarly, if a white-collar employee's first "assignment" is to study a manual during the first two weeks on the job, this can become very boring indeed. Employees need to be given initial assignments which are designed to familiarize them with the system, and provide the opportunity to develop enthusiasm and express creative abilities. There is usually no more helpful way to orient employees than to make initial assignments which are designed to reveal the issues, projects and missions of the department. This is known to help employees make the adjustment more easily.

Employee Turnover

The task of developing and training employees becomes more costly and troublesome in an industrial climate beset by employee turnover. Department of Labor Statistics indicate that approximately 50% of the work force changes places of employment annually. Restaurants, department stores, service stations, and large factories alike, have the common problem of employees quitting their jobs, getting fired, or being laid off during low business cycles. In the midst of commitments

133

to plough back a greater amount of profit into equipment for modernization and high wages, managers have the additional problem of replacing many of their skilled and experienced people with personnel, either from within the company, or from outside. In either case employees must continuously be trained in order to effectively meet production standards and deadlines.

How can a company keep employees after it has invested heavily in them through extensive training, or subsidized expensive college education? Some managers have accepted worker mobility as a societal characteristic, but become very frustrated when they repeatedly lose valued employees to other companies just when their departments begin to show good progress. They have expressed concern that their companies have become an employee training ground for competitors.

Excessive turnover should be a signal to the management that the "mobile society" may be obscuring significant internal problems. Voluntary terminations are often related to poor internal operations of the company, most of which could be improved by a better quality of work life, monetary incentives, and better leadership. Where a high turnover rate exists, the company should also examine its policies governing advancement, fringe benefits, accident prevention, hours of overtime scheduled, replacement of outdated equipment and flexibility of work assignments.

Supervisors and even upper managements are promoted into leadership positions with little leadership training. While education in human relations factors is no panacea, if it focuses on practical issues and proven principles, this type of training will surely help.

Executives sometimes expect first line supervisors to run efficient departments and produce high quality work, but fail to make certain these leaders are knowledgeable of what constitutes efficiency and how to effectively reach high quality standards. In an atmosphere where strong production commitments are made, and schedules are critical, there is high likelihood that the inexperienced or unqualified leader will impose inconsistent or unreasonable expectations on employees, with the employees leaving to find better working conditions at another company.

Where employees are already dissatisfied with their companies in a community where there is a scarcity of people for these jobs, these employees are good prospects for recruiters. People trained in unique skills are especially sought after, and thus, not only become "fair game" for zealous recruiters, but become challenges to those who are skilled at proselytism. Recruiters from companies where managers have been earlier victims of employee rustling by other companies, now attempt to find replacements for their losses. In many instances, when influential employees leave, they take with them other valued employees. Recruiters tend to paint very rosy pictures of their companies and impose great temptations on employees who already have axes to grind with their present employer. In a community where jobs are being widely advertised, and where needed skills are "available," "head hunters" are constantly on the prey for good employees.

On the other hand, if an employee enjoys his or her job, has a good working relationship with the firm, and has developed a sense of loyalty to the company, an employee usually will not expose himself or herself to temptations offered by recruiters, unless there are more pressing personal reasons to leave the area.

A Total Quality Assurance Curriculum

An increasing number of human resources personnel and recruiters are searching for graduates with a quality assurance degree, but generally without much success. Engineering and business schools have departments where one would expect to find programs in quality assurance. In reality, there are very few baccaleaurate programs to be found.

Several reasons for this scarcity of programs can be cited. First, quality assurance as a profession has only recently come into its own. While many of the disciplines which are associated with quality assurance are as old as some of the more classical professions, quality has not enjoyed an equal professional image. Second, it is believed by some that quality assurance is not a separate profession, and that traditional curricula are sufficient to deal with the subject. Those holding this view believe that (1) curriculum emphasis given to quality can be adequately dealt with through sundry undergraduate courses or by a master's degree in this field, and (2) the broad and interdisciplinary nature of quality assurance makes it more difficult to fit it into conventional curricula. Others believe, however, that quality will never be accepted as a true profession until sufficient baccaleaurate programs have been activated, producing graduates specifically educated in this profession.

If one examines the interdisciplinary nature of quality control/ assurance, engineering technology departments are a likely place to launch B.S. degree programs in this discipline. Technology departments usually have curriculum flexibility and come closer to having the kinds of laboratories needed for quality assurance. (The exception would be found in quality curricula that must be oriented toward the fields of foods, drugs and cosmetics, which are also expanding fields.)

135

Universities having an engineering technology program have an excellent opportunity to institute a quality assurance degree program for the traditional disciplines. The interdisciplinary nature of quality assurance is shown in Figure V-1.

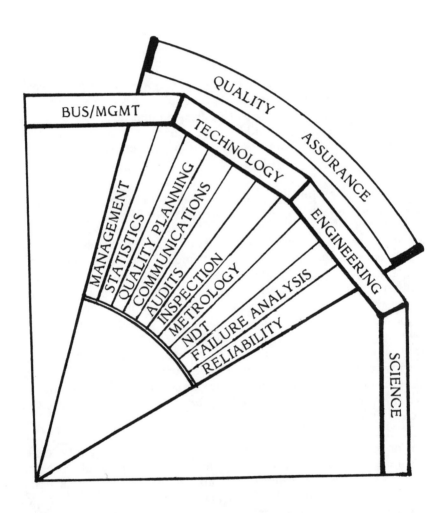

FIGURE V-1. QUALITY ASSURANCE IS AN INTERDISCIPLINARY DEGREE PROGRAM

There are five major areas of learning that graduates should encounter in a Bachelors of Science degree in quality assurance: general education, laboratory and hands-on work, management concepts of quality assurance, and the technology and engineering emphasis.

1. *General Education* subjects which are often referred to as liberal arts and the general sciences have two broad goals for a quality assurance graduate.

They will learn or acquire the following:

A. Information: the raw material for thinking, analysis, reflection, and discourse.

B. Method of inquiry: direction and practice in methodologies of the several disciplines.

C. Basic skills: the ability to analyze ideas and data, to relate these to other materials, to develop arguments both logical and cogent, to reach conclusions, and to present the results of these processes with clarity and style.

D. Qualities of mind: a respect for data and unpleasant facts; an appreciation for the arts; tolerance, commitment, a taste for learning, creativity, perpetual curiosity, and a sensitivity to ethical considerations.[10]

They will be provided with fundamental building blocks for transfer of learning. This is not only dealt with in a pattern of progressive course work, but involves a math and science foundation for continued learning and mastery of upper division course work.

2. *Laboratory and hands-on activities* are also an important part of any B.S. degree program in quality assurance. Unlike other curricula which emphasize lectures and reading textbooks, success in quality assurance requires hands-on experience with the equipment and processes that are associated with quality. A complete quality assurance baccalaureate degree program will include laboratory assignments congruent with modern quality assurance functions. For example, two fields under the quality assurance umbrella for which companies have great difficulty in finding competent people are metrology and nondestructive testing. It is not possible for a person to be qualified in these fields without first having experiential knowledge.

At a minimum the metrology laboratory should be equipped with enough equipment that the student can perform exercises in the electrical and mechanical units of measurement as well as calibration exercises. A nondestructive test laboratory should be equipped so that students can perform ultrasonic, penetrant, magnetic particle, eddy current, and radiographic tests. Emphasis in most engineering programs is in the areas of physical and chemical testing rather than nondestructive testing. In programs which are not equipped or staffed to provide education in the aforementioned areas, collaboration with industry might be a viable alternative.

3. *Management concepts* are a necessary part of a baccalaureate degree program in quality assurance. Principles of supervision, industrial organization, marketing, procurement, finance, and costs are among the broad areas that should be covered. A very important consideration is to utilize instructors who have experiential knowledge in management, and how these apply to quality fields.

4. *The philosophical and engineering concepts of quality assurance* are vital core concerns. This area covers subjects on systems, quality engineering, total quality assurance, testing of materials, statistical process control, reliability, failure analysis, audits, procurement quality control, software quality control, and general quality problem solving.

5. *Technological aspects* of the curriculum will include subjects in drafting (including true position tolerancing), machine technology (including robotics), and numerically controlled equipment, materials and processes, metallurgy, computer applications, industrial safety, production analysis, electronics and engineering economy.

This list can serve as a guide for university administrators in establishing programs in quality assurance. As a minimum more quality oriented subjects need to be included in business, engineering, and technology education and training programs across the country. Because of current and increasing interests in quality, more courses and curricula can be expected, but few currently exist which address a complete program.

There is persistent belief among some academicians and industrial managers that quality assurance engineers and managers are easy converts from other engineering or business fields. Because there have been so few complete quality assurance degree programs, there have been no other options. The conversion process is far from easy—often taking place in the midst of chronic quality problems. A vast majority of quality managers hold either engineering, or business degrees, or none at all.

There are persistent negative stereotypes about quality jobs. Professionalizing quality will mean building a concomitantly new and positive image of quality functions. The quality education gap will be closed when *industrial* personnel give this body of knowledge sufficient credibility that students will seek degrees in this field, and when *academia* realize the importance of this profession.

PART II: MEETING THE CHALLENGE

While creativity flourishes in some U.S. firms, gaining and holding a competitive edge remains an ongoing challenge to most companies. The past two decades have been painful for some industries, especially where the forces of competition have resulted in low profits and consequent layoff of employees. In some sectors, workers disdain foreign-made products because of these circumstances. Many believe, though, that international competition has served to revive the spirit of excellence and move managements' thinking toward more effective approaches. Many obstacles that once inhibited productivity gains are being carefully analyzed, splintered and eliminated.

Successful analytical methods and commitments to improve the quality of work life are having a positive impact on company cultures. Accordingly, an increasing number of people are realizing that pervasive quality attitudes are a requirement for the long-term good health of a company, and that generic affinity for fine workmanship is a concrete building block for job security.

Progress is also being demonstrated in the area of teamwork. Companies that have been the most successful have taken pertinacious actions to rid the organizations of inconsistency, indifference and Machiavellian methods. Enemies of teamwork (such as stratagems) are seldom found in the most successful companies. Companies which have the most difficulty in generating teamwork are continuously confronted with festering ambivalence about the job, resistance to cooperation, passiveness about innovation, communication chicanery, and vexatious distrust. These interrelated factors fuel adversative fires and counteract efforts to generate teamwork.

Conversion of a confrontive industrial environment into one which spontaneously calls upon teamwork processes for solutions is slow. The long-standing division of labor and management has diluted the meaning of teamwork and has made collaborative goals more abstract and remote. In a free society, oppositional viewpoints are not only natural, they are encouraged. The challenge is to harness this interactive energy and direct it toward constructive outputs, and simultaneously retard encounters that detract from meeting objectives.

Barriers which preclude cooperation are being broken down by taking *deliberate* actions to do so. Many companies have introduced organizational mechanisms called "productivity teams, quality circles," and the like, to develop and make use of employee talents which heretofore have been suppressed or lost in interorganizational wrangling.

Improvement comes in small packages from employees, as well as from major shifts in management strategy. Collectively, small changes originated at the grass roots level will result in more long-term productivity gain than from caveats and panacean approaches taken by top officials. However, in a large number of cases, workers ironically feel that they must wait for such "sounds of alarm" from the management which only feed the inertial machinery and impede progress.

With *leadership,* a working climate can be created in which employees simply *decide* to pitch in for the company. The following chapters focus on these important issues, together with ancillary factors that generally need addressing.

CHAPTER VI

The Cultural Foundation

Building A Quality Culture

Characteristics. Industrial culture describes the pattern of performances and the expectations for such performances which are developed within and transmitted by a group. Ideas, habits, attitudes and customs become somewhat standardized in an organization.[1]

A quality culture is one in which unfolding attitudes and habits are quality oriented. Genuine desires to perform work right the first time pervade the organization. Often referred to as the quality ethic, this culture comprises quality values that have been absorbed by employees and evidenced by habits of taking quality seriously.

The status of the quality culture at any point is largely a product of the past. While a company's quality culture is a changing force, past management policies and practices, outside influences, and the interaction of these forces essentially determine the maturity status of this culture. Illustrated in Figure VI-1 are two general categories of U.S. companies and the cultural positions they hold.

Companies which have positive quality cultures experience the synergism of teamwork in an ongoing cooperative work environment. With continued emphasis on improvement, effective management strategies and a high quality priority, organizations shown in Zone A will continue to show a positive cultural slope. Companies shown in Zone B have developed characteristics which negatively impact quality and are shown with negative slopes. These firms will need to unlearn certain habits, which have been built on long standing indictments against quality. Historical management practices have created patterns of behavior and associated adversarial worker climates which are adverse to productivity.

Employees of firms in this category have developed attitudes that oppose cooperation. The evolving culture promotes a combative environment in which there is a win/lose situation. Employees psychologically aggress against and exploit one another. Teamwork and mutual achievement are minimal. Improvement will begin once the managements can achieve a quality orientation and generate a team spirit throughout the organization.

Based on a solid quality foundation that only the senior managements can introduce and sustain, conditions that are conducive to quality can then be expanded within the internal systems of the company. This base will, in turn, gird additional efforts to build a climate in which productive work will be accomplished.

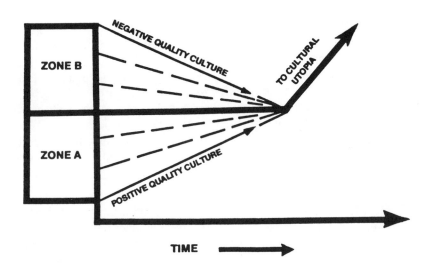

FIGURE VI-1.   STATUSES OF COMPANY QUALITY CULTURES

Learning from the Covert Culture

The *informal* systems of a company always carry intrinsic learning potential, and employees learn to identify with or adjust to the prevailing culture. If the culture is positive, the employees join a productive team. If it is negative, they must either unite with this culture, or be regarded as troublemakers, or leave the company. Industrial culture is powerful; good habits can be converted to poor ones, bad habits to good ones, or good ones can be strengthened even more. This is a learning process.

(1) *Unsaid Expectations.* In a company where the culture is shown by a steep positive slope, expectations of quality will be felt by employees without having to post slogans and caveats as reminders. This unsaid value becomes the standard with which new employees identify. The grapevine takes the high road, manifesting expressions of company growth and loyalty.

A higher degree of ambiguity about quality standards exists in companies which have negative cultural slopes. In these companies unsaid expectations are characterized by ambivalence and frustration among the work force. The grapevine usually carries negative overtones about the company.

(2) *Latent Pressure.* In modern industry latent pressure will always exist to some degree. In a culture characterized by high quality values such pressure is positive, temperate and healthy. Sufficient planning has been and is being done to avoid crises. In low level cultures, latent pressures are dominated by schedules with undocumented short cuts and communication gaps; moreover, leadership will be perceived by the majority of employees as having omnipotent, autocratic and non-listening characteristics. Pressures in excellent companies motivate high performance; pressures in a low quality cultural climate generate error and fear.

(3) *The Management Philosophy.* Where good quality cultures exist, the managements will be fundamentally people oriented. Emphasis will be placed on the leadership of people instead of management of things. In poor quality cultures management of the inanimate systems has become a way of life, with employees being regarded as instruments for results. This theme would be vigorously denied by most, but if this is a cultural trait, it is more or less an unconscious and automatic management response.

(4) *Treatment of Employees.* The character of the prevailing culture

that exists in a company is interpreted by the ways employees are treated. The managements in companies with excellent quality cultures have been and continue to be regarded as evenhanded, empathetic and consistent. They see to it that the necessary resources for the jobs are provided and expect commensurably high performances. In poor quality cultures, supervisors fix blame for mistakes instead of finding permanent solutions. Employees find it necessary to make excuses for inadvertent errors. Fear often pervades the organization.

Another characteristic of a poor quality culture is where employees' potential for improvement has become "rootbound." Their spirit has been weakened by narrow and rigid parameters usually set in place by years of development. This can take place rather quickly, however, (i.e., one year), but usually matures over a longer period. Encased by the constraints of directive leadership and of barriers fixed by organization structure, there is little breathing room and few openings for creative development. While assignments are doled out, which occasionally challenge employees, stresses and distresses of the job outweigh intrinsic feelings of achievement and pride of workmanship.

In companies where a high quality culture exists, both the anticipation and fulfillment of creative outlets abound. Employees take advantage of opportunities to innovate, and are repeatedly motivated to accomplish things beyond expectations. Employees experience the emotion of achievement and consistently convert their potential for accomplishment into meaningful results. Even in the midst of a disruptive organization change or a business slump, employees are able to perceive or anticipate that such opportunities are in the offing.

(5) *Correlation Of What Is Expected With What Is Practiced.* In excellent quality cultures, managements apply to themselves the same standards of performance they expect others to honor. They practice high standards of quality, and apply them fairly and consistently throughout the organization.

Management and employees cannot work in concert in a system characterized as having dual standards. If a company has, for example, an open door policy, it needs to be applied openly and uniformly not just as a testimonial of management's willingness to listen.

The idea behind such a policy is to "allow" employees access to upper management. In a low quality culture, however, suspicion and retaliation will prevent an open door policy from working even when upper management is sincere about its use. A company which has allowed ambiguity and hostility to creep into the organization, will reflect doubt and conflict.

In poor quality cultures, trust has broken down because employees have *learned* that hard work and high workmanship do not pay. Espousement of high quality is heard from the management, but at the first opportunity, substandard units are shipped out the back door to meet a billing goal. Accordingly, the "management" is perceived as being untrustworthy.

(6) *Perceptions Are The Children Of Company Culture.* As high quality cultures develop, so also will positive self images and good perceptions about the company. Trust and loyalty will replace both animosity among the workers and doubt about the company's future. Conversely, negative perceptions will develop as various organizations absorb values which work against quality. Leadership inconsistency, conflicting rules and nebulous standards contribute much to negative attitudes and perceptions about departments and the company as a whole.

Every department consists of unique features that have been formulated from the past leadership and customs. Especially in large companies (over 1000 employees), it is not unusual to find some departments which have a strong aversion to company-wide cooperation. Cooperation is viewed as a way for other departments to pry or obtain information that has been traditionally held sacred and confidential. An unbiased observer from the outside would conclude that some departments compete with others much like two companies compete for business. That *all* departments have as their common objective increased market share and productivity improvement, is not obvious in some companies. Where such barriers to teamwork exist, top managements need to correct the primadonna organizational syndromes where they are found and break through the "us and them" attitudes in order to get on with the business of improvement. These changes will have a positive impact on companies which are at the threshold of realizing important gains.

Effects of Culture on Improvement. To have a quality culture is to have a foundation for improvement. The quality ethic and available energy for improvement have conterminous and integral meaning. The ease with which improvement attitudes can be inculcated throughout the company rests largely on the character of the existing quality culture. A culture that is predisposed to improvement already cultivates improvement. A culture which tolerates poor quality is one in which behavior is likely to have been learned which directly or indirectly opposes improvement.

The rate of improvement can be increased by attaining a better

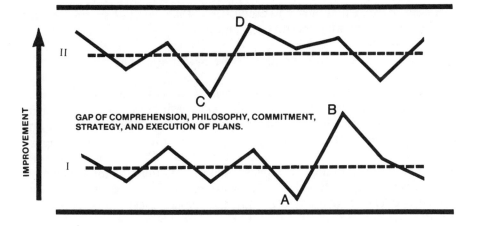

FIGURE VI-2.   THE IMPROVEMENT GAP

comprehension of pertinent issues, shifting and strengthening philosophies where needed, making stronger commitments to improvement and adopting and executing strategies that will bring about needed change. As shown in Figure VI-2, every company at any given time is at Level I. Some function at Level I too long, feeling successful when point B is occasionally reached. They unwittingly become comfortable with a moving average between A and B; as long as sales are high they are able to satisfy stockholders, keep most employees employed and realize satisfactory profits. These companies experience the usual equipment failures, schedule crises, customer complaints and business is described as satisfactory; the normal operating zone continues between A and B with sporatic highs and lows. In such cases, improvement is perceived narrowly, relative to internal operations of a plant.

A better index carries longer term and external implications, defined in terms of sales and competition. If sales and especially profit are improving, chances are senior managements are making decisions that lead to both short and long-term improvements. But, if they do not constantly evaluate the needs of customers as well as competition, or are lulled to sleep for any period of time at Level I, they are inviting trouble and have already allowed the improvement process to wane.

After systematic and sustained action has been taken to improve the company's competitive position, and when Level II has been reached and

147

operating in the C-D range, continued effort should be concentrated on even further improvement. This process should dominate thinking processes of every manager and employee in the company. Firms that do so will increase their competitive advantage.

Common Execution Errors of Management

Companies which are in various stages of cultural transition are redirecting factors which cause quality to be a driver of costs to a more solid foundation on which quality becomes a driver of profit. But, many are encountering great difficulty in executing the necessary changes. Top managers who are confronted with this quality dilemma, are serious about the matter and most are aware that quality must be improved and accomplished more efficiently. Senior officers have made commitments toward this end, and many have utilized expert consultants as *energy sources* to overcome initial inertia and reinforce their convictions.

The problem usually lies neither in a simple decision to deliver products of greater value, nor in being committed to quality; it is more a question of knowing how to translate commitments into actions and results. Two hazards that are frequently encountered are impatience and a search for panaceas. The intensity of the need to progress from Level I to II in Figure VI-2, swollen by the pressure to perform, too often causes management to take impulsive and costly actions. Three are discussed as follows:

(1) *Undertake a major reorganization.* This will demonstrate two things: commitment can be made visible by juggling team players; this is an overt and sometimes startling action that everyone can witness. "Top management means business." However, a reorganization is frequently not the cure for the "reasons" for a reorganization. A problem which festers and ultimately results in an organization change may not reside in the functions or people who are the subjects of the reorganization.

(2) *Hire expert consultants as another demonstration of commitment to action.* Consultants usually know very well what a company must do to bring it to a more profitable position. Often, exhaustive seminars on strategy and the mechanics of implementing needed change are candidly presented to top officials and other senior managers by consultants, but these efforts do not convert awareness into action. The required actions must come from a believing, knowledgable and motivated staff throughout the company. Most consultant efforts address concepts and principles that should apply, but the deeper aspects of company culture are issues which only the management can improve.

(3) *Implement quick participative programs as a panacea.* Some top executives have been sold on the concept and benefits of quality circles, slogans and colorful charts and graphs, but have no inkling as to the seriousness of the adversary relations that exist between the employees and management. Neither are they aware of the intensity of the animosity that exists at various levels and departments in the organization. When emotions run deep, such quick fixes usually do not work; they are answers to the wrong questions, and can even obviate progress.

Bridging the Execution Gap

Difficulties in creating or building a quality culture may not originate from top officials whose philosophies and decisions are thought to oppose quality. Usually all principal parties have honest intentions, and are desirous of galvanizing efforts to achieve the best possible results. Impasses, however, do inadvertently occur between the plant manager, the quality director and other members of senior management. The plant manager openly and sincerely commits his or her support to quality objectives, but results are frequently less than expected. While the quality director feels some responsibility in this matter (perhaps even under strong pressure from above), he or she is also unable to demonstrate appreciable progress. Some plant managers believe that programs which highlight quality by means of posters and exhortations will bring about desired results. Others believe that their "involvement" simply means to issue statements about the importance of quality on a regular basis. Still others assert that such pronouncements have no permanent effect on value systems of employees, and therefore they prefer to devote their energies to conducting meetings with the senior staff to find solutions. Meanwhile, the typical quality director feels that building a quality culture is a much broader company issue than his or her organization can influence, and direction and motivation for such change must originate at the top. Thus, a stalemate of sort is inadvertently created while negative idiosyncrasies of culture continue to develop and go unchecked.

There seems to be little concensus on how best to execute changes that will positively impact quality culture, but there are several methods that have worked well in the past and are still in use. Successful firms generally meet the following criteria and employ combinations of these techniques.

(1) *A Believing Management.* A knowledgeable, dedicated and involved senior management staff, including the CEO, is a necessary first step to building a quality culture and effecting desirable change.

(A) Whether or not consultants are utilized, the executive staff should have a keen insight into the relation of quality to productivity and costs.

(B) Top officials *believe* in the importance of quality, and are dedicated to the goal of improving productivity and profits through quality. This involves a commitment that will energize action from the top down. Believing carries a more indepth meaning than often does an overt expression of commitment.

(C) Executives become personally involved in the process. An active interest to the point of involvement not only at various levels in the hierarchy, but also systematic exposure and interaction with employees is important. The question of how to find the time is moot if the alternative—lower productivity—will be the outcome. Without personal involvement, the executive's role is reduced to a "cheerleader or attaboy" position, and does not provide the stimulus needed by employees.

The above three actions also need to be taken at the next lower level of management. Typically referred to as managers and directors, these people need to be even more acquainted with the cost implications of quality and possess a broad knowledge of industrial engineering principles. (These are both discussed later.)

(2) *Special Education.* Some departments have traditionally separated themselves from "quality" responsibility and have left this task up to quality assurance functions.

(A) Parochial perspectives sometimes held by finance, purchasing, marketing and design departments should be expanded to the point of belief that they, too, have a *specific* responsibility for quality and productivity. Customary views which narrowly define or associate productivity with manufacturing departments need to be broadened.

(B) First line supervisors also need to have more detailed knowledge and information about the importance of their roles in producing efficient quality. Methods principles, the costs associated with quality, and statistics of quality control are among the coffers of substantial benefit. First line supervisors should be privy to principles of motion economy, costs of rework and scrap, and how to apply statistics in controlling processes in their own departments. Lecturing to various groups for a certain number of hours is usually insufficient. Truly effective learning will include a way to achieve involvement, and provide for sufficient hands on experience so that participants will believe and accept the principles covered. Actual data from machines should be used to illustrate problem solving techniques. The learning process should reach such a level of maturity that first line supervisors are not only comfortable with the use of such techniques, but they will also be able to train their employees in the skills and procedures as well.

(3) *Use of Organizational Mechanisms.* Where attitudes and desires for improvement are in place, but strategies and actions are sluggish, better use of organization mechanisms may be needed to energize the system. Making use of an executive productivity council, consisting of representatives from the eight key areas presented on page 39 is an example of a successful approach used in some firms.

A similar technique is the use of task forces which are temporarily organized to deal with specific issues. In concert with the aforementioned methods, quality circles and variations of this concept have been found to be very effective at lower hierarchical levels to generate more cooperation and expand creative thinking.

In order to significantly increase improvement processes, employees need to be able to work freely enough to solve the problems that need to be solved. Without the use of such organizational vehicles, the dynamics of teamwork will be less vigorous and more time can be wasted through controversy and dysfunction. The executive staff should create a climate in which calm, deliberate and rational thinking can take place.

(4) *Teamwork Begins at the Top.* A basic approach to instigating productivity improvement is for key people to sit down and hash out goals, expectations, and available resources to reach these goals. Sometimes quality and industrial engineering departments have not developed productivity and quality cost reporting indices in forms that the plant manager can use to effectively demonstrate his or her support. Without accurate and readily available cost data, the top executive will have difficulty in carrying out the quality and productivity message. Such information is the basis of dedicated support and constructive action.

Completed work by the quality and industrial engineering organizations together with comprehension and involvement by the top officials are not only catalysts for improvement, but they are the resources of synergism needed to convert an adversarial climate into an enthusiastic and energetic team spirit. This process will disencumber the company from obstacles to productivity gain.

Effects of Culture on Cost

When a firm has an excellent quality culture (one in which quality is imbued and generically expected throughout the company) its organizations possess the framework to maintain low quality-associated costs. When concern for customer satisfaction permeates the system, and the spirit of quality is infused throughout the company, quality effectiveness is inherently achieved. Since a quality culture means high regard for quality and a pervasive expectancy of meeting quality requirements, people will be energized to do the job right the first time. This is the zenith of a healthy productivity posture.

The basis of large quality associated costs usually begins early in the life of a company. Managements' collective philosophy about conducting business sets the stage for the culture that is born and nourished to maturity. This developing culture either contains quality in its operating philosophy or factors that, if fed and allowed to mature, support the hidden factory where costs multiply. This is illustrated in Figure VI-3. Once the culture is well established, though it will resist change, it can be improved or worsened by the factors shown in the figure. If the positive elements are in place, quality costs will be inherently lower than they would otherwise be. Moreover, they can be made even lower with the ongoing stimulus and nutrients of these factors. However, if the negative influences predominate, costs to meet quality expectations of customers will not only be excessive, but will increase as these negative elements become integrated into the company's operating philosophy.

Institutionalizing Quality Improvement

Establishing quality improvement as an institution will require a reversal of correction action *values,* and simultaneously an attack on the "need" for corrective action. This process typically will necessitate a change in management philosophy as well as making preventive actions and teamwork pervasive components of a firm's culture.

The idea is to make quality improvement an integral part of the everyday lives of the management and employees. This will be accomplished by (1) converting the practices of *expecting* things to be done over to the beliefs and reliance on these beliefs that tasks can be done right the first time, and (2) implementing appropriate preventive actions in an environment of diligence and cooperation so that proclivity toward corrective action will be kept in check.

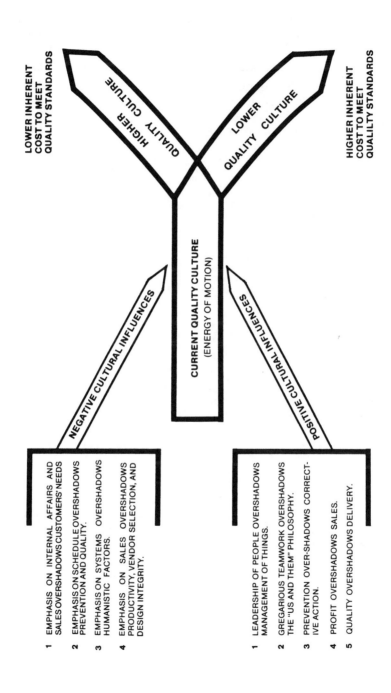

LOWER INHERENT
COST TO MEET
QUALITY STANDARDS

HIGHER QUALITY CULTURE

HIGHER INHERENT
COST TO MEET
QUALITY STANDARDS

LOWER QUALITY CULTURE

NEGATIVE CULTURAL INFLUENCES

CURRENT QUALITY CULTURE
(ENERGY OF MOTION)

POSITIVE CULTURAL INFLUENCES

1 EMPHASIS ON INTERNAL AFFAIRS AND SALES OVERSHADOWS CUSTOMERS' NEEDS

2 EMPHASIS ON SCHEDULE OVERSHADOWS PREVENTION AND QUALITY.

3 EMPHASIS ON SYSTEMS OVERSHADOWS HUMANISTIC FACTORS.

4 EMPHASIS ON SALES OVERSHADOWS PRODUCTIVITY, VENDOR SELECTION, AND DESIGN INTEGRITY.

1 LEADERSHIP OF PEOPLE OVERSHADOWS MANAGEMENT OF THINGS.

2 GREGARIOUS TEAMWORK OVERSHADOWS THE "US AND THEM" PHILOSOPHY.

3 PREVENTION OVER-SHADOWS CORRECT-IVE ACTION.

4 PROFIT OVERSHADOWS SALES.

5 QUALITY OVERSHADOWS DELIVERY.

FIGURE VI-3. MAJOR INFLUENCES ON QUALITY CULTURE

153

Such changes will be achieved by re-orienting both managements' and employees' attitudes and customs which lend credence to remedial actions, and coincidentally raising employees' sights to a higher ideal. Massive training may be required, and the top management will need to be willing to invest in this *preventive* activity if necessary.

In addition to the educational aspects, Juran has emphasized that long-term strategic planning, together with setting yearly goals toward this end will be necessary.[6] There are five steps in this process.

1. Identify units of measurement.

2. Design a mechanism to detect and measure.

3. Establish goals for improvement.

4. Implement the system.

5. Make it work.

Building Blocks of Quality Culture

In concert with the aforementioned steps, there are five cultural building blocks which will also be required for success at institutionalizing quality improvement. These are shown in Figure VI-4. Where excellent quality cultures are found, they are the result of high ethical practices, participatory leadership and provisionary disciplines set in motion by the top management.

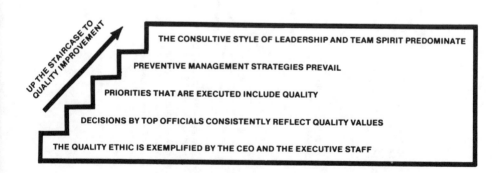

FIGURE VI-4.   BUILDING BLOCKS OF QUALITY CULTURE

The degree of influence by the hierarchy on the culture is illustrated in Figure VI-5. Examples are set and emulated largely according to the power structure of the organization.

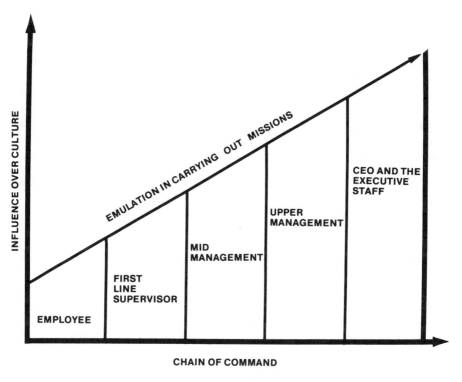

FIGURE VI-5. HIERARCHY OF INFLUENCES ON QUALITY CULTURE

Step I — The CEO and the Executive Staff Exemplify Quality

The quality ethic is influenced by countless factors most of which can be controlled by the senior managements. First, the chief executive officer sets the tenor of the company's attitude toward quality. By exemplifying quality values in both word and deed, the CEO and his or her staff establish the foundation upon which the quality ethic can be nourished. Decisions and behavior at this level will reflect the top officials' interest in quality. For example, a good test of this commitment can be achieved at lower levels when an order of parts which does not completely conform to requirements is held up from shipment by a top executive. Such a situation would occur in a company where the senior staff is attempting to turn around a poor quality culture. It should be emphasized that in a company where a mature

155

quality culture already exists, it would not be necessary for upper managements to intercede or take such actions; the material would have been dealt with earlier at the level where the authority and responsibility reside.

Actions speak louder than words. The behavior of top officials is emulated at lower levels. Integrity and trust will break down quickly if espousals of high expectations of quality are heard from the top officials, but when tough decisions about quality have to be made, options are taken which compromise the quality position. While such decisions are clearly the management's prerogative, it is perceived hypocritical of the top staff to issue pronouncements on the value of quality, while at the same time making decisions that undermine efforts of employees to uphold quality values.

Step II — Decisions Are Made Which Reflect Quality Values

Numerous examples could be given which illustrate whether or not decisions reflect quality values, but three broad categories are discussed here to illustrate this concept.

(1) *Management Philosophies Are Oriented Toward People.* Quality mindedness includes having the welfare and best interest of the employees at heart. People are recognized as the most valued asset and resource. This implies that actions to achieve participation among the work force, listening to employee concerns, invoking fair and consistent policies, together with both financial and non-financial incentives are firmly in place.

With the infusion of the features presented in Step I, quality attitudes among the upper and mid levels of management should be evidenced. The degree to which this maturing process is actually taking place will be manifested at lower management levels by the integrity with which matters involving quality are carried out. Any dissatisfaction with progress will require (1) more persistence by the executive staff to imbue quality values, (2) specific forms of education and training, and (3) identifying and finding solutions to obstacles that impede progress.

In spite of top management's strategies and insistence on improvement, old ways have a way of creeping back into modes of operation, especially if the mid managments have had many years of indoctrination to other practices. Only by repeated example, steadfast commitment, unbending standards of quality and contiguous training, can long standing ineffectual practices be effectively changed.

(2) *The Company Is Educationally Oriented.* A strong indication of a maturing quality culture is the general advocative attitude by both the management and employees toward education and training. Irrespective of how an employee development program is organized in the overall company structure, if a company enjoys an excellent culture, training functions will be highly regarded and regularly utilized by both the management and employees. A competent team of employees is one of the most important company assets. A company whose managements portend to have a quality culture will have a dynamic employee development program. A training department can exist in the absence of a mature quality culture, but no modern industrial organization can effectively sustain long-term improvement without a suitable management and employee development program.

Improvident management and naive supervision breed mistakes and can even lead to contempt. For example, the unthoughtful placement of people in situations they do not understand can produce negative repercussions and send resentful messages throughout the organization. Placing employees in "sink or swim" situations may be a challenge to those who have the required tools and skills, but may also be a source of antagonism and error to those who have not been properly prepared for the job.

Many employees will "hang on" in spite of grueling circumstances, but negative attitudes build. Insensitivity to conditions of the job by the managements, together with pressure to perform, comprise the formula for employee bitterness, error and discord. The management sometimes inadvertently places employees afloat in a sea of insecurity, with neither an oar to make progress, nor a rudder for direction, leaving outcomes essentially to chance.

Any company with a maturing quality culture will have as one of its educational objectives a strengthening of the bonds between individuals and groups and between employees and managements. An integrated program of education which reaches the more deeply implanted behavioral aspects of motivation and interest will be in use. Task oriented learning, though necessary in most instances, usually does not address needed changes in attitudes and beliefs. Changes in behavior as they relate to building a quality culture will be evidenced by an increasing degree of teamwork, company loyalty and sensitivity to matters affecting productivity.

Appropriate education must also reach the various levels of management to convert outdated customs into approaches that are known to be successful. While excellent old practices need to be woven into the fabric of new techniques, allegiances to old methods which

157

contain redundancies, inaccuracies and other inefficient practices need to be eliminated. Yoretime notions and habits built on unproved dogma are counterproductive in a worldwide network of dynamic competition.

The importance of conforming to requirements, communicating clearly, recognizing outstanding performances, and building trust and cooperation will also be dealt with appropriately when efforts are made to strengthen the quality culture.

(3) *Planning and Provisionary Practices Are High Amongst Priorities.* Two of the most basic functions of management are planning and making appropriate provisions to carry out the plans. A plan predetermines future actions. It not only bridges the gap between the position at a point in time and a desired result, but it also describes the basis for arriving at the objective. This implies that the missions of an organization can be carried out effectively only if the planning is a result of visionary and insightful top management, and if the necessary system elements are in place to effectively implement the plans.

Managements are the only people who can interpret business conditions, chart courses for the company, make preparations for the future, and make final choices. Management's principal job is to ensure that the elements for such decisions and actions are in place, in balance and function properly.

A provisionary management is also practical. Implicit in goal setting is expectation of results. Goals and plans should be reasonable and attainable, however. The continuous upward progression of performance goals under driving pressure to meet them, without some form of remuneration or reward, will ultimately be met with resistance. Employees sooner or later will interpret this process as a form of manipulation. The driving kind of manager whose style is to call all the shots without conferring with others cannot win the confidence of his or her people and keep it. This leadership style will cancel other attempts to build a quality culture.

Step III — Priorities Include Quality

A number of allusions are made about establishing quality credibility in a company. U.S. industry has had a history in which quality associated activities have been embroiled in controversy, and in some instances the real meaning of quality has been held captive. If the previously described attributes of Steps I and II are in use, quality should be increasingly witnessed as a leading factor when prioritizing important objectives or projects. Quality will assume its right to precedence when price and delivery questions arise.

Having a mature quality culture does not mean that quality must always head a list of priorities. It does mean, however, that quality will always be a key factor in setting priorities, commanding a position of importance warranted by and commensurate with the nature of impending decisions.

Quality tends to have priority significance where people respond positively and spontaneously to quality and where quality is a viable force in the company. Where a poor quality culture exists, quality will have nondescript features, and will be couched in turmoil, possessing recondite and esoteric characteristics that will make it an easy target for compromise.

Where a good quality culture exists, fewer independent quality safeguards will be necessary. Both the management and worker will take quality seriously; preventive disciplines will be widely used and camaraderie will be observed throughout the company. This suggests that the systems approach to quality shown on page 39 will have already had acceptance and has become more or less naturally integrated into the organization. Traditional tactics needed by quality personnel to block the progress of nonconforming units will be unnecessary. Units not meeting standards will have already been separated out or removed from the processes more or less spontaneously as they occurred. In such a culture quality functions are essentially delivered from the quandary of organizational change. The maturity of the system removes quality organizations from traditional adversarial positions to the more positive position of a respected partnership role.

Quality safeguards will always be necessary, however, by an amount commensurate with a company's inability to establish a quality culture. As quality values are inculcated in both the management and employees, requirements for people in protectionist roles will shift to the more productive roles of assurance.

Step IV — Preventive Management Strategies Prevail

Webster defines prevention with the use of phrases like: "shutting off possibilities of occurrences," and "acting in anticipation of an event or incident," to define the term. In the context of quality assurance, prevention means to take measures to avoid an undesirable occurrence, or merely to take certain actions today that will forestall the occurrence of an unwanted future event.

This idea obviously has merit and an air of practicality. Extension of the concept might even lead one to believe that all quality and productivity issues could be avoided by choosing and instituting the proper preventive technique. This outcome is not possible, of course, for several reasons. Not all future problems can be identified in advance so that a specific preventive measure can be applied. Some can be predicted based on historic data, analysis and best judgment. Many happen only by chance and no degree of advance preparation can stop their occurrence. This fact of nature challenges the best of minds and has denied success of many would-be prophets. Scientific approaches to prevention suggest, however, that in order to prevent something from initially occurring, it must first be anticipated. If a problem is already evidenced, cause and effect relationships can be investigated and analyzed, and its *recurrence* prevented.

Primary and Secondary Preventive Measures

Prevention, as it relates to industrial productivity, is a relative term. Ideally, *primary* prevention will yield best results, representing the greatest potential for cost effectiveness and error avoidance. Primary prevention is achieved best through the inherent ability of a person or activity to do jobs accurately. Several examples will serve to illustrate this point.

1. *Inherent process control* is gained through the accuracy and reliability of a process. A process which is capable and consistent in its ability to deliver has the innate capacity to prevent and circumvent problems. This ability can be maximized through the use of *capable* equipment, preventive maintenance, quarantine of unsuitable work and presence of the necessary tools in the hands of competent people.

2. *Design integrity* means that a design is complete, accurate and producible when it is released. This is a primary preventive activity in that an early quality base line is established which inherently eliminates the need for corrective actions from occurring later in procurement and manufacturing phases.

3. *Methods and planning* functions predetermine future actions. Therefore, properly accomplished, they prevent unwanted situations and cause desirable events and conditions. To the extent that planning is satisfactorily accomplished, inconsistency, dual standards, fatigue, down time, redundant work and corrective actions will be prevented.

4. *Education and training* also have primary preventive significance. Skills and the ability and encouragement to apply sound operating principles are mandatory for accurate performance. To the degree that people are qualified beforehand, error and corrective action are prevented. Ignorance has been proven more costly than education and training.

Secondary prevention has several levels of effectiveness, depending on the extent that additional information loops are required. There are numerous activities that have preventive qualities, but they depend on information feedback to identify causes and to prevent recurrence of unwanted conditions. For example, while design integrity was listed in the primary preventive category, design checks and reviews are critical tasks to be completed in order to achieve design integrity. In manufacturing departments inherent process control was listed as a primary preventive category, but control charts are used to assess the degree of this control, and concomitantly identify fabrication errors to trigger corrective measures, and consequent reduction of inspection and failure costs.

The milieu in which secondary prevention takes place markedly influences effectiveness. For example, in the case of design, if feedback loops to designers are marred by controversy, or broken by organizational distance, the probability of error will rise as will the number of tertiary information loops. (This concept is illustrated on page 264). In the instance of manufacturing, if the operator or inspector does not believe in the benefits of statistical process control, this secondary preventive technique will be less effective and more information loops will be needed.

Logistics also play a part in the effectiveness of secondary prevention. The more the distance increases between the function which initiates feedback and the one needing such information, the greater the chance that faulty operations or work will continue.

Long-term creeping change can also be responsible for negating the usefulness of a secondary preventive technique. A preventive maintenance program, for example, can become so large and unwieldy that the feedback system breaks down; the mechanics of response becomes so clumsy that the procedure becomes perfunctory and ineffectual.

Embodied in the functions of management—planning, organizing, leading, staffing and executing—is the concept that feedback loops should be kept simple and small. Early warnings of impending problems can then receive the kind of attention needed for effective prevention.

Much effort will be in vain if attempts are made to implement preventive measures where the foundation blocks (described earlier) have not been laid. For example, in a company culture which is exemplified by crisis management, preventive techniques will be only partially effective at best. Factors that keep the company on the crisis treadmill are the same as those that hinder the effective execution of preventive strategies.

Ironically, companies which are trying to bear up under the effects of crisis management, have the greatest need for preventive strategies. But, if crisis management has become the "way of life" for a company (and it has for many), this energy in motion will resist changes in direction. If training is regarded as "another hour wasted;" if the use of statistical controls is overtly accepted, but covertly rejected; if roles of supervisors have been reduced to coordinators, or "parts chasers;" if temper tantrums on the shop floor are common; if the designs which are released to production require a flurry of changes or waivers; if excessive rework and scrap are encountered, and if the production department is always behind schedule, a classic scenario of the long-term effects of crisis management is represented.

In companies where crisis management is deeply rooted and where managers have naively but zealously practiced it, a preventive measure such as training will likely be interpreted as yet another road block around which new detours must be developed. Prevention measures will usually be received as just another panacea contrived by an unknowing manager or consultant.

Deliberate and systematic actions taken to break the cycle of crisis management require a great deal of courage and faith. Complaints may even be voiced that a "backward" step is being taken. While prevention can result in a more profitable position for a company, it can be hindered by those who drive for greater output, with "crisis blinders" on, believing that time can be better spent striving to meet schedules. This is shown in Figure VI-6. A company which is constantly faced with month-end shipment crises should be a signal to take up-front action to smooth the flow. But such improvement will come slowly indeed if the upper managements are conditioned to believe they can continuously wring just a few more products out of the system month after month. Nonconformances, overtime, and schedule delays tend to be regarded as necessary evils rather than as symptoms of the increasing stresses of crises management. As shown in Figure VI-7, proper prevention can bring about long-term improvement.

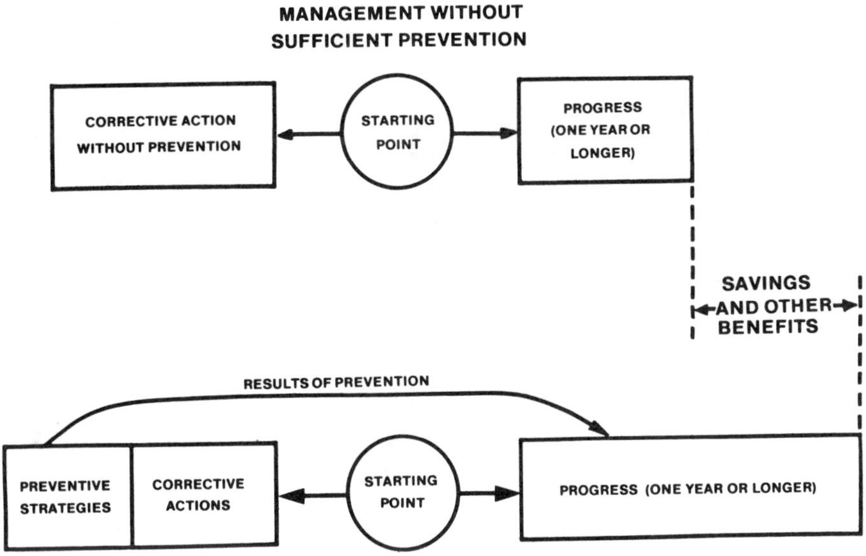

MANAGEMENT WITHOUT SUFFICIENT PREVENTION

FIGURE VI-6. NET GAINS PRODUCED BY PREVENTIVE MANAGEMENT

Another roadblock to the prevention philosophy is the difficulty of attributing improvements to specific preventive techniques. Prevention always involves a time factor between when a preventive measure is applied and when results are expected. In a society which is action and results-oriented, this prevention time factor will always be a deterrent to its use. Cause and effect relationships become fuzzy, and it is difficult to draw a clear line from a preventive action to the consequences of such action. Results are difficult to measure if improvements come in oblique forms and are not traceable to a specific preventive action.

The effects of training provide a good example of these difficulties. In a certification type program, employees are tested or observed on the job to verify competence, and cause and effect lines are relatively easy to draw between good and poor performance. However, during such training, behavioral change may have also taken place—improving cooperation and teamwork, honoring policies and procedures, or raising quality consciousness. These are very important effects which become fused in massive organizational networking. Gains in productivity are ensured, but causes will be obscure. The end result is obviously desirable; but some of the real values of training itself will not be credited to the training activity. Humble training directors may

163

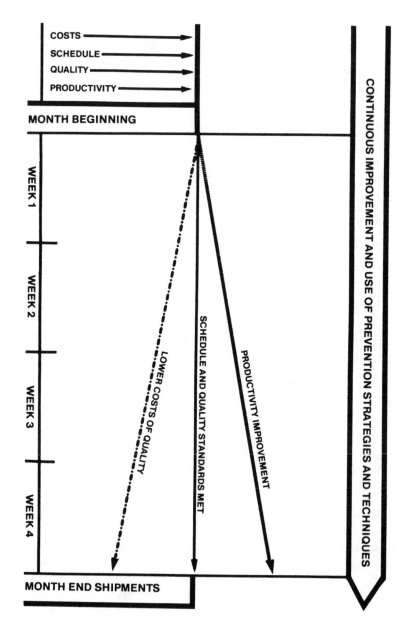

COSTS ⟶
SCHEDULE ⟶
QUALITY ⟶
PRODUCTIVITY ⟶

MONTH BEGINNING

WEEK 1

WEEK 2

WEEK 3

WEEK 4

MONTH END SHIPMENTS

LOWER COSTS OF QUALITY

SCHEDULE AND QUALITY STANDARDS MET

PRODUCTIVITY IMPROVEMENT

CONTINUOUS IMPROVEMENT AND USE OF PREVENTION STRATEGIES AND TECHNIQUES

FIGURE VI-7. EFFECTS OF PREVENTIVE MANAGEMENT ON SCHEDULE, COSTS, QUALITY AND PRODUCTIVITY

164

proclaim this as good, saying, "I don't care as long as the company benefits." The issue is not whether credit should be given to the training *department*. It is important, that results be appropriately attributed to *training* so that training continues to be perceived as a worthwhile and high priority investment.

The same can be said of other preventive methods. In statistical process control, for example, process variation is observed in real time and therefore provides the opportunity to stop a process *before* it produces defective products. While the concept is obviously valid and cost effective, *measurable* values which attribute improvement to the technique have not been sufficiently highlighted to convince skeptics that the technique is indeed a source of profit.

Prevention will gain credibility and be regarded as an important *long-term* mechanism for improvement when the following occur:

1. Boards of directors, stockholders and top executives generally need to have a better understanding of the potential benefits which can be gained through long-term strategies so that results of prevention can be realized. This comprehension will need to be manifested by overt incentives to take a longer range view of business dynamics.

2. Quality assurance, industrial engineering and training departments need to consolidate their efforts to develop measurement indices that will accurately show the effects of their respective preventive efforts. These will, in turn, be a measure of productivity gain.

3. Based on dollar analyses, managements can be convinced that up-front monies will be necessary to support preventive activities. Without such hard evidence, it is less likely that upper management, operating on the basis of management by exception, will give sufficient credence to a "principle" that it will cause a budget difference. Instead, they are happy to see good results if and when they occur.

Step V — A People Oriented Style of Management Will Predominate

Values in Conflict. This subject is addressed in subsequent sections, but is abstracted here in the context of building a quality culture.

Building a people oriented style of management in an industrial culture of paradox and conflict is difficult. Values in conflict, some of which are well entrenched in industrial fiefdoms, make progress slow. In traditional America, a paragon of success is an individual proprietor who "single handedly" realized a dream by converting a product built in his garage into a multimillion dollar business. Winning against great obstacles is a mark of success. However, individual success and *sharing in success* continue to demonstrate values in conflict. A salient characteristic of a free democratic society is that people desire to be a part of the process of arriving at the decisions that affect them.

The contradictory nature of organization is also receiving an increasing amount of attention. The linear organizational imperative under which most companies function predetermines *conformance*. As tenure in an organization continues, members are conditioned to conform. Potter alluded to this, pointing out that, "While working within an organization, we *become* what we do in the sense that personal values increasingly match those of the organization."[7] Organization conformance and standardized patterns slow creative processes. Paradoxically, organization is both a cause of ineffectiveness and an important means to become more effective. While people seek organizational devices to "win," there is increasing evidence that organizational linkages in the form of teams are converting negative stresses of conflict into motivational vehicles for improvement.

Having had over two hundred years to mature, such conflicts have been manifested in forms ranging from the unionization of workers to competition among top executives to influence decisions. Strong control, demands for fealty and the need of workers to participate, while deeply rooted in U.S. culture, tend to oppose each other in action. For several decades some of these conflicts have been largely suppressed. Management and labor coexisted; management exercising its right to control and unions distrustful of management prerogatives.

Coterminous philosophies, however, have undoubtedly contributed to productivity difficulties. It has become necessary for many U.S. executives to reevaluate their leadership styles, examine new approaches and find better ways to deal with the mechanics of organization as well as with peers and employees.

Overcoming Traditional Obstacles. Perceptions of managers and the realities of their behavior in practice contribute to difficulties of achieving successful worker involvement. Some advocates of participative management are on a "participative caravan," naively following an unidentifiable leader and never experiencing the kind of decisions and responsibilities that a typical manager faces.

In the strict meaning of the concept, participative management will dilute the power of an executive which he or she may covertly cherish. Shunting off to subordinates some of the power coveted by managers, particularly in an authoritative environment, may be a novel idea, but vastly more difficult to successfully activate. To achieve favorable outcomes considerable effort and perserverance may be required in some companies. It can be done and is being accomplished, but meeting with cogent obstacles. For these reasons, the building blocks previously described need to be honored before appreciable success can be realized in instituting effective worker involvement programs.

If the company culture exhibits a leadership style prone to strong authoritarian methods (likened to McGregor's Theory X style) efforts to inaugurate true participative management will probably be met with both active and hidden resistance. Authoritarian leaders will view true participative goals as a loss of personal power and control. Moreover, if this style of leadership has been set in motion by the top officials and "perfected" over years of indoctrination, the task will be even more complex.

Given such cultural characteristics, if top officials now choose to abandon former practices that they believe are outdated, this too can produce short-term backlashes and ancillary costs sufficient to cause some top executives to retreat from their earlier positions. This contradictory portrayal of leadership can be viewed in a similar way as some quality control departments are perceived to function. On one hand, the consultive and advisory roles of a control function implies collaboration and coadjuvancy, but in the final analysis control may take over and mean the restraint of flexibility and denial of opportunities to depart from customary methods and practices.

In the U.S., custody of authority and responsibility for results resides with the management. If there is one factor which is traditionally managerial, it is the sacredness of the officialdom, influence and attendant responsibility for results, which are vested in hierarchical management.

Desire to control is felt even more strongly in organizations driven by power motives. Since the prerogative to make decisions and the responsibility for such decisions are retained by the management, some managers rationalize their positions with the expectation or need to be arbitrary ("The justification for me being in this position is that I am not only the most qualified to make the decisions at this level, but I am *expected* to make decisions and am held accountable for results."). This process goes on with or without participation.

Participation may imply to some that those involved have a share of responsibility for results, but they do not. Involvement without accountability is actually consultation. This occurs when employees are encouraged to suggest improvement without the authority to make decisions.

In order for the consultive method to be effective, it requires more involvement by management and less assertion and exhortation. People who "participate" need solid evidence that their involvement is meaningful, and that some decisions are different than they would have been without the involvement. There is an abundance of evidence to support the management philosophy which provides for worker involvement. More and more managers are turning the corner from "telling street" to "participative boulevard," realizing that puppeteers ultimately find themselves in positions where they must make decisions about matters in which they are not properly versed. Moreover, they recognize that employee involvement builds trust and loyalty which in turn, adds long-term strength to the company.

CHAPTER VII

Quest for Teamwork

TEAMWORK: IMPORTANCE AND MEANING

Much of industries' productivity dilemma lies in the fact that executives have been so concerned with deadlines and steady increases in output, that they have unthinkingly downplayed the roles of its most important resource—people. People have been and will continue to be the driving force of industry; they are the originators of ideas and innovations, and without them the material system would soon stagnate and become meaningless. In spite of this simplistic logic, there is a strong likelihood that unwitting disregard for employee needs, interests, and ideas will continue to prevail. It is not so much that anyone plans it this way, nor that managements do not wish the best for their employees; it is more likely that managements inadvertently direct their attention to the inanimate factors of machines, materials, money and facilities because, unlike people, these "things" neither react, compete nor resist being directed.

In the early years of industry, company presidents and executives were constantly amongst the employees listening to their concerns, and oft times problems were solved on the spot. Today, it is impossible to have this level of contact, especially in large companies, because of the sheer size and diversity of functions. In some instances workers would not recognize top executives even if they saw them. It should come as no surprise that front line workers have developed the notion that the "management" belongs to another class to which they could never hope to attain, and conclude that their superiors have only one principal interest: to achieve the greatest profit possible from *their* labors. More and more managers now recognize that the growing value gap between them and their employees is a dead end productivity street, and they have stepped up their campaign to find ways to build better relations at all levels in their organizations. Among other thrusts, they are

169

emphasizing the need for better cooperation within and between departments.

Where managers in the past failed to realize the significance and impact of dealing with employees of different ethnic backgrounds, values, religions, characters, and economic statuses, managers now find it increasingly necessary to deal with the problems workers face, and solicit their contributions.

Definition and Scope. Webster defines teamwork as the joint action by a group of people in which each person subordinates his or her individual interests and opinions to the unity and efficiency of the group. Participation involves *sharing* and involvement means to *include.* Thus teamwork, participation and involvement are more than allied terms; they are integral concepts. Teamwork reaches maturity in an atmosphere of trust and unselfishness, where respect for the opinions and rights of others and open communications are always found.

Teamwork flourishes through (1) the participative processes of sharing experiences, abilities, opinions and concerns and (2) having the opportunity to be included in the process. Nothing will kill the participative process or worker initiative more quickly than an indifferent demeanor, a non-listening attitude, or a major change in work procedures designed by someone who neither sought nor received inputs from those who must live with those changes.

Society and industry function through the interactions of people. One reason that an individual belongs to a group is to attain a sense of security and belonging. No individual feels complete unless he or she feels accepted by other members of a group. A team has a much deeper meaning than a group, however. A team is a group whose members are not only committed to a common goal, but are also sensitive to the problems, emotions, ideas and concerns of other members of the team. When a group functions as a team, individual objectives are subordinated to the goals of the team. Teamwork thrives only when its members *sacrifice* in deference to team pursuits. Like a sacrifice fly in baseball, individual desires must take second place to the team goal. A very strong commitment and desire for team success are usually necessary to offset the urge a person has to compete *individually.*

Achieving teamwork in the U.S. is actually a much broader concern than can be defined in the context of industrial organization. While industry is the main thrust of this book, true teamwork eludes even the major institutions of the U.S. Raymond M. Demeré, Jr., one of Hewlett-Packard's top executives, expressed it this way: "We must break down barriers to process improvement, be it the process of education, of government or of business; be it the barrier between labor and management, or between vendor and customer. We must gain greater insight into and awareness of the other party's relation to the process. In other words, we need greater teamwork."[1]

Are Industrial Managers Ready For "Teamwork?" While teamwork carries positive connotations, the term participation (the sharing element of teamwork) has generated some concern. To some, participation implies that those involved have a share of the responsibility for results. They usually do not. Groups generally organized for teamwork (e.g., quality circles) are advisory since they have neither authority nor accountability for their recommendations. When managers are confronted with the idea of workers being directly involved in the planning of their work, or other traditional roles of management, some flinch and become wary; others reject the idea outright. Does participation mean to stop short of traditional management functions? In reality, participation is encouraged at the hardware level, but planning and decision making, per se, have always been management privileges. The potential values of teamwork are realized only if the management will provide the *opportunities* for employees to experience the emotions and results of teamwork. Organized as teams, employees can exercise creativity as well as manual skills and in doing so, experience the challenges and excitement that can be found in problem solving. The management retains its authority to make decisions based on facts and evidences brought forth by a team. But, herein lies some of the difficulty in making teamwork effectual. How far should or can managers go in the participative process?

Long-term implications of expanding participative type activities need to be appraised. Is the management prepared to deal with employee involvement in areas that customarily have been held company confidential? For example, matters of burden rates, perquisites of certain people in the company, salary structure, customer and vendor dealings, hiring and firing policies, incentive plans, financial conditions, etc., have been variously held company private and in some cases, inconsistently applied. Is the management willing to open up such areas of information? If not, will teams be content to be restrained and not be allowed certain information? What will be the managements' approach if they do? As teams are developed, and people become more involved in the quality of work life, more questions will be raised and managements should be prepared to deal with these questions.

Launching programs such as quality circles and productivity improvement teams is difficult and should not be undertaken without first building the proper foundation. This process takes time and can be a problem where the management is impatient. It generally takes longer to make decisions democratically than it does automatically, and not all decisions will please everyone.

In order for participative management to work, managers will need to resort less to manipulation, exhortation, and autocratic pronouncements and more on logic, persuasiveness and clear communication. The latter will require a great deal more effort, and usually accompanied by the need to face past mistakes. Managers will need to come to grips with the fact that a "white collar" does not necessarily hold a monopoly on creativity, knowledge and common sense. Group dynamics are excellent stimulants for these forces, and the manager can quickly face his or her own inadequacies. Some managers will successfully embrace the benefits and power of this process; others either fear the exposure, or are vulnerable because of a history of errors or a proudhearted spirit.

Once participation is established as a principle, it is often difficult to know how far democracy should be in decision making. The extra time members need to invest in meeting and in informing themselves is sometimes questionable, especially if results cannot be readily seen. In a typical U.S. plant, middle and first line managers are highly vulnerable to restiveness because they are under pressure to meet deadlines.

Needs and Conditions of Teamwork. Workers of today want and need certain benefits not previously afforded them in most companies. For example, employees should be able to have an appreciation of the business outlook of the company. Some firms practice posting regular statements about sales expectations of the company and certain financial information, etc. Yearly or semi-annual business meetings held between the top executives and employees is also a technique sometimes used. Employees need to be aware of business conditions because *they* are important elements of the process. Employees also need to have a general knowledge of the customers with whom *their* products are marketed. Pride of workmanship is strongly related to workers being able to identify with the end product and the customers involved.

When an organization is planned, manned and managed so that a team spirit is manifested both on the production floor and in office areas, it has taken an important step toward success. For a company to be successful, it does not need to be a vast industry with many thousands of employees with general offices in New York, and plants scattered internationally. Large organizations are often those that find it most difficult to stimulate team spirit, and it is these that have had to do the most extensive work in the field of developing better managers. With the small plant, it should be easier for the executives to create an atmosphere of working together and to build up a team spirit that will yield greater efficiency and increased output.

The factory team is developed not through haphazard growth, but through careful planning and guidance. Thought is given to the selection of workers; attention is given to placing them where they are the happiest and where they can do the most productive work, and pains are taken to train people for leadership. A factory formed in this way is not something that simply emerges without direction, but is rather a balanced, smooth-running, efficient production machine. Every part of it is essential; every part is in the right place.

There are four essential conditions to successful teamwork.

1. Members of the group must have an understanding of, and work toward, a common goal. This in turn, involves, (1) hearkening and assisting employees in solving problems, rather than telling and controlling answers, and (2) removing obstacles from employees, so that they can perform their jobs.

2. Team members must be adequately educated or trained in the jobs they perform, or are expected to perform. This means (1) establishing a climate for innovative outlets, (2) helping employees to find better ways of doing the work, and (3) taking actions to contribute to employees' development.

3. The organization must be designed so that (a) authority and responsibility are clearly defined, (b) the people best fitted to perform tasks are assigned to them, and (c) clear instructions are given in advance and fully understood. This means also that suitable resources for the jobs are provided.

4. Freedom to experience teamwork emotion must also be provided. This involves (1) demonstrating trust in employees by allowing them to pursue goals without close and anxious supervision, and (2) soliciting employees' ideas on how to do the job better, rather than projecting the image that "my way is the best way."

Management Roles. Highest on the priority should be the management's desire and commitment to increase the quality of teamwork throughout the organization. This requires an awareness of the degree that it presently does or does not exist among and between departments. Gaining this appreciation may in itself be a knotty problem. Because of the variety of leadership styles used by the managements, a good many executives are less informed than they might be as to some of the goings-on at lower levels. They receive filtered information which tends to carry messages of what subordinates perceive upper managers want to hear. Especially if fear and anxiety exist, reports will carry omissions, distortions or concealments of important information. In medium and large size companies "executive distance" tends to amplify this problem, and thus should be tackled as an area for improvement.

Some top managements have regular *rap sessions* with employees to demonstrate their desire for teamwork and to help close information gaps. These are meetings arranged by the CEO with a group of about 20 randomly selected employees at least once a month simply to listen to employee concerns and suggestions. In turn, the CEO is able to explain certain important matters and attempts to establish presence and rapport. As one CEO put it, "I am often surprised to be asked questions that I have answered to my staff some months before."

Attendees must feel confident that all information discussed in rap sessions will not be used against them. This is a test of leadership skills of the senior officer. Whatever technique is used, if the mood of the company is one in which groups and individuals feel free to express their concerns and ideas without fear of reprisal, this is strong indication that conflict and employee grievances will be kept at a minimum, and the ingredients for building even greater teamwork are present. Organizational mechanisms may be needed to foster the team building process. These include productivity teams, quality circles, task forces, quality councils and so forth. Each kind of team has a specific purpose for being created, but properly administered, all can be excellent vehicles for increasing teamwork.

The belief that workers generally will respond favorably to participation must precede specific efforts to increase it. This does not mean that all workers will be immediately impressed with the idea and render spontaneous cooperation; it means that the management should (1) be convinced of the value of participation, (2) provide employees the opportunity to assume more responsibility and express ideas, and (3) consult employees about matters in which they are involved. It is expected that managements will maintain control while participation processes are being increased. Loss of control is incompatible with successful participation.

Genuineness and candor are also requisites for effective participation. Employees will recognize very quickly when the management is not sincere, and will become indifferent or even angry when they perceive participative "programs" to be phony. Honest and sincere *expectancy* produces results. If high performances are expected in an environment where managements are concerned and interested, and where ideas are considered and used, there is a very good chance that the employees will give their best.

Triads of Teamwork

While individuals need to feel that they are viable and contributing members of a team, departments also need to function as a team. Some organizations have a special need to work collaboratively not only for the welfare of the departments, but also for the company as a whole. The four triads illustrated in Figure VII-1A through 1D depict a number of functions which have deeper need for teamwork than is usually found. Trust, cooperation, and joint ventures are especially important for these functions, and coadjutant efforts need to be generally expanded in these triads. While it is possible to create additional interconnecting links and form additional tripartite groups, a vast amount of potential for improvement exists within these four groups.

QUALITY CIRCLES

The number of quality circles and their attendant popularity have increased in the United States at least up to now. The concept of circles gained momentum in Japan during the 1960s and 70s, and now at least 10 million Japanese are involved in circle activities. They have been so successful in Japan that many leaders in the United States during the last 10 years campaigned hard to implement them in U.S. companies. If one considers the objectives and why they are created, circles *should* contribute markedly toward the improvement of a company's productivity posture. However, some U.S. leaders have persistently opposed the idea, believing that circles cannot, in the long run, be successful in the U.S. Pros and cons, as well as factors influencing them, are discussed in this section.

Characteristics of Circles

What Is A Circle? A circle is a team consisting of between five and ten people who meet regularly (typically one hour per week) to identify and solve problems. The circle is a means of allowing and encouraging people on the production floor (as well as white collar workers in some instances) to participate in making and implementing decisions that will improve quality and/or reduce operating costs.

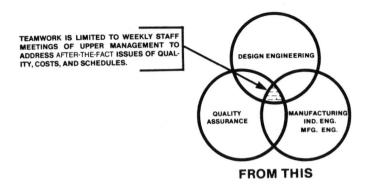

TEAMWORK IS LIMITED TO WEEKLY STAFF MEETINGS OF UPPER MANAGEMENT TO ADDRESS AFTER-THE-FACT ISSUES OF QUALITY, COSTS, AND SCHEDULES.

DESIGN ENGINEERING

QUALITY ASSURANCE

MANUFACTURING IND. ENG. MFG. ENG.

FROM THIS

TO THIS

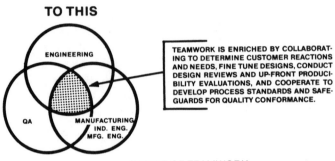

ENGINEERING

QA

MANUFACTURING IND. ENG. MFG. ENG.

TEAMWORK IS ENRICHED BY COLLABORATING TO DETERMINE CUSTOMER REACTIONS AND NEEDS, FINE TUNE DESIGNS, CONDUCT DESIGN REVIEWS AND UP-FRONT PRODUCIBILITY EVALUATIONS, AND COOPERATE TO DEVELOP PROCESS STANDARDS AND SAFEGUARDS FOR QUALITY CONFORMANCE.

FIGURE VII-1A. TRIADS OF TEAMWORK

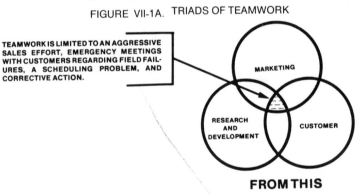

TEAMWORK IS LIMITED TO AN AGGRESSIVE SALES EFFORT, EMERGENCY MEETINGS WITH CUSTOMERS REGARDING FIELD FAILURES, A SCHEDULING PROBLEM, AND CORRECTIVE ACTION.

MARKETING

RESEARCH AND DEVELOPMENT

CUSTOMER

FROM THIS

TO THIS

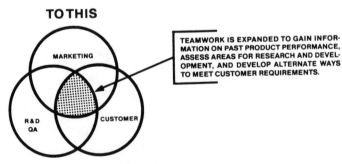

MARKETING

R & D QA

CUSTOMER

TEAMWORK IS EXPANDED TO GAIN INFORMATION ON PAST PRODUCT PERFORMANCE, ASSESS AREAS FOR RESEARCH AND DEVELOPMENT, AND DEVELOP ALTERNATE WAYS TO MEET CUSTOMER REQUIREMENTS.

FIGURE VII-1B.

TEAMWORK IS LIMITED TO RANDOMLY SELECTING A SOURCE FROM A LIST OF SUPPLIERS, AND DEALING WITH QUALITY PROBLEMS AFTER RECEIPT OF THE MERCHANDISE.

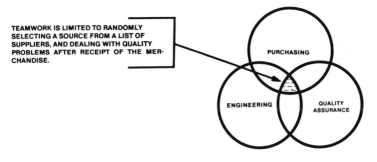

FROM THIS

TO THIS

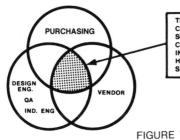

TEAMWORK IS EXPANDED TO ASSURE PURCHASE ORDER INTEGRITY, DEVELOP GOOD SOURCES - QUALIFYING THEM BEFORE PURCHASE ORDERS ARE RELEASED, AND WORKING WITH SUPPLIERS DURING FABRICATION, HAVING SCHEDULED CONFERENCES AND SHARING TECHNICAL INFORMATION.

FIGURE VII-1C.

TEAMWORK IS LIMITED TO PERIODIC MEETINGS WHERE THE DESIGN IS QUESTIONED, A DESIGN WAIVER IS REQUESTED, A QUALITY PROBLEM OCCURS, OR WHEN A MACHINE FAILS.

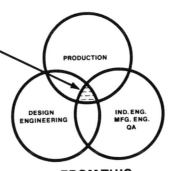

FROM THIS

TO THIS

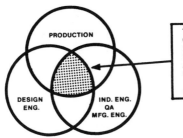

TEAMWORK IS EXPANDED TO PROVIDE GREATER ASSURANCE THAT QUALITY IS BUILT INTO PRODUCT BY HAVING: (1) A FINISHED DESIGN TO WORK WITH; (2) APPROPRIATE METHODS, TOOLS, AND STANDARDS; (3) EQUIPMENT THAT WILL PRODUCE THE EXPECTED QUALITY, AND (4) COMPETENT PEOPLE TO DO THE JOB.

FIGURE VII-1D.

177

The most commonly used title, "quality control circle" does not accurately describe the true function of the team. Quality, while it is a major consideration of the circle, is only a part of the total area of circle involvement. Every idea worthy of implementation must be justified on the basis of cost savings in some way and most improvements, although quality oriented, have strong *productivity and methods* overtones. Many of the problems that are encountered by circles have a corresponding relation to safety and industrial engineering disciplines. This has caused some confusion about what circles should be named: Should they be called "productivity circles," "methods circles," or just plain "circles?"

Objectives of Circle Teams. The fundamental purpose of establishing circles is to improve productivity. This is done through the team efforts of circle members to reduce the costs of quality and otherwise improve productivity.

In addition to the direct problem solving nature of the circle, other important objectives and benefits can be identified. If circles are *properly* functioning, they will:

1. Be an indication that managements are serious about workers' roles in the improvement process.

2. Improve worker morale.

3. Remove biases and other bases of unhealthy conflict.

4. Develop creative skills of members.

5. Improve communication and leadership skills of members.

6. Broaden the knowledge and functional bases for problem solving.

7. Improve attitudes of both management and circle members.

8. Assist in union avoidance programs, or improve union relations.

Circle Organization. Originally, members of circles came from the front-line, blue-collar work force. Now, a mixture of employees is found to be even more effective in a number of cases. A broader range of talents can add efficiency to the problem solving process, and build better relations between departments.

Outside members from specialist organizations also can be included in the membership, either as active members or as contributing guests. Effective leadership of circles, however, irrespective of circle composition, is always a critical factor. Such people are highly respected and are known for their evenhanded and unintimidating qualities.

The *facilitator* is another important person in the circle organizational structure. He or she is specifically trained to coordinate multiple circle activities, oversee circle progress, document results, and train circle members in their assorted duties. The position of the facilitator usually constitutes a full-time position, but may be only half-time until the number of circles grows to approximately 8 to 10.

To be successful in this role, the facilitator should have an understanding of the activities discussed in circle meetings although he or she does not report to the supervisor/leader. The facilitator is obliged to support the leader and coordinate circle activities. Because of the scope of involvement of the facilitator, he or she should possess a number of attributes that will help circles to be successful. To the degree that these "credentials" are manifested in the facilitator, circles will have a greater chance of reaching their full potential.

Training of Circle Members. It is unproductive to place people in situations in which they are expected to perform, but without the provision of the necessary tools. Training is to circle members as knowledge of blueprint reading is to inspectors. In both instances, these tools are fundamental to their success.

Following are the general categories in which circle members should be given training. It is beyond the scope of this book to analyze each discipline, thus major areas are simply listed.

1. *Operations Analysis*
   — Value Engineering

— The Problem Solving Process
— Work Simplification
— Plant Layout Principles
— Methods Principles
— Safety
— Brainstorming

2. *Data Gathering and Analysis Techniques*
— Pareto Analysis
— Charts and Graphs
— Cause and Effect Diagrams

3. *Principles and Application of Statistics*
— Frequency Distributions
— Histograms
— Scatter Diagrams
— Control Chart
— Variation

4. *Presentation Techniques*
— Use of Audio-Visual Techniques
— Communications
— Selling an Idea

Making Circle Meetings Productive. Provided that circle meetings are held in a democratic setting where members feel free to openly share, there are four factors that must be considered in making effective group decisions.

1) Advocacy of personal views should be played down. Ones position should be presented as logically and lucidly as possible, listening to other reactions and considering them carefully before pressing a point.

2) One need not win or lose when strong opinions are voiced, or when the discussion reaches a stalemate. Instead, these should be used to generate viable alternatives.

3) Bargaining or taking a majority vote to avoid conflict should be avoided if it has compromising effects on the spirit of the *team*. If a dissenting member finally agrees with the majority, it should not be done with the expectation of getting "ones way" the next time. Quick and easy agreement in some instances should be viewed with skepticism. Changes of opinion simply to avoid conflict and reach harmony should be avoided.

4) Differences of opinion should not only be expected, but

encouraged. Controlled disagreement is vital to the generation of sufficient information, opinions and alternatives upon which good judgments and decisions can be made.

Why Circles Succeed or Fail

Circles have had varying degrees of success. They have flourished in some companies, have been attempted and failed in others, have been unsuccessful and dropped in some and have been only a topic for discussion in others.

What Makes Circles Succeed? Though others could be listed, there are three major reasons for their success.

1. All levels of the management give more than passive support. While top managements may institute the idea, the mid managements are enthusiastic about making them work. The real stimulus for circles comes from the mid managements, for it is at this level that circles are provided the essential support. Circles succeed largely because these managers are convinced that circle time away from the job is time well spent; and that both direct and indirect results will be of specific value to their operating units.

2. The circle procedure allows all members to communicate and deal in a higher plane of intellectual endeavor than the regular job usually provides. This is a form of job enrichment which allows an employee the opportunity to share in the problem solving process of the job. In addition, since members meet each week away from their normal work areas to work on problems different from their normal activities, circles are also a form of job enlargement. Job enlargement is the provision whereby employees are cross trained in other jobs. This will help them be challenged by a greater scope of work and reduce monotony as well.

3. The concept of circles is supported by modern motivational theory:

A. Maslow's higher levels of human needs (satisfying ego and self actualization needs).

B. McGregor's theory Y which recognizes the worth of an individual (that all people can be creative, responsible, and contributing human beings).

C. Herzberg's theory that true motivation is found in the work itself. (Learning, having the feeling of achievement, communicating, giving and receiving feedback, and having more responsibility and receiving recognition for it.)[2]

Why Do Circles Fail? At least five general reasons can be given.

1. It may be considered trite to say that circles fail because of the lack of management support. If this is the case, how could they have been implemented successfully in the first place? Ironically, after circles have enjoyed considerable success they still are known to fail because of waning support. This is manifested in at least three ways.

A. Early emotionalism of the new wears off. Circles may not have cured as many of the problems as initially believed or hoped.

B. True negative feelings of certain mid managements can surface after several months of circle operation and be the delayed cause of circle demise.

C. Circles have been known to be operating very successfully until new leadership takes over. If circles were neither the idea, nor the desire of the new management, they become very vulnerable indeed.

2. Panacean expectations of upper managements have caused some circles to be introduced without adequate preparation. Building a solid foundation of generic psychological acceptance through training, together with the promotion of the concept, is time-consuming and time is a precious commodity. In spite of warnings, impatience and restiveness of managements continue to be the cause of decay of many potentially sound, long-term ventures such as circles.

3. When circles of hourly employees are attempted in a climate and under circumstances not conducive to involvement, such attempts are an indication of more extensive and latent shortcomings in a company. Top management may recognize the need for more teamwork, but the networks involving preparation, training and conditioning have not been given proper attention. The proper groundwork must be laid before circles can be successful.

4. Paradoxically, circles can expose conditions under which they cannot survive. During circle meetings, for example, a manager may be continuously brought up as a deterrent to needed change, being responsible for many of the projects where improvements are needed. If certain people who have considerable influence in the company privately do not think kindly of the circle idea, circles will meet with political obstacles. While "personalities" are not supposed to be addressed in circle meetings, if certain influential people hamper progress of major projects, this becomes a gnawing issue anyway.

5. A circle is not just another weekly "meeting"; it is a team

organized to solve problems. With this idea in mind, the conduct and demeanor of a circle should provide for smooth flow of information and the free exchange of ideas, heard attentively. Around the circle, knowledge, ideas and open dialog are the objectives. New concepts flow best in a heedful atmosphere which dominates the character of such meetings.

The practice of pretending to listen only long enough to find an opening to insert ones own opinion needs to be unlearned or throttled. A potentially fine idea may never be allowed to surface if a reticent circle member is not given the chance. Being an effective listener is a personal characteristic that should be *enjoyed* by others, but is an asset that too few seem to possess. Hierarchical authority or other types of dominance also have no place in circle meetings. This serves to silence ideas and quell participation; no one should be perceived as the *boss* in circle meetings.

Considerations to be Given Before Organizing Circles. There has been an abundance of information in circulation about quality circles. There is good reason for this. Not only have there been phenomenal interests and growth in the kinds of circles introduced, but proponents have done an excellent marketing job. In addition, a certain amount of controversy about the subject has also generated interest and additional opinions.

Circles have been credited with being the source of substantial business gain. The fact that they have withstood the test of time in many companies is a testament of upper managements' commitment to improvement through people. Even if questions are raised about *measured* value, strong belief in the circle idea will direct attention to the need to improve the quality of work life for employees.

In order to provide greater assurance of success, several considerations should be given before embarking upon circles programs. Is the climate in the company right for circles? A company's "personality" did not evolve overnight, nor did it develop in one year in most instances. Present ingredients that indicate the extent to which teamwork currently exists are a product of past occurrences, and one simply or suddenly does not erase these evolving characteristics. If a cooperative and mutually respectful environment already exists between the management and worker, circles will be a natural addition, and if the groundwork for teamwork has been laid, with collaborative elements already in place, a company will probably reap quick benefits.

Some of the factors that need to be addressed before beginning circles, or resolved early on are as follows: (These are obviously relative, and companies will have been variously successful at accomplishing these goals).

1. Is quality placed in the right perspective with cost and schedule? (This usually means more emphasis on quality in all phases of work.)

2. Are practices of consistent imperious management being corrected?

3. Are indifferent management attitudes, wherever they exist, being converted into ones which are steeped in empathy and sincere concern for employees?

4. Are dual systems of standards, conflicting authority and ambiguous procedures and methods being addressed? (while some of these factors can be problems that circles address, they can also be instruments which thwart circle success if they are not dealt with).

5. Do first line supervisors have the authority which should be vested in this position?

6. Have budgets for training and circle leadership, etc., been adequately considered and approved?

7. Have strong measures been taken to convert a pervasive corrective action and an urgency style of management into a viable prevention philosophy?

8. Are the top managements willing to occasionally drop in on circle meetings as a testament of support?

It is usually better to select divisions or departments which have attributes that are known to lead to success. In every company, certain departments possess more chemistry for circles than others. This is defined in such terms as responsive leadership, desire by employees to participate, and the existence of good problems to solve. If there is neither a strong desire for circle success, nor commensurable belief that they are beneficial by influencial people, it will be only a matter of time before enthusiasm and support will wane.

The Circle Paradox

The amount of benefits to be gained from circles will vary inversely with the probability of their being successful. In other words, companies that are unable to achieve success with circles tend to need them the most, and companies where circles can be organized "naturally" need them the least. This is illustrated in Figure VII-2. It would be very unlikely that companies, which function under the management style shown on the left side of Zone I could successfully implement circles.

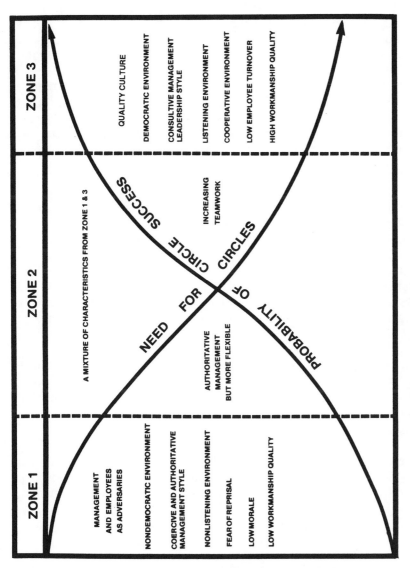

FIGURE VII-2.   CIRCLE EFFECTIVENESS INDEX

Actually, firms with these characteristics and attendant management philosophy probably would not want circles anyway. While organizations in this category need them the most, managements in these firms consider circles a waste of time and generally perceive them as opening up Pandora's box of conflict with which they do not wish to encounter or cope.

Companies falling on the right side of Zone I may have attempted circles, but even these usually have great difficulty in surviving. They are sometimes started by an isolated department, or an enthusiastic executive who realized the need. But, lack of support from senior managements, insufficient preparation and education, prevailing exigent management, and the covert internal destructive machinery that is usually entrenched in these organizations become formidable obstacles. There can be and probably are some success stories in this zone, however. Through dedication to the idea, pertinacious efforts, re-education and tenacious coordination, a healthy and longevous change can be realized.

Zone II is the category in which the probability of success and benefits of circles are optimized. The mixture of attributes in Zones I and III create a balance which on one hand represents opportunities for circles, but contains characteristics that make complete success still difficult. For example, some managers may strongly advocate circles while others have a lukewarm attitude, or qualms about the philosophy. Also, some managers are prone to giving schedules first priority and work under the influence of crises management without knowing how serious it is. These conditions will continue to impose severe hardships on circles.

Employee participation means more than merely *having* quality circles or other vehicles for employee involvement. Introducing "programs" which can be advertised as participation, and inferring success by the *number* of small groups in operation, may be far from any semblance of fruitful participation and measurable improvement.

Any group of people meeting with the common purpose of problem solving will probably show progress, if only through the synergism of group processes. Little beyond this level is reached in some companies, because the management remains focused on achieving quick recovery. In such instances, circles are *allowed* to be implemented either out of desperation or hope that something magical will occur.

At the position far right of Zone III, the elements of teamwork, spirit of cooperation and democratic leadership are already in place. Circles, in these companies, are not a challenge, but a natural extension of the philosophy that is more or less inherent in the organization. Firms having these features tend to have stable employment, be non-union and boast of circle success. In these companies there is some tendency to render blind faith in circle activities and be complacent about circle effectiveness. While all the elements for circle success are in place, and they are more or less natural additions to the organizations, their productivity also needs to be conscientiously assessed.

A part of the American genius is couched in non-conformity and some managers have chosen not to adopt quality circles formally because they would rather do it "their way!" Some firms have had remarkable success without the use of circles. Their internal communication networks and management styles offset the need for circles, per se. These companies are indeed successful, and are appropriately found in Zone III. Unlike circles in Zone I where they function to help *build* teamwork (if they survive), in Zone III circles serve to *enrich and maintain teamwork*.

The question often arises, "Can circles be the instrument to build participative processes in a company where the culture opposes participation?" The answer is maybe. If the objective of circles centers myopically on quick and measurable cost savings, many will fail. Given this narrow management expectation, circles will never make an appreciable impact on company culture. They will remain a duty to be fulfilled *for* the management and perceived as being instituted *by* the management, even though they are "voluntary." If this scenario develops, the management apparently does not fully understand the potential values of utilizing teams of people.

Management-worker conflicts that have been maturing for many years cannot be immediately desolved with the use of circles. Jumping on the circle bandwagon in an effort to find a quick solution to problems of historical origin and development is indicative of the type of decisions that have brought the company where it probably is now. Where a great deal of the creative energies of employees are spent on ways to "beat" the system instead of making it work better, the sudden adoption of circles will likely be viewed as just another management gimmick or trick. In a company where the management and employees have been polarized, for quite some time, factors that contributed to this adversary condition which are probably still in place, will make circle success very difficult to achieve.

The more meaningful and longer term values of teams can change the direction of a company's culture. Not as easily measured, but more important than gaining rapid and cursory cost savings, are those benefits which reach the deeper emotions and belief systems of employees.

Everything else being equal, loyalty, creativity, teamwork, enthusiasm, cooperation and learning, all of which can be acquired from participative processes, have more sustained *long-term* value to the company than specific improvements that evolve simply out of situational togetherness. As deeper quality values among circle members grow, so will the effectiveness of the circles increase.

Suggestion Programs vs. Circles

A manager once pointed out that while he agreed that quality circles were needed, their formal establishment included training which would be too costly. He could not afford the time for employees to be away from their jobs. Instead, he preferred to formalize and strengthen the existing suggestion program and develop new extrinsic rewards of buttons, pins, and plaques. This improvement included better administration of the suggestion program and higher financial awards.

The initial thrust and employee involvement were impressive. Monetary "payoffs" to employees were substantial. After several months, the *obvious* improvements had been implemented with employees duly rewarded. Then there was a marked slowdown of activity. Three difficulties arose and became apparent: (1) employees lacked the knowledge and creative skills to identify the less obvious problems and arrive at solutions, (2) a framework or forum was lacking to develop ideas, and (3) the participative value could not mature. Even with the financial incentive, interest could not be maintained. Productivity improvement efforts need to have a sustaining and long term connotation if they are to be truly effective. Typical suggestion programs go through cycles of revival and depression because they tend to become a burden to those who must review them, and lack the spirit of teamwork that provides synergistic energy.

The management cannot acquire teamwork and a quality culture by "purchasing" them. Employees will gladly receive payment for an idea, but their more deeply rooted attitudes about the management may not be changed by any appreciable amount. While the value of an idea may be far greater to the company than payment for the idea, this is neither a warm nor effective way to gain employee confidence. Of far greater meaning, is winning the trust and loyalty of the employee with the assurance that employees will give their abiding allegiance to company goals. This is accomplished through deep concern for employees' welfare and sincere actions.

The Circles Movement Continues

During the late 1970's and early 1980's the subject of quality circles was a hot topic. Advocates and consultants were both in the arena, enjoying camaraderie and a sense of purpose. At last, the message of employee participation was getting across.

There are signals, however, that quality circles, like value engineering and the consumerism movement, have "matured" into their operational phase. There appears to be less advocative emotions expressed, and only token testimonials of new adoptions are heard. This is not an indictment against circles; it is a part of a normal life cycle and a characteristic of American industrial culture. Waves of interest and fancy come and go, but their effects endure. The value engineering and consumerism movements also made their marks of progress; albeit, given less published notoriety now, they are not only well entrenched, but also subtly and securely fixed.

The quality circle movement in the U.S. was necessary to achieve additional employee participation, a higher order of expression for employees and to generate new ideas for improvement. These have been largely accomplished, even in the wake of daunted and opposing customs and traditions found in most U.S. companies.

Although the *glamour* of the circle movement seems to be waning, the concept lives on. Those who are championing the causes of quality circles have repeatedly expressed that circles will be met by varying degrees of enthusiasm and acceptance, but the learning and new values of teamwork which result from circle experiences, will remain impervious to entrepreneurial change.

EXPANSION OF THE TEAM CONCEPT

White-Collar Teams

Many companies have broadened the circle concept, moving it into higher hierarchical levels. In some instances a much greater potential for improvement can be found *between* organizations of unlike roles than *within* departments where people have like duties. Where conventional circles have concentrated on blue–collar employees in manufacturing functions, some companies are now organizing white-collar employees in circles that cut across organizational lines. They have recognized that many costly problems relate to organizational barriers between the eight key functions illustrated on page 39. For example, with the rapidly advancing technology of computers, robotics, etc., new communications and producibility challenges are being faced. This does not mean that these challenges were not present before; they are merely being exposed more now than before.

Some companies are realizing great benefits from utilizing teams which operate like customary circles, but with the membership comprised of people from such departments as manufacturing engineering or planning, production control, quality assurance, design engineering, industrial engineering, purchasing, and certain production supervisors. In cases of producibility problems, equipment capability concerns, design specifications inconsistencies, vendor obstructions, etc., such a team can deal with these difficulties on an ongoing basis, meeting regularly on a weekly or bi-monthly basis. Other successful teams are composed of sales or marketing representatives, design engineers, quality engineers, and others who might have important inputs to e.g., quality issues in the field or new product development undertakings by the company.

Another kind of group that has proved to be successful is a team organized *within* a department other than production. For example, key designers who need to brainstorm about major design changes, or develop a better change control system, etc., may find it more beneficial to meet regularly to solve such problems than to have them be continuously put off.

This type of circle is able to define a list of major projects it wishes to accomplish for which time had previously never been allocated. These projects usually have preventive overtones and are accustomed to "back burner" positions, but should occupy places higher on the list of priorities.

Task Forces

Unlike circles, task teams are temporarily organized to carry out specific projects to their conclusion, but are disbanded when the job is completed. Successful task forces possess the following characteristics.

1. There are usually no more than 10 members, organized temporarily to deal with specific issues, or solve special problems.

2. The reporting level of its members is in relation to the importance of the problem.

3. The task force is pulled together rapidly when needed and usually does not have a formal charter.

4. While being results oriented, they also have an informal demeanor and are not burdened by formal paperwork.

5. They have quick response time.

Task forces have the disadvantage that they may not be organized into action until they must become agents for corrective action. The organization of a task force tends to be delayed until serious problems have already occurred. They are, of course, needed at this point to prevent further delays or costs, but the element of prevention may not be addressed since they are organized for a specific purpose and disbanded after a problem has been solved. Also, they may not last long enough to experience real teamwork, nor receive the training that would maximize their effectiveness.

Productivity Improvement Councils

Some companies have recognized the advantages of maintaining a high level productivity improvement council. Such councils should consist of the heads of the major functions shown on page 39, or comprise the following minimum membership:

Directors of departments of:

> Manufacturing
> Engineering and Research
> Marketing
> Quality Assurance
> Industrial Engineering
> Purchasing

Responsibilities of the council are to:

1. Define major productivity quality improvement goals and establish priorities to maximize efficiency. These include those which have both short-term and long-term impacts.

2. Provide a mechanism to achieve the necessary resources to solve the major productivity issues in the company.

3. Direct the activities of productivity improvement task groups responsible for the implementation of the improvement projects defined by the council.

4. Evaluate and monitor progress of the task teams toward achievement of the stated projects and report progress to executive management.

Unlike the task force, the council is a continuous unit meeting bimonthly or perhaps monthly, based on need.

The council should identify advisors from other principal functions such as purchasing, field service, finance, personnel, safety, manufacturing, engineering, and training so that they can be available as needed to assist in problem definition and resolution. Though these functions may not be represented directly on the council, heads or specialists in these departments are usually privy to relevant and critical information needed by the council for decision making. The council should not assume direct responsibility for any department line or staff function. Neither should it provide specific direction or coordination for implementing productivity improvement department activities. Rather, it should function to support and delegate authority where needed to implement changes to achieve desired results.

Councils are "circles" operating at the highest functional level in the organization. With the quality assurance and/or the industrial engineering head chairing the council, and a member of lower management from the manufacturing or engineering organization, acting as a facilitator for the council, quality and productivity's problems and solutions will become less evasive.

There are several major benefits of such a council.

1. Quality issues are raised to a level of authority where definite action can be taken.

2. Upper management is exposed to more of the facts surrounding certain issues.

3. Actions by the council are concrete indications that the top management is serious about productivity/quality matters.

4. Council members will be more confident that decisions they make will be the best under current circumstances.

5. High level brainstorming takes place which helps to place the proper emphasis on issues and seeing these in the right perspective.

6. Both strengths and weaknesses of, departments, together with the reasons for these will be better understood so that needed adjustments can be made.

7. Just as important as the aforementioned points and probably less tangible is the demonstration of better teamwork between major departments. Root causes of conflict will be exposed and addressed. Conflict between organizations that sometimes originates at this level and felt at lower levels should diminish. Teamwork inherent in the

actions of the committee should help to build respect for each others views with the results that more attention should be focused on issues instead of personalities. If the management at this level cannot get together on issues, there is little hope that personnel in lower ranks can.

With a perspective of the future, feedback from actions will determine variance from goal achievement. This qualitative review will serve as an aid to decision making that will improve future achievements and further progress. This process is a way of gaining predictive control that is ultimately better than after-the-fact variance analysis and management by exception. If action plans are well conceived, weekly or monthly results will indicate performance measured against goals.

CHAPTER VIII

Operations and Systems Effectiveness

Up to this point, the emphasis has been on quality and the behavioral aspects of productivity. While these are fundamentally significant and have an important impact on productivity, the methods and systems used to coordinate and control work also are primary influences on output. Without specific responsibilities for the monitoring and updating of methods and systems, problems tend to develop and grow, sometimes unnoticed, until serious and expensive inefficiencies are created.

A better trained work force will help to alleviate this situation. Employees are not routinely taught about (1) where hidden inefficiencies can be found and how they occur, (2) cost consequences of these factors, and (3) problem solving techniques that can be used to correct deficiencies and prevent their recurrence.

This chapter is devoted to techniques that are being successfully used to creatively accomplish productivity gain. While these techniques have been given different labels during the past 50 to 75 years, the central themes are much the same and have certainly withstood the test of time. And, they should be fully exploited before calling in the consultants.

Operations Analysis

Five vistas of waste and high cost are summarized here in the context of design and production systems. These are intended to serve as an illustration of deeper issues which lead to compounding costs.

1. People acquire habits and attitudes which correlate with past and ongoing organizational characteristics and environmental conditions, and make decisions based on what they believe to be true, and not necessarily on fact. Some people *learn* their jobs through self-taught, trial and error methods. Both managers and employees tend to accept work situations in an unthinking and unquestioning way, allowing

creeping avoidable inefficiencies to become a way of life in their departments. (For example, replacement of poor tools or machines is always easy to postpone 'til better times, or it is the subject of problems for the wrong reasons; inspection is always required; causes of quality problems are unique to manufacturing departments, etc.) Honestly held wrong beliefs often block good ideas and decisions, and delay progress.

2. The common thread in many problem situations is the lack of facts. This includes job functions or processes, and honest quality standards.

3. Inefficient temporary circumstances sometimes become legitimized by repeated use. For example, decisions based on urgent requirements, tight design parameters, or production limitations, can force a person to initiate temporary solutions or "fixes" to satisfy a requirement without due consideration of quality and cost consequences.

Creative Problem Solving

Steps of the problem solving process are variously applied to operations analysis, methods analysis, and value analysis. The difference between these uses will be found in a few key words and applications.

The steps taken in the traditional problem solving process are:

1. Describe the problem.
2. Get the facts.
3. Define the problem.
4. Develop alternatives.
5. Select the best alternative.
6. Implement the solution.
7. Follow-up.

For several decades these elements have been tweaked, twisted, revamped, and glamourized, and have become the bedrock of some successful consulting firms. But, the essential elements have remained simple and effective, and have withstood the test of time. They always work when properly applied; if they fail it is due to the environments and conditions under which they are used. Ingredients which lead to success are few: collaborative effort, patient leadership, helpful sub-cultures and informed and willing employees. The following are examples of situations that tend to occur in the use of this problem-solving model.

Describe the Problem, Get the Facts, and Define the Problem. Once a problem has been properly and completely defined, 50% of its solution will be apparent. This implies that problem definition is vital, and sufficient energy should be spent on gathering and sifting data to reach a solid conclusion that the isolated problem is indeed *the* problem. This is why complete definition usually cannot take place before this stage. The real problem may be quite different from the one originally described. In carrying out Step II, erroneous or biased information may slow or stop progress. If the problem can be construed to represent personal shortcomings on the part of the person supplying information, bias and oblique accounts are likely outcomes. Similarly, information or data sources who stand to gain from the results can consciously or unconsciously bias his or her contribution. The amount of substantiation is inversely proportional to such intangible factors as self-confidence, trust and cooperation. Where the culture begets clashes between people and organizations, straight-forward and accurate information may be difficult or even impossible to acquire.

Reports themselves can be misleading. Many financial statements, for example, account only for scrap and rework, leaving out inspection, reinspection, lost time and other nonconformance costs.

Infatuation with a "technique" can also contribute to the difficulty of problem resolution. A reliability or quality engineer, for example, may know just enough about statistics and probability to camouflage important information. (This can go on for months or even years!) Passion for the technique itself can supercede judgment about its usefulness as a *tool* for control and decision making. Statistics for judgment purposes are especially hazardous if there is a gap of comprehension between those who supply the information and those who need it for decision making. With the limited number of people who typically understand the "high math" of statistics, low management confidence tends to exist, even if the data are accurate. A result of such misleading information is the tendency to find fault with employees instead of machines, processes, or vendors. When problems are improperly defined, there is greater proclivity of finger pointing.

Verbal and written instructions also have historically been a fertile source of inaccurate or slanted information. Communication gaps, grapevine news releases, language barriers, and urgency all tend to produce their characteristic difficulties. Problems which are highlighted for immediate attention are often incomplete descriptions of symptoms. It is important but not easy to recognize the difference between the problem symptoms (which usually draw first attention) and the underlying causes. In short, until a problem is properly defined, the situation may seem overwhelming, but once the underlying issues have been identified and clarified, effective corrective measures become more obvious.

In the U.S., such a high value is placed on results that managers often feel pressed for immediate solutions. It is unfortunately axiomatic that the less time spent in effective problem analyses, the longer the solution will take. Some find solace in being incredibly active at attempting solutions to problems which frequently do not have assignable causes. Some problems simply "go away;" they are lost causes which create work for trouble-shooters. This is more likely to happen in the absence of a problem solving style which systematically isolates and defines problems that are worthy of investigation, and warrant concerted effort.

Pareto's Law of Maldistribution. In the problem solving process, it becomes very important to know which problems deserve a greater amount of attention. The question that usually needs to be answered is: How can a person distinguish the *significant* problems from trivial situations? There is a technique called Pareto's Law of Maldistribution that many people use to avoid the time thief of misguided emphasis. This method of revealing important problems is also sometimes referred to as the "significant few" versus the "trivial many."

A person who can classify and rank the most costly problems in a department or process, and solve the top 20% of the causes, according to Pareto's Law, will have eliminated 80% of the problem impact. For example, if the defects in an area totalled 1000 with 25 types recorded, the Pareto analyses might look something like this:

Kind of Defect	Rank	No. of Defects	% of Total
Surface Blemish	1	220	22%
Burrs	2	210	21%
Wrong Molding Contour	3	190	19%
Uneven Hole Pattern	4	182	18%
Total significant few-4 causes		800	80%
Total trivial many-21 causes		200	20%
Total		1000	100%

One can see by the distribution that only 4 of the 25 possible defect types accounted for 80% of all defects. If those situations found in the significant few of approximately 20% were corrected (the top four in this distribution), then approximately 80% of the defect problems will have been solved. On the other hand, 21 causes were attributed to only 20% of the total problem situation; thus these comprise the trivial many.

Studies show that in practically all cases where errors are occurring in a department, they are occurring primarily in a particular sector (machine, process, person, material, etc.) within an area of activity. An appropriate cost-conscious program requires not only the encouragement and nurturing of people or activities which are producing good results, but also the continuous analysis of each work unit to determine those areas where inefficiencies and mistakes are a drain on resources and a drag on department energy and vigor. This analysis should yield continuously improving plans for improvement.

Determine Alternative Solutions and Select the Best One. Several ideas normally must be examined and perhaps enlarged upon before one best solution can be identified. Sometimes the final choice between several "best" solutions is appropriately left to the managements to decide.

Creativity, a necessary factor in effective problem solving, has been defined many ways, but the central theme focuses on thought processes which produce or stimulate the flow of ideas. In the problem solving process, it is often desirable to advance a large number of ideas, then converge on the solution. Techniques such as brainstorming are used to increase divergent thinking. When a group is encouraged to function this way, ideas multiply geometrically; as divergent thinking takes place, each idea forms the basis for stimulating new ideas and so on. An additional advantage of this activity is a myriad of options that otherwise would occur too late, by chance, or perhaps not at all. An idea that is never stated, for whatever the reason, is one less building block on which final choices can be made.

Evaluating alternatives is an important part of creative problem solving, but it is not decision making. The process of evaluating begins with the grouping of possible solutions into categories and eliminating irrelevant segments and ideas. Whatever method is employed, the group should gather enough data to permit an accurate evaluation of the alternatives. A list of criteria such as availability of resources, possible side effects, costs "nice to have" vs. "must have" features, etc., can be generated and the alternatives evaluated against the criteria in an orderly fashion.

In decision making, it is important to know who will have the final word, and to agree up front on what is expected from the group. Will the boss make the final decision, or will there be consensus? Group processes can be reduced to a perfunctory exercise if the boss intercedes or uses political judgment to overrule the recommendations of the group. If there was an expectation that choices were to be shared, management zeal can dampen the spontaneous commitment to the solution, and probably contribute to indifferent involvement in future problem solving ventures.

Implement the Solution and Follow-up. Companies seem to experience difficulty in executing decisions once they have been made. Momentum of tradition and resistance to change, are often cited as reasons. Other reasons emanate from uncontrolled situations that generate barriers. Managers should include group dynamics as a healthy and non-manipulative way to involve people in the planning and execution of projects. While this is only a partial solution, and one ingredient of the recipe for success, it is one with proven merit.

Change is much more palatable and therefore has a far greater chance for success when it is carried out participatively. Less time will be needed to make progress when all the players have participated in and understand the change. Where the culture is not conducive to accepting change, more follow-up efforts will be needed in enforcement of change, and delays and backlash are likely. Follow-up is nearly always needed to detect newly emerging difficulties and unpredictable circumstances.

Value Analysis

Quality vs. Cost. Value analysis is a "discipline" which helps to establish appropriate quality and cost levels. This implies that a careful analysis is made of customer requirements, materials, designs, and manufacturing processes.

The design and fabrication of unnecessary quality characteristics into the product seldom add value; usually, they only increase the cost of manufacture. Designers sometimes inadvertently incorporate tolerances into component designs which afford greater precision than needed to meet all performance requirements. Unnecessary design exactitude can result in the necessity to fabricate the work elsewhere, in using scarce resources, or in excessive inspection time and equipment. These unnecessary costs can become a significant liability.

Eventually these practices, and other problems can add so much cost to a product that managers are driven to press for cost reductions. This action is manifested in budget cuts, reorganization, reduction in personnel strength, etc., which aggravates instead of alleviates the situation. It is in this phase of the business cycle that there is an especial temptation to compromise overall product reliability. The primary goal is to produce deliverable units that meet customers' expectations of quality, yet produced at minimum cost. This is the important concept in value analysis.

The Value Analysis Procedure. The value analysis procedure follows the problem solving process very closely, except that value analysis is the cost quality oriented discipline of questioning, evaluating and analyzing for the express purpose of improving product quality and productivity. This goal is met *effectively* by completing all design and specification work, then fabricating and assembling units that conform to these specifications.

Utilizing an analytical process as its basis, value analysis involves the identification, selection, development, and implementation of an idea that will result in products of higher reliability, or of lower cost with no sacrifice of quality.

Specifically, the value engineer seeks to:

1. Select the best materials for the job,

2. Select the best manufacturing processes and equipment for product fabrication,

3. Identify and select the best design concepts,

4. Identify all cost and quality factors that reduce produce value, and

5. Replace poor design, poor methods, and inadequate specifications with ones of greater value.

In order to accomplish the objectives cited above, the value engineer must get factual answers to six basic questions:[1]

1. What is the part or function?   (Identify)
2. What does it do?   (Function)
3. What does it cost?   (Cost)
4. What else will do the job?   (Alternative)
5. What would the alternative cost?   (Alternative Cost)
6. Would the alternative improve quality? (Alternative Quality)

While the value analysis discipline is frequently applied to design factors, it can also be used in operations where methods have become inefficient.

Methods Classified

Included among the important areas where productivity improvements are being made are the elimination of unproductive practices and the development of better work methods. Developing better methods requires the application of a body of knowledge, principles, and disciplines for this purpose. Unproductive practices are broadly defined as unnecessary or wasted motions and activities that are inadvertently or naively introduced into the job. Although methods are accepted as having a significant influence on output, their importance is widely ignored in practice, and usually are not the result of a careful investigation. Many methods have simply evolved over a period of time and are assumed to be satisfactory. Dedication and hard work are usually squandered where the methods are inferior.

Every operation in a business enterprise may be performed in a number of ways, and it is evident that all are not equally efficient. As a rule, even casual investigation would yield exceptional results, and many methods would be disgarded at once. Many managers and employees have been uninformed about what constitutes good methods and have not been given the training or the time needed to improve methods of work.

Macromethods. Macromethods pertain to the interaction of people, machines, equipment, time and money *between* the operations which are used to carry out the missions of the company. Subjects for analysis in this category relate to the movement, storage and other activities encountered during the conduct of business. Described in Figure VIII-1 are the symbols that are commonly used in the analysis of macromethods. Shown also are two additional symbols which signify major areas of productivity concern, namely corrective action and paperwork. Traditionally, the first five (operation, inspection, transportation, storage, and delay) have been the center of focus for study. In recent years, an increased amount of emphasis has been placed on paperwork and quality factors. Quality usually has "freeway" significance to improvement while the others have only "side street" importance.

Nevertheless, all seven areas are inseparably entwined. For example, corrective action always involves movement, inspection, reinspection, storage and delay. Corrective action also involves additional operations and labor which would otherwise be doing profitable work. Moreover, every rework and scrap action requires additional paperwork, its completion and its movement through the system. These activities are among those referred to as the hidden factory, giving rise to additional "needs" for handling, movement, separate storage, delays, with

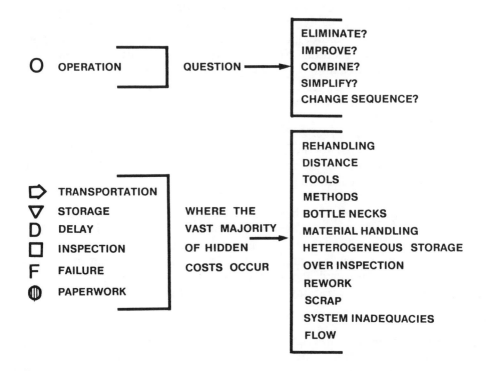

FIGURE VIII-1.   SYMBOLOGY AND SOURCES OF HIDDEN COSTS

attendant bottlenecks, lost parts, and so forth. The best contrived systems succumb to confusion when contaminated by rework and scrap. If the company does not enjoy efficient networks, quality issues serve only to compound the problem, adding more hidden obstacles to productivity improvement. If the high cost of such problems were accurately exposed, most knowledgeable executives would likely be energized to change their priorities.

It is beyond the scope of this text to cover the details of material handling and storage, etc., but the reader's attention is directed to some areas where room for improvements can generally be found.

Micromethods. Micromethods are those that are confined to an individual work center where an operator or assembler performs a *cycle* of work. For example, a cycle of work may be a drill press operator who, in the beginning of the job, repeatedly follows a series of elements which comprise the cycle.

Elements

(1) Get part from box
(2) Place in jig
(3) Drill hole   — One Cycle
(4) Remove from jig
(5) Dispose of part in box

The above sequence of elements illustrates how a cycle can be broken down into elements for analysis. During the performance of the elements, certain questions can be raised: (1) Where are the parts located with respect to the operator? Is the quantity correct? And what kind of box or material handling device is used to stage the parts? (2) Is the jig designed properly? Is there a risk of defectives being produced? Does the jig need to be fool proofed? Should it be designed to take multiple parts, etc? (3) Is the work done on the proper machine? Is the proper drill bit used, etc.? (4) Can the part be easily and quickly removed from the jig, etc.? (5) What type of box, pallet or cart is used to transport parts? When will it be moved? How far is it from the operators, etc.?

Ergonomics and Motion Economy

The science of ergonomics is concerned with the health, physiology and efficiency factors of employees in relationships to their environments. The effectiveness with which work is accomplished is regulated in great part by the appropriateness of ambient conditions. For example, the effects of lighting and temperature on the quality and quantity of output are obvious but are continually overlooked.

Color and noise also sometimes markedly influence output. The abundant use of either dull, monotonous colors of low contrast, or bright, clashing colors of high contrast are known to negatively impact ones psyche and despiritualize efforts. Similarly, startling noises also disrupt concentration and psychophysical balance. Variety, without extremes, and consistent with the kind of work involved, is generally considered the most desirable and healthy work environment.

Another ergonomic factor is the use of proper furniture. The seats provided for employees obviously should not cause back pain, or physical or psychological fatigue. Adjustable chairs with back rests should be provided, especially if the job necessitates long periods of sitting.

A supervisor or manager may need to assume the duties of an employee for a day or two to discover the inconvenience of the work station, or the extreme discomfort an employee is consistently experiencing. It often takes this level of involvement to convince a manager that changes in work areas need to be made. Conscientious effort to adapt people psychophysiologically to their work stations, is an important step toward productivity improvement.

In addition to the "conditions" of the work place, principles of motion economy should be considered in the design of work stations. Here are six important principles.

1. All unnecessary operation, activities, steps or body motions should be eliminated from the job. Work should be arranged so that the best balance of body members can be achieved. Figure VIII-2A illustrates the best layout for two-handed work. The most desirable situation is where parts, tools, etc., can be located in the normal work area, (see figure) requiring less use of body members and muscles. Sometimes it is necessary to arrange work in the maximum work area because of the nature of the work, or the number of parts required for the job. However, tasks that necessitate reaching beyond this area should be avoided because of the excessive motions and fatigue involved.

2. Fixed positions for tools, parts and assemblies should be provided. If items are *prepositoned,* a job will be easier to learn, better organized, less motions will be needed to perform the work and the jobs can be done more quickly with less frustration. Any degree to which this is not accomplished will result in employees having to search for needed parts, tools and materials. These are classified as hidden costs because they are often assumed to be "normal" and undetected. Such occurrences increase the risk of taking shortcuts which frequently result in error and corrective action.

3. Work places should be arranged so that both hands are as free as possible to complete the task. If one hand must be used as a holding device, for example, it is not free to perform productive work. Frequently a foot operated fixture can be used to free a hand as shown in Figure VIII-2B.

4. Work should be organized so that activities can be done concurrently. For example, in the above situation both hands performing concurrent work will produce nearly twice as much as when one hand must be used as a holding device, etc. Also, where the cycle of work involves a team of operators, segments of the work need to be balanced fairly among the team and sequenced so that idle time is minimized during the cycle. Work done in a series of activities will always take more time than if it were accomplished with simultaneous activities.

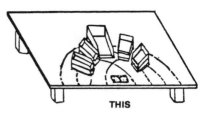

Bins are arranged close
in and for two handed work.

THIS

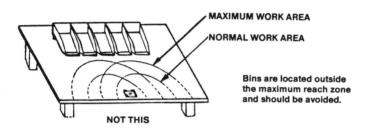

→ **MAXIMUM WORK AREA**

→ **NORMAL WORK AREA**

Bins are located outside
the maximum reach zone
and should be avoided.

NOT THIS

FIGURE VIII-2A.   GOOD VS. POOR WORKPLACE ARRANGEMENT

A. Foot operated fixture is
built into the work place.

B/C Parts are located for
easy access.

D. Proper lighting is
provided for the work
to be accomplished.

FIGURE VIII-2B.   FOOT OPERATED FIXTURE

5. Proper tools and bins should be provided to allow for optimum efficiency. Semi-automatic tools, for example, sometimes offer a great deal of opportunity for savings. Bins which allow for gravity feed and proper quantity of parts can also be a significant source of improvement.

6. Work centers should be arranged so that foot motions and awkward movements can be minimized. Work center layout essentially "fixes" the method the operator must use. In bench assembly work, the work place arrangement establishes the motion patterns to be followed;

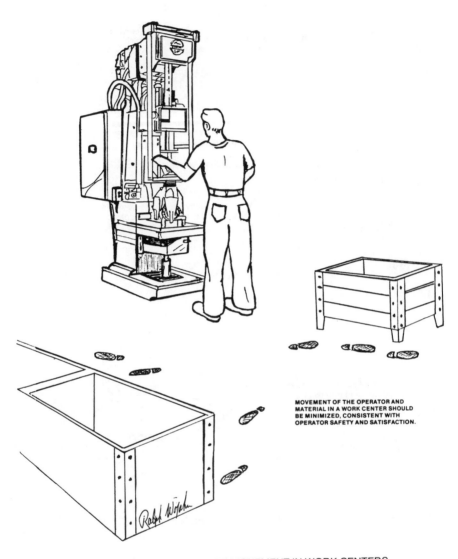

MOVEMENT OF THE OPERATOR AND
MATERIAL IN A WORK CENTER SHOULD
BE MINIMIZED, CONSISTENT WITH
OPERATOR SAFETY AND SATISFACTION.

FIGURE VIII-3. REDUCE MOVEMENT IN WORK CENTERS

in heavy manufacturing work, the work center layout predetermines the amount of movement needed by the operator. This is illustrated in Figure VIII-3.

Companies like Xerox, IBM, Hewlett-Packard, and Atari are demonstrating productivity gains through the use of ergonomic principles. The following photographs illustrate ergonomics equipment which is in use in these companies.

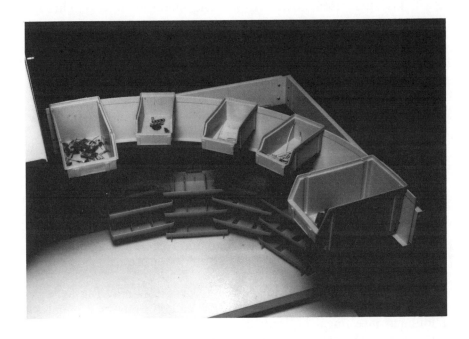

Courtesy Ergo-Tech Systems; Costa Mesa, California

There are 10 methods violations which persist in many factories:

1. Improper work height. (The work height should be approximately elbow height or just below.)

2. Inappropriate positioning of materials and tools at the work station.

3. Excessive movement within and between work centers.

4. Lack of instructions.

5. Improper tools (this includes fixtures and lifting devices).

6. Safety hazards.

7. Reverting to old methods once better ones have been introduced.

8. Disorganized or heterogeneous storage of materials, increasing "search" time.

9. Bottlenecks of materials.

10. Insufficient quantities of tools and materials to carry through a time period.

Costs of Methods Improvements

Methods improvements can be generally classified into three cost levels. The first level includes changes that may run as high as approximately $200 each. These are improvements that normally can be made quickly without the need for a great deal of investigation or justification. Based principally on violations of principles of motion economy, such improvements may involve: a simple rearrangement of a work place to allow for better use of body members, the provision of a hand tool or holding device to make a job easier, or even a bin for parts. The benefits should be obvious; however, such "small" improvements are sometimes considered inconsequential and passed over. No matter how small it may seem, every poor method represents some amount of avoidable cost and is therefore an opportunity for profit.

The second cost level of methods improvements may run as high as $3000. This level involves the uses of principles of motion economy, but additional investment in designing, constructing or purchasing devices will increase the costs. For example, an electro-mechanical device for holding or turning a part can reduce an operator's or inspector's cycle time by as much as 50 to 75%, but design and fabrication hours will probably be needed. When consistency is needed and human inconsistency is involved, investments in mechanical devices should be easily defended.

Methods work often inadvertently yields to items that upper managements believe are more important. Ironically, efforts to improve methods will usually help to accomplish the tasks that have been given the higher priorities. If the company does not set aside specific functions or allocate resources to this work, it will not likely get done.

The third and highest cost level of methods takes place when it is necessary to purchase special equipment, which requires a high capital investment. This covers anything over approximately $3,000. The purchase of special equipment may be overlooked as a "methods" improvement, but such equipment usually represents improvements in both methods and quality of output. Repeatability, high accuracy and the release of people to perform thinking roles are important gains. Where continuous production is involved, a company cannot afford not to have automatic or robotic equipment.

Making the best choices usually requires deliberation, skill and pooled information. In many plants, the detritus of past mistakes is everywhere—machines purchased, but never really placed into service. Inadequate information and bias can lead to investment disaster. Industrial engineers who normally have the job of justifying such purchases can be swayed by persistent production personnel with an emotional attachment to a certain machine. The lack of participation by production personnel in a procurement decision can also lead to determined resistance to cooperation and change.

Another reason that new equipment may not be utilized well is the long lead time for delivery of many machines. During a period of six months or one year, requirements for a certain machine can change enough to render it less useful by the time it is delivered. According to textbook explanations, this should not happen; organizations charged with procurement planning responsibilities are supposed to be able to plan far enough ahead to avoid these situations. With the rapid rate of change of technology, some machines may be obsolete by the time they are delivered. This, coupled with the growing number of equipments from which to choose, make it even more important to be systematic and certain during the evaluation of alternatives and selection of the best alternative.

In spite of everything done to avoid problems with new equipment, few major purchases are without pitfalls. Most can be eliminated during early phases of use, but in some instances, "debugging" does not solve all the problems. New automatic or semiautomatic machines may create the need for secondary operations that originally were not considered during planning. For example, a machine may be ideally suited for producing parts which meet critical tolerances, but may produce burrs which have to be removed subsequently. This is an unpredictable "rework" activity that has to be accomplished, but can result in considerably more labor hours than planned.

Creeping Change

Creeping change and how it effects productivity is a constant challenge. Change can be a boon to improvement, or a productivity swamp. When a company is first established, its organizers have a market vision. They acquire the necessary elements of capital, equipment, people, facilities and materials to carry out their perceived mission. As the company grows, it will have acquired a large number of characteristics that make management much more complex.

If change is properly managed, it can be the leading edge of productivity improvement; foresight into market changes, research and developmental work and ongoing sensitivites to market shifts are managed well by firms which have good productivity stances. Better managed companies also take advantage of technological opportunities, effectively control equipment depreciation and obsolescence and facilitate needed personnel and methods changes. Firms which have not been successful at managing change now find themselves in a reactive crisis management mode, ill equipped to deal with the dynamics of competitive markets and technological progress. Managements' attention should be balanced between those aspects of change which affect productivity rates and those which impact on market strategies.

Undesirable creeping changes have the insidious characteristic that, while they may be questioned at the time they occur, many are dismissed and ultimately forgotten when other priorities enter the picture. This problem is generic to most companies today, and the only solution is a thorough, systematic and deliberate problem solving effort. Creeping change can be illustrated by comparing facility changes over a specific period. Shown in Figure VIII-4 and VIII-5 are two flow plans before and after a company experienced 20 years of "change." Flow lines of the two products, A and B which were originally manufactured by the company, are shown in Figure VIII-4, and flow lines for the two primary products now produced by the company are shown in Figure VIII-5. While many small changes also occurred during this 20-

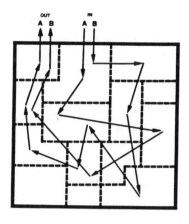

FIGURE VIII-4. INITIAL FLOW OF PRODUCTS A AND B

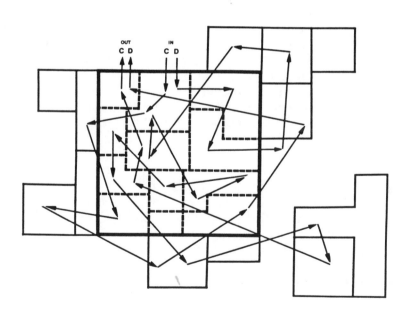

FIGURE VIII-5. FLOW AFTER 15 YEARS OF CHANGE

year period, the company, as it is now arranged, is at a disadvantage to effectively produce the new products C and D. Changes in facilities and equipment tend to lag market conditions and product line changes, gradually and systematically adding to the list of hidden factory costs.

Standards Integrity

Standards vs. Improvement. Another fruitful question is related to the credibility of a company's standards. Many companies, new and old alike, do not have an honest and reliable basis for calculating manufacturing costs. Accurate decisions and predictions about capacity and output cannot be made without accurate standards, but it is frequently tried.

On the other hand, while accurate standards are necessary for cost control, they also can be abused and cause negative outcomes. Performance standards are sometimes set and administered in a way that indirectly precludes higher and *better* performance. In some companies, standards are perceived to be used against operators who are below normal and provide no incentive for improvement for those who are consistently high performers. While standards are usually set analytically, their effects are sometimes viewed subjectively, producing unintentional outcomes. Meeting a standard which purports to be optimum makes some slow operators believe they can never win favor of their supervisors, while others believe they are "satisfactory" and regard this effort as sufficient. Others are content with their performances because they are consistently above normal, even though they could improve. Still others, not having received feedback, have no notion about the quality of their performance, even though the standards have been consistently applied. In some cases standards *follow* unplanned change, while in others, they remain unchanged long after creeping change has taken its toll on the methods that were in use when the standards were originally set.

Are standards in reality expected quantities of output based on historical trends? Do standards challenge operators to produce higher quality? Is there an incentive to increase output? Do standards include a mechanism to draw attention to workmanship as well as quantity? An ongoing method of review should be established to make certain that standards are kept current and maintained so as to provide a quality incentive. Such a program will take into account quality, methods, creeping change, training and motivation.

Methods vs. Standards. The two major phases of setting performance standards—methods improvement and calculating the standard—should be accomplished in that order, but setting the standard is typically given a higher priority. The use of best methods has profound affects on productivity and which should be of great concern to management. It is widely accepted that both quality and quantity of output are influenced considerably by the methods employed, and companies must strive to establish performance standards based on methods which are known to be effective.

The concept of methods improvement is illustrated in Figure VIII-6. The average and range of output of an operation, before methods improvement is compared to the output after proper methods work,

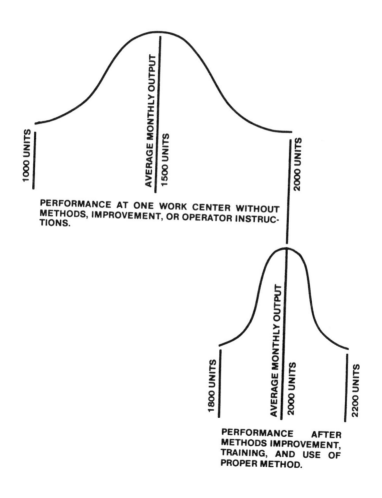

FIGURE VIII-6. OUTPUT BEFORE AND AFTER METHODS IMPROVEMENT

instructions and operator training. Output is not only higher, but control is also predictably easier and forecasts of output are more accurate. It is a basic law of production that time (labor cost) is a result of the motions and speed with which work is accomplished. Ironically, while time is cherished and held in high regard, it is inadvertently squandered through the use of poor methods.

If the importance of methods improvements and standards is as obvious as described, why have some companies not done a better job of dealing with such an important productivity subject? Several factors can be cited. The most obvious is expediency. Results-oriented managements want output and capacity numbers for their divisions. In this milieu, the "details" are left for others to ponder over with attendant neglect of a cornerstone of productivity. Industrial engineers are often required to quickly set standards without the resources to examine and improve methods first. In addition to being time consuming, methods analyses frequently lead to expenditures for material and labor. Neither of these are pleasant subjects to bring up to senior managers who believe things are moving along satisfactorily, and "just want some numbers."

Another reason that performance standards sometimes precede sufficient methods study can be traced to organization. Methods analyses traditionally have been associated with industrial engineering departments, but in many companies, methods work has become splintered with this responsibility diffused in other organizations. While this division can be satisfactory, difficulties arise when organizations lack the skills to deal with methods issues. In some companies, methods responsibility may be limited to only one person; in large companies auxiliary methods groups are sometimes organized under industrial or manufacturing engineering. In other companies this function is nonexistent, leaving methods work that is done to a manufacturing engineer who also is responsible for production planning, tooling, ordering equipment and working out producibility problems with design engineering people.

There is an education gap contributing to the methods dilemma. Some methods engineers who have come up through the ranks, and some graduate IEs have not been educated in the "earthy" techniques of methods analyses. The principles and applications of Methods Time Measurement (MTM), work simplification and plant layout, for example, are not widely understood. Even some graduate industrial engineers have missed the practical side of these subjects in their college training.

When insufficient knowledge in industrial engineering is coupled with an aggressive production superintendent, the risk of problems is very high. One can ask nearly any production or operations manager about matters of methods or plant layout and most have ready suggestions. But, their notions are often based on opinions about what "has worked," and not on facts and data about what will work better. A well-trained methods and plant layout organization, its size consistent with company needs, should help training departments educate others to cooperatively incorporate better methods. The full scope of this activity requires top management support and involvement.

Supervisor's Responsibilities

It is part of the supervisor's responsibility to see that methods improvements are utilized, and that the operators are trained and competent. The supervisor should also help the analyst in identifying the correct use of tools and techniques so that proper analyses can be made. Although a methods analyst should have a practical background in the area of work studied, he or she could hardly be expected to account for all the details of the various operations and processes. Supervisors who accept and carry out these responsibilities, even though they can never be assured of returned cooperation, will find that in the long run, their cooperative attitudes will make improvements in their departments more effective.

Having an adequate appreciation of the importance of the human approach is needed by both methods people and supervision. When performing methods work, the supervisor and the analyst should take time to talk to operators and solicit their ideas and reactions. The work progresses much more smoothly and effectively if the operator becomes a "part" of the team. This cannot occur unless he or she is asked to *join* the team. Operators are closer to the operations than anyone else and they usually have more specific knowledge about the operations. It is important that this source be realized, respected, and utilized.

Any program to improve methods must also consider workers doubts and fears. Fearing the unknown, workers tend to be hesitant about participating in improvement ventures that they perceive will work against them, and only benefiting the management.

Tooling and Inspection Planning

There is also much potential for productivity improvement in the way most companies handle the jobs of tooling planning, manufacturing planning and inspection planning. These benefits originate in the organizational and functional cadre of personnel who carry out these missions. Tooling planners, quality control planners and industrial engineers or production planners have a common bond; all perform tasks of problem *prevention* which, when properly conceived and executed, will lead to further improvement.

Tool planners determine the nature and kind of tooling that will be designed in tool design departments. Between the tool planners and the tool designers some degree of preventive efficiency is achieved. Can tools be designed for multiple tasks thereby reducing individual set ups? Have the right judgments been made about the kind of tooling for a particular machine? When tooling is planned, is it done with full knowledge of machine capabilities? The job of tool planning is variously relegated to manufacturing engineering, production supervision or tooling departments depending on the company's organization.

Effective tool planning will produce combinations of the following benefits.

- less set-up time for operators

- less defects produced at a work center

- less machine cycle time

- less inspection time

- consistent output

Inspection planning also carries considerable potential for improvement. In some firms this activity is done by manufacturing planners, in others by quality control personnel, and in others this function is dealt with only superficially or not at all. The person or persons who have the best information should determine inspection points in the manufacturing sequence. Illustrated in Figure VIII-7 is a segment of an operation process chart depicting a specific sequence of operations and inspection points. The one shown in Figure A was planned by a manufacturing planner without the benefit of quality control data. Inspection points at (a) and (b) were established because no information was available to conclude otherwise, and no questions were raised to the contrary. The sequence pictured in Figure B was the result of joint inputs from manufacturing and quality planners. Together they realized that the inspection task of measuring the milled slot could be easily accomplished by the machinist. While the standard had to be adjusted to allow time for the additional inspection activity, one-third of the total time was cut from the overall inspection task. It was also determined that the second inspection could be entirely eliminated.

216

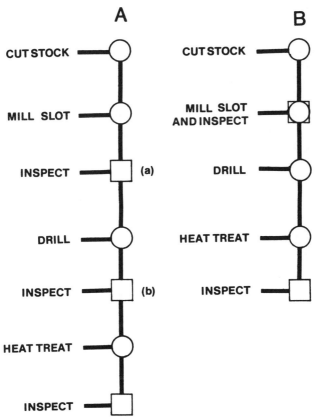

FIGURE VIII-7. MANUFACTURING AND INSPECTION PLANNING BEFORE AND AFTER ANALYSIS

Inspection data revealed that less than .1 of 1% defectives were produced from the drilling operation and an inspection point here would be perfunctory and wasteful.

This example illustrates an important productivity point. Production planners and quality control planners need to work closely together to share information in which each is a specialist. Production planners may not be privy to historical data about the quality produced by certain machines. This information is vital to whether or not inspection should be employed after or before certain processes. The quality control department should be able to provide this information via inspection results. Similarly, quality control planners may not have current information about machine loading, schedules and other production demands placed on certain machines. These criteria also are variables with which production people must deal.

Several criteria should be considered and questions answered when deciding how much and at what point inspection should be conducted.

1. What do process capability studies reveal about a given process?

2. What is the history of defectives from a process?

3. Is a succeeding operation particularly difficult or especially costly to operate? Is jamming of a machine by defectives from a preceding operation a factor?

4. Is it too costly to burden a process with even a few defectives produced in prior processes?

5. Will an operation result in defectives being covered up, making it necessary to determine quality levels before this process?

The answers to these questions ultimately must be resolved through cost comparisons. Without the use of good judgment, productivity will be impacted in the following ways:

1. Unnecessary labor and machine time may be devoted to defectives already produced by previous operations.

2. Machine down time can be caused by defectives from prior operations.

3. Unnecessary or redundant inspections may occur through lack of information or biased notions.

4. When unneeded inspection points are planned or performed (1) unnecessary labor and equipment burdens are placed on the system, (2) the number of communication loops is increased and (3) additional opportunities for controversy are created.

Pitfalls of Industrial Engineering

Over the years people have developed different perceptions of industrial engineers. Some people associate IEs with productivity improvement, some with work measurement and setting standards; others perceive them primarily as "job eliminators."

Irrespective of this colorful but not particularly helpful imagery, one of their most important missions is to institute changes in direct and indirect functions that will increase productivity. Most of the difficulties that IEs seem to experience is seated in their fundamental missions of planning and implementing change. The identity of IEs as advocates of change can generate negative perceptions. One significant reason for resisting change is the very human and understandable fear that the personal costs of change will be greater than the benefits. Employees function in a "comfort zone" and any threat to this security base is likely to be met with resistance in some form. Because change is an inherent objective of their work, industrial engineers should strive to improve the human relations aspect of their jobs. Real success as an IE may bear heavily on the degree to which causes of resistance to change are understood and resolved.

Ironically, the industrial engineering profession has sometimes inadvertently helped to build resistance to their roles. For example, a new graduate industrial engineer, in a three-piece suit, overflowing with enthusiasm and filled with textbook knowledge, is directed to the shop floor, counseled about the need for courage and sets out to put theory into practice. His or her first encounter may be with a rough shop steward or a burly forge press foreman whose initial thought is, "Here is another young college graduate for me to train!" The novice IE draws out his clipboard and stopwatch and red flags go up all over the shop floor. Such situations are of course more severe in shop cultures which are distrustful of management.

That some IE departments have earned negative stereotypes about their roles is an indictment against their effectiveness. Where this has occurred, the management should take every opportunity to support legitimate causes of IEs and bolster efforts to generate camaraderie between organizations. The IE should try to obtain "buy in" to a change and sell it on the basis of its merits so that it will have wholehearted acceptance. Early efforts to gain cooperation and team work will usually pay off in carrying out IE assignments. Gaining participation by those affected will greatly help to achieve acceptance after implementation, and make the jobs of all involved parties much easier. In some companies, the long standing stereotype that IEs eliminate people's jobs still exists. Efficiency studies can result in the reduction of the job scope or even the elimination of certain activities, and the IE department can become the scapegoat for personnel reductions which are already planned or in progress. Reduction or reassignments of people may need to be made, and IEs are sometimes perceived as the culprits who not only conceive of the idea, but are responsible for the action. This is seldom true.

Quality Factors

As previously pointed out, quality professionals have been known to accuse the management and production personnel of having strong biases toward delivery dates or *quantity* of output, at the expense of quality. This notion is strengthened if tight standards have been established without proper regard for quality, and if pressure is exerted to increase output based on these standards. Those directly responsible to meet standards become increasingly frustrated as they (1) witness the equipment they must use become more and more obsolete, (2) encounter increasing quality problems with materials, and (3) work in an atmosphere of growing resentment among employees. Senior managements, from positions on the sideline, cheer operators on to work smarter, do the job right the first time, and cut costs. Simultaneously, posters are tacked up around the plant to motivate employees to get into the "quality spirit." Meanwhile, industrial engineers under pressure of management to "fine tune" standards, attempt to locate additional "avoidable" delays so that further cuts in allowed times can be made.

The overall philosophy and content of performance standards must embody three important features: (1) Time for *quality care* needs to be incorporated into the standard by an allowance or other means, (2) methods must be sufficiently analyzed to ensure that quality characteristics are designed into the work place and job cycle, and (3) workers should not be given performance goals that are in conflict. The management team (including quality engineers, industrial engineers, manufacturing engineers, safety engineers, and the like) in its anxiety to improve productivity, exerts pressure to build quality into the products. But the workers who are on the receiving end of the plans and administrative actions are unable to take pride in their jobs when management expectations grow, without providing for the flexibility or allowances that are commensurate with the expectations. As discussed in Chapter II, some companies are entering into the phase in which operators are being trained to inspect their own work. But, if the management expects operators to take more of the responsibility for the quality of their work, the description and the allowed time for the job must account for the appropriate use of certain measuring devices, or other quality related features, and allow sufficient time for the operator to make qualitry assessments or adjustments. Managements will not be perceived as being serious about quality and productivity improvement until they convince the employees of their evenhanded practices, and allocate the necessary resources to meet all the objectives that *they* have established.

Meeting all workmanship standards can take more time than otherwise would be required where methods improvements have not been implemented, and where inconsistent practices are being followed by operators. It is incumbent on IEs and quality control personnel to work together to incorporate time factors for quality in standards where this need exists. Moreover, quality and industrial engineering managers should jointly try to educate the upper management about the realities of this issue and search for other areas to increase output that will not compromise quality. Some industrial engineers have not fully digested the quality message. They continue to perceive their roles as standards and productivity analysts, motion and time study engineers, and indirect work measurement or plant layout engineers. These are among the traditional roles of an IE and are obviously important. However, the industrial engineer with his or her special talents can be an even more effective member of the productivity team by working more closely with quality personnel. Jobs such as equipment capability studies, writing justifications for equipment replacements, providing for adequate equipment repair and studies of manufacturing processes and methods to eliminate problems of high scrap and rework should be undertaken jointly by quality, industrial engineering, and manufacturing engineering personnel. Confidence and teamwork need to flower between production supervisors, industrial engineers, manufacturing engineers and quality control engineering groups. The management of such issues as schedules, scrap and rework, inventories, performance standards, equipment capability, and producibility of hardware from design drawings and specifications will be incomplete without cooperative effort. Only a veneer of efficiency can be created without teamwork between these organizations.

Need For Quality and Industrial Engineering Teamwork

Quality cuts across every activity in a company. While the cliche, "Do the job right the first time" might be over used, it does express the need to view quality from a very broad perspective. Any error is counter productive; every significant error involves scrapping resources or doing something over. This initiates the spiral of costs. Nearly every job of the typical industrial engineer is coupled with the preventive disciplines of operations analysis, equipment purchases and repair, work place arrangements, and plant layout. Quality engineers perform process capability studies, help to justify equipment purchases, design control charts, perform a variety of quality planning tasks, qualify vendors and participate in design reviews.

While both disciplines perform functions that are critical to productivity improvement, they often appear to misunderstand each other and appear to be even in competition. Quality managers are heard to complain that work methods and equipment are causing quality problems, and capital monies are earmarked for the wrong things. On the other hand, industrial engineering managers assert that when capital equipment must be justified, IEs are unable to obtain the cooperation of quality personnel. Whether there is redundancy of effort, lack of pooling of information, or whether the "us and them" attitude is present, *effectiveness* is compromised. This is a management issue.

Quality and industrial engineering departments function well as a team in many companies. Senior managements have placed organizational teamwork high among the priorities with the result that the evolving cultures embody this value. In these companies quality and industrial engineering departments have become jointly actualized in their efforts to find better ways for employees to work in harmony. Historically, industrial engineers studied the way people worked in factories and the relationships of those workers to their machinery and tools, toward the goal of efficiency. Quality organizations in the past placed quality at the forefront, taking whatever actions that they deemed necessary to deliver units according to design requirements. Both organizations, while essentially retaining their past duties, have now enlarged their missions to include more of the human relations aspect of running a business. They have come to realize more fully that long-term productivity gains are based on better utilization of *human* resources. Although quality and industrial engineers are not concerned with social science, per se, they cannot avoid establishing contact with that field inasmuch as production, even in a highly mechanized shop, depends largely upon people. Since technical problems are interlaced with human issues, it becomes a part of the quality and industrial engineering challenge to resolve the equation between the technical and the human problems as they arise in business environments. Behind every machine or desk is a human being which calls attention to the relationship between people and their jobs.

CHAPTER IX

Productivity Analysis and Measurement

In Chapter I productivity was defined simply as output/input. This leaves a lot to the imagination if the purpose is to classify outputs and inputs by type or importance.

Productivity is a dynamic process. The goal, of course, is to stimulate an increase in the rate of growth of productivity. Progress (or lack of it) can be seen by comparing productivity ratios covering a given time period.

$$\text{For example,} \quad \frac{\dfrac{\text{output}}{\text{input}} \ (1983\text{-}1985)}{\dfrac{\text{output}}{\text{input}} \ (1980\text{-}1982)} = \begin{array}{c} \text{change in} \\ \text{productivity} \\ \text{posture} \end{array}$$

There has been some confusion about productivity "measurement," partly because there are so many ways in which inputs and outputs can be grouped. To illustrate this diversity, several examples are listed.

1. $\dfrac{\text{Projects completed}}{\text{Projects planned}}$

2. $\dfrac{\text{Actual machine hours}}{\text{Scheduled machines hours}}$

3. $\dfrac{\text{Sales}}{\text{Operating costs}}$

4. $\dfrac{\text{Actions taken resulting from meetings}}{\text{Hours in attendance}}$

5. $\dfrac{\text{Machines operating}}{\text{Machines not operating}}$ 6. $\dfrac{\text{Value of quality circles projects completed}}{\text{Time devoted to circles meetings}}$

7. $\dfrac{\text{Designs completed}}{\text{Design hours used}}$ 8. $\dfrac{\text{Improvement in workmanship}}{\text{Cost of training}}$

9. $\dfrac{\text{Rework and/or scrap}}{\text{Costs}}$ 10. $\dfrac{\text{Skills exercised}}{\text{Skills trained for}}$

After output/input categories have been defined, improvement objectives can be set and trends observed. Methods of measuring productivity vary with the type of industry and the kind of work involved. In manufacturing companies where hardware is produced, the effectiveness with which *quality* requirements are met is an important measure. Although it is common to find performances measured in blue-collar areas, it is an important and often neglected principle that the quality and productivity performances of white-collar workers should also be assessed. In service type industries, work is essentially accomplished by white–collar personnel, and the definition and measurement of the appropriate work units become the issues.

Irrespective of the kind of business, productivity is a "consequence" of at least five interrelated variables. These are effectiveness, efficiency, timeliness, quality and leadership. *Effectiveness* focuses on making the best and most accurate decisions; *efficiency* is the ability to economically produce the desired results (the ratio of work to the energy expended in producing it); *timeliness* pertains to reaching the goal within a predetermined time need; *quality* is the variable that involves (1) understanding and planning for the customers' needs and (2) understanding and managing the variables which affect output; and *leadership* is the constancy of purpose and philosophy which create an environment in which people succeed and outputs are economically generated.

It is important to understand that productivity does not have to be "measured" to improve it. In fact, significant productivity gains can be achieved through intangible factors which are integrally tied to *faith validity*. Faith validity is placing ones confidence and trust in principles, the credibility and integrity of which have already been established. This is done without allowing doubt to influence benefits. For example, the value of problem prevention as discussed in Chapter 6, is generally known. Its value lies in the execution, not in its measurement, per se. Good leadership is another example. Leadership is *known* to be positively correlated with productivity gain. Individual desire and commitment, together with group devotion to the cause of improvement, are synergistic forces which inspire and generate productivity. Doubts

224

can be raised about the value of known precepts, and the importance of these truths can be diminished by waiting for proof or measured results.

Some additional maxims are listed as follows:

1. Up front plans and strategies predetermine future results, and therefore should be freely exercised.

2. Teamwork begets loyalty and trust.

3. Prevention is less costly than corrective action.

4. Training is less costly than error.

5. Management involvement is directly proportional to teamwork.

It is not meant to imply that measurement is not important or needed. In fact, measurement is mandatory for productivity *management*. Its benefits are found in five principles.

Measurement:

- provides the basis for recognizing cause and effect relationships,

- gives an indication of the potential return on investment,

- provides for the establishment of accurate priorities,

- energizes managers to take action, and

- provides a basis for sound decisions.

If the *uses* of measurement do not contribute, or are not traceable to at least one of the benefits above, the measurement activity should be seriously questioned. Moreover, if measurement becomes an obstacle to the exercise of established truths, it should also be questioned.

White-Collar Work Measurement

Work cultures of white-collar personnel vary from continual panic situations to busyness without purpose. On balance, significant opportunities for productivity improvement can be found in indirect functions where people perform jobs of supervision, planning, coordination, and those involving data and reports. Opportunities for waste exist where "normal" work involves telephone calls, visitors, crises situations, meetings, paperwork flow and other activities where human interaction is required. Meetings to study problems and generate solutions, for example, have become a way of life and demand an increasing amount of many managers' time. A vice president of a Fortune 100 company told me that he had two people devoted almost entirely to scheduling conference rooms and coordinating meetings.

In service type organizations as well as indirect functions, performance measurement usually focuses on system effectiveness and leadership. Performance measurements of indirect work are usually more subjective and qualitative than those found in blue-collar jobs. Increases in productivity are generated largely through the removal of hindrances to effectiveness. Such obstacles include poor leadership styles, inadequate tools and equipment and cumbersome or incomplete systems.

One difficulty encountered in measuring indirect work is discerning the degree to which an activity is really productive. There are two well-entrenched myths or cultural traits that influence success in measuring performances of indirect personnel.

MYTH #1. White-collar employees are the "thinking" class of the work force, and have non-repeating work elements which carry an unmeasurable connotation.

This notion is not well-founded. If a job cannot be defined, there is no need for the position. If the job can be defined, performance can be measured. In fact, the definition of the job itself can be used as the basis of performance measurement.

MYTH #2. Indirect employees should not be questioned about efficiency factors because their work requires freedom, flexibility and creative expression.

White-collar personnel need some level of leadership and control, without which there is an unacceptable risk of undetected inefficiency and low productivity. However, one of the difficulties in managing white-collar workers in the context of performance measurement is that a "conflict of interest" is sometimes created.

Some managers of indirect functions find themselves in the uncomfortable (or even competitive) position of supervising people who have more expertise in a field than they have. To avoid conflict, these managers often allow so much free reign that the effectiveness of the organization is questionable. While a certain amount of freedom is necessary to generate white-collar productivity, a general "country club" style of management is known to be ineffective. Usually left unsaid, but clear standard operating practice in some companies, are the slogans, "you've got to conform to get along here," or "don't make waves; Charlie may soon become your boss." Such inhibiting expressions reflect attitudes that are well entrenched in white-collar cultures, especially in some large companies.

Management by Objective as a Performance Measurement Tool. One of the most widely used methods for assessing performances of white-collar employees is Management by Objective (MBO). While this method embodies other principles, it involves primarily the appraisal of work accomplished and measured against previously established objectives or expectations. (This subject is covered in more detail in the following chapter in the context of "how to," but is included here to identify pitfalls that are encountered when performance measurements are undertaken).

MBO methodology has enjoyed widespread use among American managers. Most managements are accustomed to structuring and prioritizing activities into objectives in order to achieve desired outputs. For many managers this method has become the brick and mortar, as well as the foundation for carrying out the missions of their organizations, particularly where work is accomplished by white-collar people.

The omnipresent existence of the white–collar myths previously discussed, and the "normal" confusion which surrounds white-collar jobs, often combine to make the effectiveness of MBO less than popularly believed.

The notion that measurement of white-collar employee performance is a precarious task and that it carries repercussive connotations are the basis for the lack of *discipline* needed to make MBO effective. Ironically, lack of discipline and hesitation to evaluate performances are causes of employees' disenchantment. The problem of performance measurement usually lies not so much in being unwilling to conduct appraisals, but with the frequent changes in priorities and the myriad distractions and false starts which typically confront both managers and white-collar employees.

White-collar personnel are vulnerable to creeping confusion in their jobs, or perplexing job variables beyond their control. As a result, objectives frequently have diminishing clarity and meaning. Sustaining the integrity required to make MBO effective as a measurement tool is difficult for many managers. Unquestionably, firms that are enjoying the most success with MBO are those where the managements are committed, skillful, patient, disciplined and devote sufficient time to making it work. This is found most often in companies which are predisposed to cooperation and coadjuvant attitudes.

Work Sampling. Another method used to evaluate indirect functions is work sampling. Work sampling is a commonly used method for studying work where work units are difficult to define or measure. By making random observations of activities, contents of a job can be classified, studied, and improved.

This technique has as its basis the laws of probabilities. If a *random* or *representative* sample of an activity is taken over a sufficiently long period, it will reflect the characteristics of the population. A sample is random when it is obtained from a population from which each item drawn has an identical chance of being selected. In the context of this discussion, the population is the 480 minutes of a work day. In a work sampling study, it is imperative that observations be made so as to insure equal opportunities to observe all activities. In other words, the observation times or sequences must be randomly determined.

Randomness may be insured by assigning numbers to each individual or time interval and then referring to a random number table to establish the sample and sequence of observations. Random number tables may be prepared by drawing numbers from a bowl, providing each number occurs the same number of times and that the numbers after being drawn are placed back in the bowl. Comprehensive random number tables are usually prepared on electronic computers, and are available commercially.

The larger the number of observations, the greater will be the probability that this sample will infer true characteristics of the population. However, inaccuracies are inherent in any technique which depends on chance. This is a "risk" that must be accepted unless the population can be observed continuously. Usually, the risk is evaluated in terms of the cost of a more accurate answer. The accuracy of the technique increases with the length of the study, but reaches a point of diminishing return after the confidence has been reached that no further significant statistical change will be experienced.

To illustrate the use of work sampling as it applies to the job, a secretary's job will serve as an example. It is desirable to first set forth duties that go with the job. Even if there is no job description, one can normally list the expected or perceived duties, and use these as a starting point.

Those listed in Figure IX-1 approximate those performed by a typical secretary together with some that are atypical.

Expected Activities	Random Observations	Minutes	Percent
1. Typing			
A. Status reports	XX	19.2	4
B. Memoranda, etc.	XXX	28.8	6
C. Forms and the like	XX	19.2	4
2. Appointments, visitors, etc.	XXXX	38.4	8
3. Filing	XXXXX	48.0	10
4. Telephone work	XXXXXX	57.6	12
5. Dictation	X	9.6	2
6. Coordination	XXX	28.8	6
7. Idle time	X	9.6	2
8. Break	XXX	28.8	4
Unexpected			
1. Typing for another supervisor	XXXXX	48.0	10
2. Searching for information	XXXXXXXXX	86.4	18
3. Filing for another secretary	XXXX	38.4	8
4. Miscellaneous	XX	19.2	4
TOTALS		480 min.	100%

FIGURE IX-1. RANDOM OBSERVATIONS OF A SECRETARY'S ACTIVITIES

Illustrated in the above example are fifty random observations of activities performed by a secretary. Of the total activities sampled, 40% were observed in the unexpected category. This finding is probably significant for several reasons. If 40% of the secretary's time (or for that matter any other job) is devoted to activities other than what is expected, this general area probably should be evaluated for improvement.

The category, "searching for information," definitely deserves some attention, since a greater amount of time per day (86.4 min.) is devoted to this activity than any other.

This hypothetical example illustrates how work sampling can be applied to other indirect activities. Inspection functions, shipping and receiving departments, test laboratories, management activities, design engineering are also examples of where work sampling can be beneficial, either in studying a group of people, or a specific job.

Difficulties Encountered in the Work Sampling Procedure

Like other studies where probability and statistics are applied, there is an ever-present danger of procedural abuse. Biased results can be easily obtained, and several precautionary measures should be taken.

(1) Randomness of the observed times must always be achieved. Any circumstances other than chance that influences the time an observation is taken should not be allowed in the study. Therefore, it is imperative that in the design of the study observed times have been predetermined with the use of a table of random numbers.

(2) Another temptation is to jump to conclusions before sufficient evidence has been generated to warrant a conclusion. A study must be sufficiently long to be certain that all work units have been witnessed in the investigation, and confident that trends and percentages have stabilized. If the work units of a job have been difficult to define, there is greater likelihood that unforeseen activities will occur. During the course of the study, it may be necessary to reclassify certain work units to encompass activities that were not anticipated, making the study longer than expected.

(3) Anticipation by the observed person or group is said to bias the results. However, some believe that those being studied become accustomed to the analyst and his or her presence will make no difference in the accuracy of the study. The cultural climate of cooperativeness in a company figures heavily in the degree to which this might occur.

The ability of the analysts to classify what he or she observes into the proper category will also affect accuracy. It may be necessary to ask people what they are doing or where they have been, etc. Thus, the accuracy of the study can bear significantly on the cooperation and attendant attitudes and honesty of the people involved.

Other Performance Measurement Indices. While MBO and work sampling can be applied to almost any kind of work activity, they are more often used as a tool in measuring indirect jobs where work units are obscure or difficult to identify. Where cycles of work are easy to quantify, as in most blue—collar areas, several techniques for measurement are common. These include comparing various predetermined time standards or standards arrived at by conventional stop watch techniques with actual outputs. Scores of excellent management and industrial engineering books are available which cover the general subject, of manufacturing standards; thus it is only mentioned here.

A less understood productivity measurement index, and an important variable in the productivity equation is *quality*. Most companies define quality in terms of either *conformance* or *fitness for use*. When it is defined in terms of conformance, productivity can be shown by the following equation.

$$P = \frac{\text{Conformance (output)}}{\text{Total Quality Costs (input)}}$$

Use of this formula implies that the cost accounting network is set up to report prevention, inspection and failure costs.

When expected outputs are defined in terms of conformance, measurable objectives can be defined. If requirements of the customers and design parameters, etc., have been nailed down and clear, conformance assessments to these requirements are measurable. However, where conformance is the output goal, this method of measurement can carry short-term and narrow implications. For example, research and development activities which connote new products and product improvements also need to be addressed. Meeting the "requirements" of customers today can be the demise of the business tomorrow, if marketing implications of quality have been inadvertently down played. While internal productivity is a major concern, if companies equate conformance with internal effectiveness, the dynamics of market conditions may not be given the attention they deserve.

There is important advantage in defining outputs in terms of conformance in that many of the in-house and vendor oriented productivity variables become measurable and thus more manageable. People and groups have a "standard" against which they can be held accountable.

When long-term productivity improvement is the goal, some prefer fitness for use as an output indicator. This criterion embodies the customer "change" factor and connotes effectiveness in making marketing decisions and implementing long range strategic plans. In order to achieve continuous productivity gain, the equation must encompass the dynamics of the marketplace, competitive standing and the potential for price recovery. Price recovery can be thought of as the degree to which input cost increases can be passed on to customers in the form of higher prices.[1] This ability is highly correlated with customers' satisfaction, and is a measure of both short-term success and long-term health. Customer satisfaction and good will are outcomes of strategic quality planning which, (1) help the company to maintain a competitive edge, and (2) build a long-term cushion for price recovery should internal efficiency begin to wane.

Quality Associated Costs: An Overview

A.V. Feigenbaum has pointed out that quality cost systems are leading more and more corporations to view quality as a fundamental way of managing a business.[1] Measuring, controlling, managing and reducing quality associated costs are a basic and valid technique for fostering productivity gain. However, this approach has proved to be more difficult than sometimes anticipated.

Quality associated costs are those incurred while developing, designing, building, and marketing products which will result in customer satisfaction. The challenge is to quantify and control *unavoidable* quality oriented costs, and to eliminate those which can be prevented. Mounting concern about quality costs has caused managers to seek various measurement indices in an effort to better discern between those that are truly unavoidable and those that can be prevented. This process remains an elusive goal for many firms; they continue to pay for lost machine and labor time, rework centers, scrap, overinspection, failure analyses, overprocurement, material review boards and tracking customer complaints.

While an increasing number of companies are making progress, quality cost measurement still tends to be confused, misused, abused and often fraught with inertia. There are several reasons for this struggle.

(1) Top management has not taken the subject seriously enough to cause the establishment of a workable system;

(2) Some unit managers perceive such reporting as a personal threat and may foster indifferent support, or even covert or visible resistance;

(3) Improperly conceived plans and methodology have led to

confusion and in some instances, backlash;

(4) Cost accounting departments have been territorial about how the books are kept and sometimes are less than cooperative about what they perceive as a heterodox approach to costs' reporting.

These obstacles all point to the fundamental importance of management involvement. They also imply the need for education and understanding of the quality cost reduction concept in both finance and in lower levels of supervision. As in most management situations, punitive actions are likely to create covert resistance and prevent long-term positive results. Quality cost reporting integrity is often witnessed where methods of rewarding improvement are used.

The reduction and control of quality associated costs is a predominate and visible objective of senior management in firms which are given high marks for productivity improvement. These managements boldly attack the rolling "unquality snowball" before it overwhelms them.

Major Sources of Quality Associated Costs

There are three principal sources or reasons for quality associated costs. These historically have become more pronounced at certain stages of company development, but all are variously experienced.

1. Failure to take quality seriously—not comprehending the enormity of the cost impact that "cradle to grave" quality has on profits.

2. Incomplete or inadequate definition of quality requirements.

3. Failure to conform to requirements.

The real origin of most of these costs is found in managements. The value, and cost implications of quality should be sufficiently understood by the managements and the employees so that quality values can permeate the organizations. Producing things right is not the result of luck; it is directly related to knowledge and conscious effort to avoid making mistakes. Good leadership and provisionary qualities of the management release the energy to realize this potential.

Conversely, the basis for expansive costs which are associated with poor attitudes and indifferent workmanship begins with antithetical and apathetic behavior about quality issues by managements. If the management pushes for an obscure entity called "quality," without defining standards and specific expectations, employees will emulate this neglect and progress will be foiled.

Definition of Quality Requirements

Quality requirements do not begin with contracts or purchase orders. In the aerospace business, companies compete creatively and conceptually before contract award. Past track records of quality and productivity, together with innovative technology, form the foundation for new business. In some cases, a concept is all the company has to go on. It is up to the research and development people to convert the "requirement" into a realistic and producible product that will ultimately meet or exceed customers' expectations of cost, quality, and delivery.

In the consumer products industry, up front requirements are sometimes not well understood. Definition of requirements tends to be more dynamic, hinging largely on R&D creativity and the company's ability to correctly assess customer needs. Misinterpreting customer requirements or misreading market conditions at an early stage can start a stampede of quality associated costs, the long-term effects of which can be disastrous or even final. Poorly defined quality expectations within marketing, research and development, purchasing, design, or manufacturing will cause immediate errors and result in confusion, delays and redundant work later. These factors will also cause good product lines to yield low profit margins and result in invincible competition.

This type of "quality cost" can be avoided through effective marketing, management and administrative controls in which quality is a strategic agenda item. Contract clauses, drawings and specifications, purchase orders, and quality planning documents are examples of communications where quality parameters need to be explicit.

This principle of quality management carries the full message about customer requirements from the drawing boards to the locations where products are placed into service. Customers' needs must be satisfied in the research and development phase and totally and accurately set forth in all released designs and specifications. This means that accelerated life testing or qualification testing has taken place to assure or verify the reliability of design. It may involve building models for test purposes to verify that the items can be properly fabricated and assembled by production personnel with production machinery, or sub-contracted to outside sources.

It appears to be very difficult for some managements to fully appreciate the fact that "requirements" set forth in the design and ancillary specifications are frequently the sources of avoidable quality costs. There is the tendency for some design departments to create designs which are "almost" right, but contain known uncertainties. These uncertainties encompass factors such as incomplete information about reliability or performance, unspecified prototype or production test programs, vague appearance standards and the like. Changes due to sundry doubts about clearances during assembly, expected but unresearched interchangeability problems, and doubts about producibility factors often arise at the last minute. There is less uncertainty about these factors in some companies than in others; the amount is inversely proportional to the management's tolerance for error, and directly proportional to the management's understanding of the cost consequences of unfinished design work in the shop.

An example might involve a component made of expensive material. If the design error resulted in scrapping the part, there could be a very large number of parts made before the problem was detected. Material losses immediately come to mind. However, many additional losses are also incurred; while this is not an exhaustive list, included are, lost machine time on the parts, lost production man hours, lost inspection time, time lost in writing and issuing nonconformance reports, costs of material replacement, investigation time, time for engineering evaluation and writing the change order, lost time in the original design, lost checker time, lost time in the drawing release system, lost time in blueprint control, and so forth.

Design errors or omissions can also set the stage for exhorbitant or fatal liability suits. The number and size of the awards have steadily increased during the past 20 years. All such suits are costly even when the manufacturer wins the case.

There is a common misconception that if the design is not totally accurate and complete, details can be identified and rectified later through the design change order system. Operating under the quality philosophy of no tolerance for error and under the true concept of prevention, all design change action after the release of the design package is actually a form of rework, even if it is a paperwork change only, and does not result in hardware change. The most serious cost implications, however, are found in the components which are found to be inadequate after production is well underway or failure after delivery.

Failure to Conform to Requirements

For at least two decades, a distended focus on costs of

nonconformances has diverted managements' attention away from up front quality matters. Nonconformance costs, particularly those associated with manufacturing, can be readily identified and measured; a simple count of the items reworked or scrapped can be made. This carries with it, however, the inference that all corrective action lies somewhere in the manufacturing departments. Conclusions are drawn that *production* people should be better trained, apply statistical process controls, and become involved in quality circles, etc. While all this probably has real value, attention is diverted from some of the most significant causes of quality problems rooted in design engineering, procurement, and indirect technical support functions.

A number of avoidable nonconformance quality oriented costs can be traced to the lack of direct management action. Poor quality of work life, high expectations of output with low quality provisions, and a general management philosophy that supports a negative quality culture ironically need decisive action by the management who steered the company into its predicament. Some productivity costs are not management controllable; they are either government and society invoked, or are unpredictable due to the dynamics of the work environment with their origin attributed to chance factors. Some are mandatory for productivity improvement, but the vast majority are reduceable through good management practices.

Successful nonconformance cost avoidance and control depend not only on the cooperation of design engineering, quality engineering and production departments, but also in great part on cost accounting and industrial engineering groups. While industrial engineering and finance departments have indirect assignments, their involvement in the collection, analysis and reporting of cost information is a key factor in successful nonconformance cost avoidance and control. Breaking through long established methods and roles that these departments have had in the past which have precluded a good measurement base may be difficult. A redefinition and restructuring of certain functions may be necessary. In traditional programs, costs are reported against performance standards which become an important guide for managment decision. Traditional approaches to cost accounting provide little or no visibility of costs of nonconformances vs. costs of prevention and other productivity associated costs. Most cost reporting methods do not categorize these costs in such a way that cause and effect relationships can be seen directly through cost comparisons. The achievement of an accurate ongoing accounting of productivity improvement has escaped many companies; such information is usually buried in accounting networks with the result that nonconformance costs cannot be correlated with preventive costs. This important index can be known when a *base line* of prevention and nonconformance costs is established for each major reporting unit. This analogy is shown in Figure IX-2. After a base line of costs has been established (approximately after one year of reporting), Pareto distributions and other problem solving techniques can then be applied to systematically eliminate situations that obviate productivity improvement efforts.

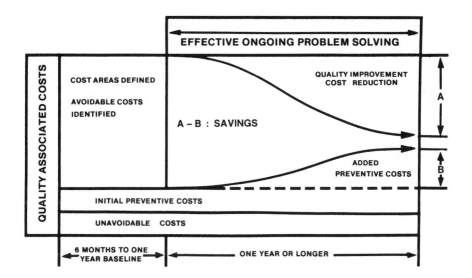

FIGURE IX-2. EFFECTS OF PREVENTION ON NONCONFORMANCE COSTS

Illustrated in Figure IX-3 is a cost comparison made between companies which have established and use quality cost systems and those which have not. By establishing a base line against which to measure improvement, and taking the appropriate preventive actions, a concrete basis for controlling costs can be achieved, and a substantial overall reduction in nonconformances can be realized.

The best managed companies enjoy 92 to 97% of their income from sales for other purposes than screening for and taking care of nonconformances. Some poorly managed companies devote as much as 25% or more of their revenues to sundry corrective actions. In some cases this problem is concealed because cost data are not available in a form which permits identification of causes.

Quality Associated Costs for Productivity Improvement

Mandatory Costs. Certain management controllable costs are

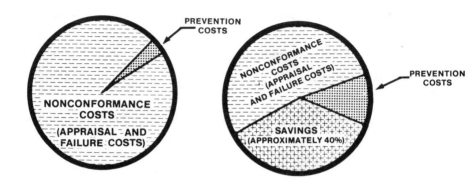

MINIMUM PREVENTION (3-5%) PRODUCES EXCESSIVE INSPECTION AND FAILURE COSTS (NONCONFORMANCE COSTS)

OPTIMUM PREVENTION (20-25%), *WELL EXECUTED,* PRODUCES MINIMUM NONCONFORMANCE COSTS

PREVENTION COSTS

NONCONFORMANCE COSTS (APPRAISAL AND FAILURE COSTS)

NONCONFORMANCE COSTS (APPRAISAL AND FAILURE COSTS)

SAVINGS (APPROXIMATELY 40%)

PREVENTION COSTS

FIGURE IX-3. SAVINGS THROUGH PREVENTION

required to improve productivity posture, satisfy customers, and increase market share. Monies and attention are needed to effect productivity improvement, and the management should boldly earmark resources to meet this goal. Following are the principal areas where management involvement and action are necessary to prevent consequent burgeoning costs of nonconformances, delays, and other lost time situations. Properly planned, administered and controlled, an up front investment in these activities can pay back multifold dividends later.

A. Costs to sustain or build a quality culture:
   1. Organize and utilize teams of people;
   2. Execute specific measures for improvement;
   3. Humanize the job;
   4. Adopt a provisionary philosophy of managing; and,
   5. Improve the quality of work life.

B. Costs to accurately and completely define quality requirements:
   1. Conduct adequate market research;
   2. Conduct appropriate research and development;
   3. Fulfill customer expectations;
   4. Release accurate and complete designs which are readily producible; and,
   5. Verify that this has been accomplished.

C. Costs to achieve conformance goals by:
   1. Providing the proper equipment, materials, methods and tools;
   2. Execute ongoing improvements in quality and methods;
   3. Institute appropriate training to assure competence; and,
   4. Establish process assurances and controls.

These are referred to as "productivity costs" to give impetus to the point that these are necessary to sustain or build a productivity improvement program. The costs of operating a successful quality program must be planned, budgeted and controlled to optimize benefits. Those who are convinced that there are "no" quality costs are likely to find their nonconformance costs rising. Without proper attention to these foundation costs, subsequent compounding costs will be incurred as shown in Figure IX-4.

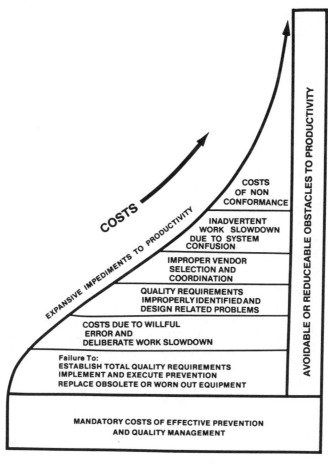

FIGURE IX-4.   MANAGEMENT CONTROLLABLE FACTORS IN
PRODUCTIVITY IMPROVEMENT

The costs of running a quality program will require up front attention; budgeting for the resources with continuous normal management activities will be necessary to realize the inherent longer term benefits. These efforts are "free" in the sense that they will return a profit if successful. But, they can add even more to an already high cost situation if the managements are unwilling to participate in the change of direction, or are unable to inaugurate them.

Avoidable Quality Costs. The most publicized and tangible quality associated costs pertain to scrap, rework and inspection. These costs are said to occur because manufacturing people do not "make it like the design." As a result, an inspection force is needed to protect the company against the high cost of defective work.

What is not usually apparent or acted upon is that as soon as everyone outside the manufacturing department has done his or her job, a decline in scrap, rework and other nonconformance costs will be seen. Equipment operators will inevitably succeed if they have an accurate design to work with, are properly trained for the jobs, have proper equipment to perform the work, are provided with acceptable materials and have a suitable performance standard. Most manufacturing nonconformance costs are actually caused by functions or circumstances beyond the control of production departments, but the boss' inclination is to fix blame and attempt to correct the problem by shaking up the shop. In many manufacturing operations, it is not unusual to find that a drawing is missing; a machine will not hold tolerances; a batch of material has to be sent back to a vendor; or a priority change necessitates a quick tear down and a hasty set up. All these situations contribute to high costs and are beyond the control of the production departments. Such problems are manifested in the manufacturing phase, but are actually caused elsewhere.

Another category of productivity related costs is willful error or deliberate work slowdown. In a culture which is not conducive to taking quality seriously, or within which people develop and harbor resentment or mistrust, malingering and errors occur more than they would otherwise. It is estimated that this cost may skin as much as 10% off the top of income from sales in a company where there are severe adversarial relations between the management and the employees. This is a difficult problem to assess since subtlety and concealment are part of its nature. Deliberate slow downs are usually associated with a history of management and employee confrontations. This kind of environment becomes a breeding ground for accelerating difficulty and a holding tank for both cost and despair.

There is another reservoir in which quality associated costs can be recovered; this is in a company's dealings with suppliers. Logistics, sheer numbers, mistakes and delays all add to the cost of raw materials, parts and services. If supplier assurance is accomplished effectively, costs associated with this activity as well as subsequent nonconformance costs will be appreciably held down. The following general rules are universally helpful:

1. Vendors should be qualified *beforehand* as having the wherewithal to produce at the required quality level and on schedule.

2. The number of suppliers should be as low as possible, consistent with the law and needs. The longer the list becomes, the more difficult it is to effectively control quality.

3. Once a purchase order has been issued, the company should continue to educate vendors during the course of the contract to assure quality, cost effectiveness and timely delivery. This will increase the odds that a high return on this investment can be gained by avoiding subsequent quality and schedule problems.

4. Supplier assurance and controls should involve establishing and maintaining incentives to make it profitable for a vendor to deliver all the required quality the first time, and unprofitable not do do so.

Vendors sometimes have an incentive not to initially deliver reliable items. Companies sometimes follow practices which enable suppliers to be rewarded with repeat sales, spares or "aftersales." This practice contains a built-in incentive to disregard quality on original deliveries, if repeat sales can be expected to replace those items which experience early failure. Firms which are "out of quality control" in their own plants, usually do not have vendors "under control."

As with design assurance, the costs and delays associated with vendor assurance may appear to be high at first, but if the job is done *effectively,* there are few investments which can produce a better return.

Conventional Quality Costs

Many theories and descriptions of quality costs accounting programs have been put forth in the last quarter century. Most of them center on the traditional four categories of prevention, appraisal, internal failure and external failure. Many companies have found these to be adequate and helpful. While they vary somewhat from company to company, the following are representative of those most commonly used.

I.   *Prevention costs.* These are functions and activities, including wages and salaries of people whose efforts focus on anticipating and planning to achieve established quality objectives and avoiding unwanted costs.

A.   Training provides the employees with the competence needed to achieve quality objectives.

B.   Process control techniques allow statistical predictions to be made about future events so that intelligent choices can be made. (This also includes equipment capability studies.)

C.   Special equipment is purchased to provide the desired and consistent quality.

D.   Design reviews are conducted to assure the integrity of design packages before they are released for production.

E.   Vendor assurance is achieved through pre-award surveys to verify in advance that a prospective supplier is qualified to produce the required quality.

II.   *Appraisal costs.* These include the wages of people who are involved in inspection and test functions and activities. They do not include reinspection and retest after rework. Here are the principal categories:

A.   Clerical and supervisory jobs of inspectors.

B.   Laboratory and test analysis of purchased items.

C.   In-process and final inspection labor hours.

D.   Gage calibration and repair of instruments used for inspection.

E.   Quality audits as a second order verification of systems operations and inspection integrity.

F.   Source inspection conducted at the vendor.

G.   Receiving inspection of purchased parts.

H.   Field inspection is conducted at the customer's site after delivery.

III. *Internal failure costs.* These are all losses (including shop overhead) due to problems in in-house engineering, manufacturing, quality or similar errors during production.

A. Scrap costs include all material and lost machine and labor time due to chance failure, operator error, purchase parts failure, lost parts, mishandling and process error. These should not include obsolete units or overruns.

B. Rework costs include labor used to rework items (bring an item up to the acceptable quality standard) due to in-house engineering, manufacturing, quality or similar error.

C. Failure analysis of units which fail before delivery.

D. Vendor analysis charged by vendor.

E. Sort or retest of reworked items including additional machine time.

F. Failure investigation.

G. Evaluation of corrective action.

H. Material Review Board activities.

I. Down time due to:

1) quality problems
2) insufficient preventive maintenance
3) lack of equipment capability

IV. *External failure costs.* These are quality costs that develop after shipment of an order.

A. Customer complaints, investigation and service.

B. Allowances which usually include customer abuse or misuse.

C. Machine replacement or repair and installation, if applicable.

D. Field costs including material associated with handling costs.

E. Negotiation and analysis costs.

F. Associated vendor costs.

G. Product liability costs.
   1) legal actions
   2) insurance and warranties
   3) safety claims
   4) consequential damage

H. Usage and carrying costs of spares.

Steps in Implementing a Productivity Cost Accounting Network

1. *Overcoming the Executive Pitfall.* Executives will need to accept the possibility that a productivity cost reporting system could reveal inefficiencies in their own organizations. If this occurs, they will need to resist the temptation to censure subordinates, or take defensive positions. The exposure and control of hidden costs will call for special leadership qualities which will place the company's welfare above that of a particular organization. A good cost report will indicate high cost areas and these should be the focal points of attention, not the people who may have been victims of circumstances.

2. *Construct Productivity Cost Reporting Indices.* After fully realizing the need to report quality associated costs, the executive staff may need to hold a series of regularly scheduled productivity council meetings in order to define major cost elements to be reported. This top level group should be able to define categories that reflect areas of major concern, in addition to the traditional quality cost categories. In achieving this objective the top executives will need to be able to hold down personal desires and enlist the aid of other staff members who have unique information vital to these definitions. When the issue of costs is the subject, only mature and conscientious people are able to place self interests second to the betterment of the company. Getting participation and generating teamwork at this early stage are the keys to the effectiveness of this cost reporting endeavor. It may also be advisable at this stage to utilize a consultant who has helped other companies to make improvements in cost reporting methods.

This step involves the classification of costs into two broad categories: prevention and avoidable costs. Every major system contains elements that should be eliminated or substantially reduced. And every undesirable or avoidable activity has one or more corresponding preventive measures that can be applied against it.

Avoidable costs include inefficient, redundant, or otherwise excessive costs that contribute to productivity drain. As pointed out earlier, in addition to costs which originate from the myriad nonconformance activities and which are typically associated with the blue-collar worker, other origins of these costs are found in systems and procedures design, organization voids or duplication of effort, and indefinite job descriptions and assignments, the majority of which are the responsibility of white-collar people. Some companies have been very successful at implementing a cost accounting network which solves the lion's share of the cost reporting dilemma. In these instances, quality costs are essentially reported in the aforementioned four major cost categories. Although some firms have had difficulty in classifying certain costs, it makes little difference how those having double meanings are classified. Quality audits, for example, are sometimes found as an appraisal cost and in other instances, a prevention cost. Calibration can also be found in either of these categories.

The important question is not whether a specific cost should be placed in a particular category; these questions can be answered in terms of company procedures and idiosyncrasies. A much more serious mistake is not making the attempt at designing and executing such a system. Accurate productivity measurement will be impossible or unduly costly if there is no central cost reporting method which shows ongoing costs of unwanted activities or functions, compared against preventive actions taken against these factors.

3. *Reporting the Avoidable and Preventive Costs.* Once these costs have been categorized it will be necessary for the cost accounting department, together with the quality and industrial engineering departments, to break these down into activities for hourly reporting. For example, if time cards are used, hours devoted to an activity can be reported against codes or numbers assigned for the activity.

The problem some have expressed is the discipline factor of accurate reporting. This will always exist, but it is not as great a problem as some seem to believe.

If a 70 to 75% accuracy can be achieved, this is sufficient to reveal trends and major areas of concern. After several months of reporting, a base line will have been established which will characterize the status of the company's productivity posture.

With preventive costs charted against unwanted costs, and after the base line has stabilized, Pareto analyses can be applied. This point was made in Chapter VIII. After the vital few have been identified, a specific preventive action can be applied to these high cost areas. This may entail higher sporatic preventive costs until the problems are solved, but if the actions are effective, the net savings generated through nonconformances reduction can be four to ten times this amount and in some cases even higher. The improvement cycle should be continuously repeated, constantly questioning why and under what conditions a cost may be considered unavoidable. Operating under the dynamic situations that companies normally encounter, what is considered unavoidable today will be avoidable tomorrow.

The only way the management will be convinced that certain problems are indeed costly is to report cost trends which will emphasize the importance of situations in need of improvement. Several examples follow.

Reports may indicate that low workmanship resulted in high corrective action costs. Responses to prevent their recurrence may take the forms of specific training or recertification. Another example might be an unusually high number of costly defectives occurring in a department where an unusual amount of scrap, rework, and inspection are consequences. Prevention may be in the form of the purchase of a special tool or new machine. The defectives might also be caused by process incapability, necessitating that certain work be done elsewhere in the plant, or the result of a design error which was revealed in an assembly operation. Each of these sources of nonconformances has a preventive action: better methods, tools, or special equipment purchase, training of operators, calibration of tools, process capability studies, with the use of statistical control charts, and better design review.

The closed loop improvement process shown on page 92 is applied in such situations, making certain that efforts do not fall back into the treadmill cycle shown at the top of page 92.

A major concern that senior managements should have is the *efficacy* with which problem solving and preventive measures are carried out. Preventive jobs are accomplished for the most part by white collar people, wherein room for improvement may also lie.

If a company plans to increase its preventive measures based on the theory that substantial unwanted costs can be prevented, it follows that the consequent reduction in costs must be greater than the investment in the preventive measures. If a company discovered that it devoted only 5% of its quality oriented costs to prevention, one might believe that by doubling preventive costs a fourfold reduction of nonconformances could be gained. This is entirely possible provided that (1) the company had adopted a well conceived cost reporting program that is tailored to its system needs, and (2) that the preventive measures undertaken are carried out effectively. To increase preventive measures with only the *hope* that they will magically solve nonconformance issues is a fantasy.

Questions regarding how much and by whom quality planning should be done, when and by whom design reviews are conducted, where and by whom process capability studies and control charts should be instituted are questions that may not be readily answered, but deserve good answers.

CHAPTER X

Activating the Productivity Message

For several decades behavioral scientists have advocated a better balance between listening and talking between managements and employees. If the number of programs designed to increase employee participation is a measure, egalitarian values are definitely on the increase.

A modern perception is to consider business and industry as economic and social institutions that should contribute to the quality of life of employees, in addition to providing goods, services and employment. The inference is that employees should receive satisfaction from their work in addition to compensation.

In the real industrial world, however, while these are viewed as laudable goals, many find these an intimidating challenge. Managements are caught up in the inescapable trauma associated with increasing output, improving productivity and keeping employees happy at the same time. In this chapter, techniques that have been used by successful managers in pursuit of these objectives are explored.

U.S. industry has not institutionalized ways to group people who represent different sides of an issue and place them in situations to work collaboratively toward a win/win solution. Normally, out of confrontation must come a winner and a loser. While mediation is available for getting two parties to negotiate a solution, bargaining tends to be foreign to and may even inhibit teamwork. Where adversarial relations between the management and worker have not become cultural traits, companies (if they choose to do so) will find it easier to progress from negotiation to true teamwork.

Leadership

If there is one word which adequately describes the prime variable in productivity improvement, the word is leadership. No system of organization, no aggregation of manpower, and no set of procedures, reports, studies or analyses can be an adequate substitute for the vigor, involvement, enthusiasm and drive which are generated by leadership. An organization must conscientiously nurture the employees who make up the organization because the bodily and mental development of its membership are important factors bearing upon the long-term economic output of the organization.

In simple terms leadership in the industrial scene can be defined as the art of motivating, guiding and directing employees, or simply getting results through subordinates. Short-term results can be gained by imperious and heavy-handed tactics, but such a style invariably carries severe long-term penalties. Like quality and productivity, viewing leadership on a long range basis is difficult, but necessary. This involves constancy of purpose and tapping into the talents of employees.

Qualities of Good Leaders. Countless descriptions of effective leaders have been documented, and it may appear as effrontery to attempt to describe characteristics of successful leaders. Everyone has an opinion; even the experts do not totally agree. Nevertheless, research and observations lead to several conclusions.

The purpose here is to focus on certain leadership characteristics which will likely be needed as industrial cultures change. Some of these attributes are described in the following statements which analogize a boss and a leader.

1. The boss uses people; the leader develops them.

2. The boss never has enough time; the leader makes time for things that count.

3. The boss is concerned with things; the leader is concerned with people.

4. The boss lets his people know where he stands; the leader also lets his people know where they stand.

6. The boss works hard to produce; the leader works hard to help his people produce.

7. The boss depends on authority, the leader on teamwork.

8. The boss generates fear; the leader inspires enthusiasm.

9. The boss says: "Get here on time"; the leader gets there ahead of time.

10. The boss fixes blame for a problem; the leader finds solutions to the problem.

11. The boss says "Go"; the leader says "Let's go."

12. The boss commands; the leader consults.

13. The boss drives his men; the leader coaches them.

14. The boss dwells on today; the leader plans for tomorrow.[1]

Qualities of good leaders, of course, extend far beyond such analogies. Leadership is the source of inspiration that causes employees to reach for excellence, constantly using past accomplishments as a springboard to further achievement. Leadership carries with it a spirit that transcends the pitfall of comfortable mediocrity. A modern leader cannot afford to accept performance measurements that are based on ordinary output; rather, performance expectations should be founded on objectives designed to stretch one's effort and on relationships structured to synthesize energy.

A leader who fails to ask for or expect any depth of commitment discourages such commitment. The poor leader sets objectives which lead subordinates to believe that they should perform at a level that is lower than could be reasonably expected. In the long run, this institutionalizes medocrity in the organization. No person wants to be identified as a mediocre worker, but anyone can find himself in this posture without being aware of how it happened. Leadership leads people to be committed to excellence and to strive to achieve it.

Leadership effectiveness is broadly measured by the degree of cooperation managers/supervisors get from subordinates in achieving organizational objectives within cost, quality, and time parameters. Effective leaders are able to identify with and relate to those with whom they interact. They are adept at applying verbal and nonverbal techniques to influence others. They also do not lose their sensitivity to the needs of subordinates. Constantly striving to improve the quality of work life for employees, they are evenhanded in their dealings. Leaders also take risks and face the possibility of failure. However, if failure occurs, good leaders are able to analyze and learn from the failure and renew their efforts to reach a goal. Poor leaders sooner or later ask the question—why bother? Effective leaders also accept responsibility for their actions. They are able to absorb information, assess courses of action, weigh the risks, make the decisions, and assume the responsibility.

In this period of burgeoning technology and growing heterogeneity of the work force, certain leadership qualities not given much attention heretofore will become increasingly important and beneficial to those in charge. One such attribute is *forbearance*. Even today, patience and being slow to boil are qualities not found often enough among those who manage.

Many companies are experiencing communication difficulties because of language barriers. The need for forbearance will grow as miscommunication annoyances increase between levels of management and between management and the worker. For example, responses by first line supervision to directives from management are sometimes slow or at variance with expectations; reasons can often be traced to poor communication. At the management/worker level, management tries to communicate concepts and objectives of the organization to the workers through various written and verbal methods established by the management. Workers on the other hand, attempt to express to the management their concerns, needs, reasons for difficulties, and how they might be more effective through whatever channels are available to them. Too often communication from neither the management nor the worker is effective because of organizational barriers and comprehension gaps. Questions on both sides are naively perceived as irrelevant or even obtuse because neither is attuned to the other's needs. Forbearance is a virtue that leaders will find even more important in areas where people with different ethnic and language backgrounds infuse industrial culture.

Another characteristic of good leaders that will continue to have special meaning in the years ahead is *persistence*. Persistence without aggressiveness and pugnaciousness, exercised in cycles with patience, is a virtue that few leaders seem to have fully mastered. Maintaining the persistence to overcome the red tape and bureaucratic networking which befall most managers will continue to be a key leadership trait. Successful leaders know that perseverance, persistence and forbearance are effective fighters against burnout and are among those essential leadership qualities that must be constantly guarded and nourished.

Throughout this book, allusions are made to the importance of managers addressing subordinates' needs. Nothing is more effective in suppressing a spirit of endeavor than a leader who exerts strong pressure on employees to produce more and high quality work in a system where the ingredients and recipe do not exist. Unless the management is sufficiently involved to be sensitive to the needs of the worker, what can a worker do, for example, about a machine that will not hold tolerances, or a supervisor who will not or cannot correct problems? The effective leader invites enthusiasm and confidence to grow by ensuring that effort and understanding triumph over manipulation and indifference.

The importance of leadership is well known among good managers. While it is not fully understood whether leaders are born or made, certain principles are known to have credence. Here are a few that successful leaders apply.

1) They make certain employees know how their jobs fit into the total organizational picture.

2) They let employees know why their jobs are important. Every employee should be cognizant of what will happen if he or she does not perform properly.

3) They set worthy examples for employees to follow. Employees identify with practices and objectives that are based on quality, but become confused when confronted with directives which contain conflicting parameters, or ones which differ from prevailing practices.

4) They let employees know what is expected of them. They discuss and agree on the key factors in the job and set specific performance objectives. The majority of people want to receive honest and forthright feedback about their work.

5) They present a challenge to the employees. They have them help to overcome difficulties in the operating unit since they probably are directly involved in the issue and have a need to participate.

6) They let employees help by not only assigning them meaningful work, but also involving them in the decision process. Out of true participation comes dedicated effort.

7) They give credit where it is due—and accentuate the positive. Others will follow this example because it works.

8) They give recognition when it is earned or deserved. In addition to a verbal comment, they provide written recognition for outstanding work. They recognize that insincere or undeserved praise or reward does more harm than good.

9) They show personal interest. They know that employees respond in kind to heartfelt appreciation and interest in them, their problems, their future, and their well-being.

10) They are effective communicators in listening, writing and speaking. They share information freely, keeping people informed and fostering teamwork.

11) They provide opportunities for training, growth, and promotion. If the intrinsic reward of achievement can be experienced, employees usually will want more responsibility and seek advancement (There are exceptions, however).

Managers on the Move. Americans live in a society which prizes success and winning. Such victories in industrial cultures mean reaching the top and being successful at this level. Leadership ability, more than any other factor, determines this success.

The higher leaders advance, the more they seem to find themselves the subjects of controversy and targets for criticism. Stronger leaders, nevertheless, recognize such pitfalls and are buoyed by the challenges of their positions. They are actively involved in the organizations to build teamwork, and are able to sift criticism, using the good for improvement and discarding that which dulls enthusiasm. Managers on the move tend to possess four key attributes which set them apart from other leaders.

1. *Intellect and Self-assurance.* Studies on this subject indicate that outstanding leaders have above average intelligence, and possess a good deal of knowledge about operations and human interaction. Victorious leaders are most often noted and recognized, however, for their strong belief in what they can accomplish through their own abilities. While they are capable of genuine humility, managers on the move are extremely confident of and comfortable with their own resources and power. They possess a high degree of self-approbation and hold the ability to arrange conditions to bring about expected outcomes. Their aplomb is manifested by courage and endurance.

2. *Energy.* People blessed with extraordinary leadership ability usually manifest more energy than do typical leaders. They are known to visualize the outcome of their efforts, which continuously inspires them to achievement. They possess an inner motivational spark that constantly ignites them to action, and seem always able to muster the energy needed to reach their goals. They are the last to throw in the towel. At the point where good leaders quit without guilt or blame, great leaders plod on.

3. *Charisma.* Outstanding leaders have a remarkable ability to "attract" followers. They possess the distinctive quality which not only produces a listening audience, but gains for them the respect of followers. They have a knack for knowing when to listen, when to speak, how far to press a point, and how to accurately assess the mood of a group. These leaders possess a special intangible power which gives them influence and authority over people.

4. *Winsomeness.* Not the least of the qualities of a great leader are his or her engaging manner, attractiveness, presence, and strength of character. However, managers on the move are known for their toughness when the need arises.

Great leaders may not be known for all of these traits, but they are endowed with a sufficient number to offset shortcomings they might have in others. Usually possessed with a keen sense of judgment, these leaders know when, how much and under what circumstances these qualities should be applied.

Motivation

Why do some individuals seem capable of endless renewal, rising to an occasion, learning and applying new resources of energy and spirit, while others come to defect early? All too little is known about the remarkable differences in motivation and the ardor with which work is accomplished.

Researchers do not always agree as to the best style of management to motivate employees. There is general agreement among behavioral scientists that accomplishment, together with earned recognition for such achievement are strong motivators, especially in a climate where sensitivity to employee needs exists. Other authorities maintain that monetary incentives are equally effective motivators, and advocate bonuses, profit sharing, and other incentives that are tied directly to salary. Still other studies have shown that workers respond to leaders who exert strong power over the organization and employees in meeting objectives of the company. Can these philosophies be integrated into one effective leadership style? Even if the proper chemistry is present, no single style will fit every situation and employee all the time. Great wisdom and discernment on the part of the leader are dynamic requisites.

There are some practices which are fairly broadly accepted as being helpful or counterproductive. A doctrinaire management style and a listening attitude are incompatible in action. Imperious control over an organization, coupled with an unswerving passion to make unilateral decisions, have negative effects on attempts to create an environment conducive to listening. The management style of peremptory authority, which drains the dignity from a subordinate or position, is neither felicitous nor effective. One cannot *tell* and *listen* at the same time.

Many of the most successful managers ascribe to a *consensus* style of leadership (listening and getting inputs from others in a participative setting). This has the advantage of the leader *sharing* the responsibility for a decision and avoiding such possible repercussive statements as, "I knew it wouldn't work, but he wouldn't listen." When employees participate in the decision process, they experience a spontaneous vested interest in the successful outcome of the enterprise.

Advocated some thirty years ago by researchers, participative decision making has been largely resisted by managers, and dismissed as impractical and unworkable in their environments. But, a variety of socio-economic factors have emerged since 1950 which have caused some managers to take a second look at participative management styles. Concomitantly and perhaps more dramatically, a new reason for re-examining management strategies is the changing texture of the international marketplace, and the attendant need to compete more effectively. It seemed that only after U.S. productivity began to decline and after Japan demonstrated its phenomenal success with teamwork, that U.S. executives began to seriously examine their own traditional methods of management.

In 1960, Douglas McGregor introduced Theory X and Theory Y in his book, *The Human Side of Enterprise*. McGregor observed that most organizations and managers operate under what he termed Theory X or Theory Y assumptions. Theory X assumptions suggested that people dislike work, that they must be threatened, controlled, and directed to achieve organizational goals. Thinking this way, managers attempt to control the behavior of employees through a system of external constraints. Employees, on the other hand, attempt to make the organization aware of and responsive to their needs by withholding their total commitment and producing at a lower level than their potential. In turn, additional constraints are exerted, anxiety is increased, and tighter controls are exercised by the management. When employees behave in terms of the assumptions of Theory X, managers point to this behavior to justify additional force to get satisfactory performance.

McGregor found that performance and productivity appeared improved by managers who acted in concert with the principles of his Theory Y. Theory Y is characterized by selective adaptation of management techniques rather than a single absolute form of control. It recognizes people as resources with substantial potential rather than uninspired skills. Theory Y managers integrate the personal needs and goals of the worker with those of the organization.[2]

Some believe that the behavior of a manager which flows from a set of assumptions about people, has a self-fulfilling effect on the behavior and performance of subordinates. The behavior of managers then becomes the determinant for the behavior of employees. This is an example of the Pygmalion effect that comes into play in the relationships between management and the employee. Managers who expect their employees to dislike working for them are most likely to use coercive leadership methods which tend to create a self-fulfilling prophecy of resistance and less work. Conversely, managers who believe that employees are quite willing to seek responsibility and are capable of skillful self-direction towards rewarding goals, can also create a self-fulfilling prophecy.

Can McGregor's Theory Y, Herzberg's job enrichment concept, and other similar theories, hold up in today's complex industrial environment? There is growing evidence that they are valid and working. Companies which have directly or indirectly applied these theories together with other sound strategies for operating business are demonstrating success. While dictatorial practices are still alive and well in some of the best managed companies, people-oriented styles of management advanced by behavioral scientists are gradually becoming more commonplace and manifested in the following beliefs.

1. The work place should represent a challenging and growing experience for employees, providing an environment in which friendship and achievement can flourish, and providing for both financial and recognition rewards for such achievement.

2. Improvement in the quality of work life is positively correlated with productivity.

3. Sincere and empathetic involvement of managers directly in the shop culture helps the cause of productivity improvement.

Attitude Surveys

Attitude surveys are conducted to determine true feelings of employees. Communications are among the most difficult tasks facing all levels of management. Notions and perceptions of employees about the management and supervision are often different from management's perceptions. Managements frequently naively believe that correspondence is reaching employees and being comprehended. In reality, the intent of messages sent may be distorted through the hierarchical system or simply misunderstood. Most studies in communications show a substantial degree of filtering of information when it passes through several levels of hierarchy. The feedback loop (from employees to management) is usually the direction which contains the most bias or misrepresentation.

Some companies make extensive use of employee attitude surveys to bridge the communications gap between management and employees. Such surveys help the management to establish credibility and raise upper management's understanding about how employees really feel— provided, of course, that the surveys are properly conducted. Without some mechanism to by-pass the chain of command, there is no way for upper management to know exactly how employees really feel.

A recent attitude survey in a medium size company disclosed a great deal of employee unrest and dissatisfaction with the management. Following brief investigations, senior management dismissed the survey results as invalid. A few months later a labor union filed a petition for recognition, showing that 53% of the employees had signed union cards. While it may be difficult to separate cause from effect, there is no denying the value of this type of advance notice.

Attitude surveys are increasingly utilized by non-union companies which desire to continue to be non-union. Following are some points that should be considered in conducting attitude surveys.

1. Every employee is a candidate for an attitude survey.

2. Attitudes are like perceptions—they do not have to be factually based to be real.

3. Involvement by senior executives is very important.

4. Attitude surveys can usually be structured in a 20 question format.

5. Top management should avoid overreacting to negative feedback about certain departments by taking immediate punitive action against certain managers. The survey will indicate problem areas which may take careful analysis before corrective action. Impulsive corrective action may address only symptoms and miss the real problem entirely.

6. Attitude surveys are not a one time venture, but should be an ongoing tool for the assessment of employee morale.

Making Effective Decisions

Decisions are expected of a manager because they are the universal hallmark of managing. Whether decisions are made collaboratively or individually, they have to be made. However, the question is how best to carry out this responsibility.

Decision making always involves making choices from alternatives. Frequently, there are differences in opinion, circumstances and information concerning these choices. The process of converging on best choices and converting these into effective action requires skillful leadership.

It is generally agreed that flexibility must be maintained as a factor in one's leadership style. Correspondingly, there is a growing trend among leaders to seek a middle-of-the-road style as a normal practice. This is illustrated by the continuum in Figure X-1 which also shows the relationship of one's leadership style with decision making.

	Zone A	Zone B	Zone C	Zone D
DECISIONS	Made totally by the boss	Made with screened and biased inputs	Made with open communications and emloyee involvement	Decisions fall out at random
	No participation	Little participation	Listening environment	Participative free-for-all
	Non-listening	Listens to loyal subordinates	Encourages Participation	Listening without purpose
LEADERSHIP STYLES	<u>Coercive</u>	<u>Essentially Autocratic</u>	<u>Democratic Process</u>	<u>Free Reign</u>
	Theory X	Selling style—after the boss has made the decision	Theories Y and Z	Country Club style
	Telling style		Consultive style	Lack of direction
	Exercise of power			
		Strong control	Delegates authority	Loss of control
	Close and anxious control		Maintains control	

FIGURE X-1.   RELATIONSHIP OF DECISION MAKING TO LEADERSHIP STYLE

Most managers would like to believe they function in Zone C, which contains all the classic "do's" that researchers describe as best practices. Within most companies, especially larger ones, Zones A through D can all be found. At lower levels of supervision, particularly in blue-collar shop areas, characteristics of Zones A and B often predominate. In white-collar areas (which include the management hierarchy as well as the divisions of engineering, marketing, personnel, industrial engineering, and quality assurance), more of the characteriscis listed in Zone D will be found. The existence of these two extremes (A and D) should not be too surprising. While a "laissez faire" style tends to be overused in white-collar departments, dominion and strong control over employees are excessively exercised in many shop environments. Shop superintendents still argue that if they were not authoritive, and even threatening sometimes, they would quickly lose control. "I've got a job to do out here. If you're nice to those guys they'll take advantage of you!" Unfortunately, the messages in such comments are apt to be accurate where severe crises and Theory X management cultures exist.

In such cases, a negative style of leadership, distrust, and resistance to direction become a self-perpetuating vicious cycle which can be broken only through deliberate and systematic efforts. Reactive and combative shop cultures are transformed through persistent, long-term, and fair treatment of every employee. As pointed out earlier, once the work culture has matured to the point where the system is resolved to accept confrontation as a way of life and is designed to expect and deal with destructive discord, positive change is slow to come. (It is important to glean from this discussion that while it is possible to select an optimum style, it is also true that style should adapt to the people involved and to the management situation.)

In white-collar organizations, while many exceptions can be found, it is generally accepted that professional people require less direction and should be given free reign. A majority of white-collar jobs are non-specific in nature and require problem-solving, coordination, and follow-up. Little would be accomplished without freedom and flexibility to accomplish such jobs. In certain instances, because of the nature of white-collar work, there is the tendency to favor the management style described in Zone D. In a country club atmosphere, happiness of employees can become the focus of the organization. In this zone, output expectancy and energy to meet project objectives tend to receive less attention than attempts to make everyone comfortable and happy. Ironically, loyalty, respect and long-term allegiance to the company are by-products of feelings of success and being contributing members of the team.

All employees need to understand the boundaries within which their organizations must function, as well as the expectations that relate to job performance. Whether these are drawn up through consensus, prescribed individually, or communicated in staff meetings, output objectives should not only be comprehended by all employees, but prioritized accordingly.

That leadership and ability to motivate people are among the most important attributes of successful managers is a well accepted fact. There are several other key factors which, when effectively executed, will contribute to productivity gain.

White-Collar Time Management

The management historically has emphasized managing the time of production operators. This is evidenced by the emphasis on performance standards of shop personnel, with less attention given to the "details" of how white-collar people use their time. In recent years, more attention has been directed at how white-collar workers are using their time. Ranging from office workers and the clerical staff to the managements and other indirect functions, outputs per input dollar invested reportedly has gradually slipped away in these functions. Analyses and recommendations by both consultants and internal specialists have been made, but making the best use of ones time is typically not what white-collar employees do best.

In a U.S. Chamber of Commerce, Gallup Poll, a large population of American white-collar/professional workers were asked how much of their energies were devoted to their jobs while at work. The figure was a surprising 50 percent. Given a forty-hour work week, one might legitimately ask where are the other twenty hours going?

Productivity concepts are frequently foreign to white-collar managers and supervisors, and these leaders may need to develop new ways to manage their departments. To produce an effective and long-lasting productivity program, it will be necessary to initiate changes in both the *style* of managing and the emphasis on *what* is being managed.

White-collar ineffectiveness creeps into an organization like creeping change enters shop areas, except even more subtly. Among other things, fuzzy job definitions, system confusion, and searching for answers to problems not yet well defined prevent the effective use of one's time.

Studies indicate that on an average, more time is wasted in white-collar activities than by people on the production floor. This converts into billions of dollars every year. Is it reasonable to expect that white-collar workers can find and institute ways to correct a problem of which they are a significant part?

Much has been written on time management, and it is not the purpose here to delve deeply into this subject, but rather to summarize some pertinent points that have been found to be beneficial.

1. *Paperwork is often inefficiently handled.* Paperwork can be sorted into two categories—those items that have to be answered and those that do not. Then action items can be arranged in priority.

2. *Better utilization of a secretary can be an important source of efficiency improvement.* Proper organization of the files, screening telephone calls, monitoring visitors, etc. can be extremely beneficial especially to an executive who is vulnerable to these situations. Many details should be delegated to a good secretary.

3. *An early morning list of things to accomplish during the day can help the manager do a better job of organizing projects.* Making such a list will help to establish priorities and place tasks into their proper perspective.

4. *Delegation should be fully exercised.* The martyr manager who complains of never having enough time and having to work late hours is most likely the person who is unable to delegate effectively. Both burnout and inefficiency are results of poor delegation.

5. *Difficult and important tasks should be accomplished first.* By first categorizing those projects that need accomplishing, then developing the discipline to follow through, more time can be accumulated to accomplish tasks further down the priority list. Procrastination and trivia are felonious time thiefs.

6. *The manager should be aware of how his or her time is spent.* Most managers are victims of the "fire fighting" syndrome, not fully realizing how much time they are devoting to perfunctory meetings, idle conversations, long lunches, and so forth. Individual company cultures range from an open stamp of approval where abuses can be clearly observed, to those which have low tolerance for such activities. However, the aforementioned "activities" are more or less accepted as normal practice in the American business world for white-collar and management personnel. These areas have been identified, however, as being a significant source of low productivity among white-collar workers.

There is an inverse relationship between how effective a supervisor can manage his or her time and the prevalence of crises situations in overall company systems. Where methods of management must accommodate prevailing "emergency" situations, these actions will take precedence over one's ability to manage time effectively. To the degree that crises dominate internal communications, decisions, and actions, a manager's time is driven by the system with less time being available for crisis prevention.

Corrective action management and management by exception are closely allied terms and their predomination in a company will transcend specific efforts by a supervisor to be efficient. As the management philosophy and the direction of expended energy increasingly exemplify a corrective action mode, less time can be found by a supervisor to complete tasks which will yield a high rate of return on his or her investments of time.

Effective Planning and Control

The planning and control functions of management are sometimes misunderstood. Planning is the systematic process of selecting and developing the best course of action to accomplish objectives. It involves determining the what, where, how, why, and by whom, events will take place in the future. Good planning predetermines future actions, which when taken, will effectively meet objectives.

Commitment to action is part of the decision process. No decision has been made unless carrying it out in specific terms has become someone's assignment and responsibility. The leader must make sure not only that responsibility for action is clearly exacted, but that the people responsible are capable of performing properly.

Thus, a plan must be complete and it must contribute in a positive manner to the realization of the objectives of the organization. The following six suggestions are offered to make planning effective.

1. Take planning seriously; it should not be left to chance.

2. Communicate planning objectives sufficiently.

3. Exemplify the planning process from the top down.

4. Be aware of the need for change.

5. Integrate long-term with short-term plans.

6. Avoid planning that lacks concreteness.

Complete planning encompasses a means of gaining control which involves three principal steps: Establishing criteria or standards, measuring performance against these criteria, and correcting deviations from the established plans and standards. These steps can be effectively achieved only if they are done with a closed loop information system and attendant feedback. This closed loop concept is illustrated in Figure X-2.

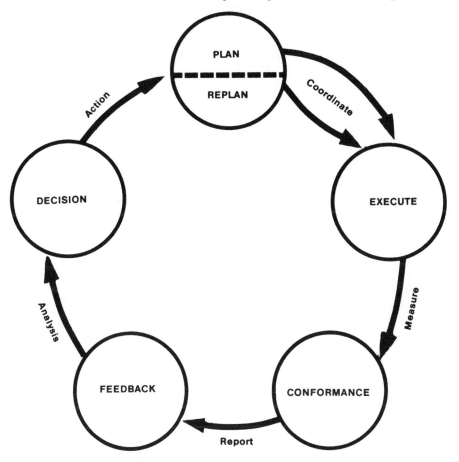

FIGURE X-2. THE PLANNING AND CONTROL CYCLE

When plans are carefully formulated, they are communicated to appropriate people, actions are taken according to the plans, assessments of conformance are made, this information is fed back to responsible and cognizant people, and finally, new decisions are made based on this information. There can be neither control nor effective decisions without accurate feedback.

Effects of Open Loops. A true test of whether or not an information system is working well is how many secondary or tertiary loops must be generated before proper information is obtained and actions taken. Best systems close loops the first time which prevent error and the need for further information gathering. Illustrated in Figure X-3 is a schematic of a closed loop information system. It represents primary prevention, if the intended messages are received. The figure also illustrates how added information must be generated when original loops are not closed. This information takes the forms of meetings, discussions, memoranda, and even special documents designed for the express purpose of effecting closure. This process is a source of compounding costs; as more loops are needed, there is growing risk of misunderstanding and error. If unnecessary loops can be avoided, more confidence about information integrity can be generated.

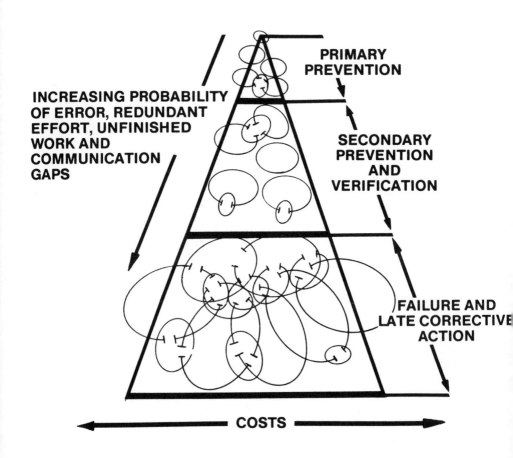

FIGURE X-3. COMPOUNDING EFFECTS OF OPEN LOOPS

Examples and Consequences of Communication Gaps. The following
story of a plumber illustrates how misunderstandings can occur with the
use of inappropriate verbage.

A plumber who was using hydrochloric acid in pipes noted
that the pipes were being eaten away. So he wrote a large
chemical lab for advice on the use of hydrochloric acid.

He received this reply:

*"Dear Sir: The efficacy of hydrochloric acid is indisputable,
but the corrosive residue is incompatible with metallic
permanence."*

The plumber was happy to see that the chemical lab endorsed
his use of hydrochloric acid and continued to use it. But when
trouble developed again, he again wrote the lab for advice.

A young chemist, seeing the problem, sent this note to the
plumber:

*"Dear Sir: Don't use hydrochloric acid—it eats the hell out
of the pipes."*

Author Unknown

Another less ludicrous example is how deviations from designs
exceptions are approved. The design engineering department usually has
the final word about the acceptability of departures from the design. If
anyone should know how a product must go together and function, the
designer should. The problem does not stem from whether or not a
department has the authority to make the decision, but in how the
decision is carried out and the ambiguity and confusion that surrounds
the decision. For example, is a *verbal* waiver by a design engineer
acceptable? If so, under what conditions? At what point does a waiver
become the responsibility of a committee or a material review board? Is
there a clear policy for handling design waivers? If so, is the policy
enforced and understood by those who are involved? Such questions and
how they are answered and executed are a measure of closed loop
effectiveness.

Another example can be found in communications between
production and inspection people. The wrangling that sometimes takes
place between inspection and manufacturing employees as well as
between the managements of these departments is frequently rooted in

communication gaps. Standards or measurement criteria are sometimes indefinite, giving rise to differences of opinion. As a result, inspectors are inconsistent from one time to the next. This is the basis of dissention and further communication problems between the two departments. It is difficult for production operators to take quality seriously when they witness what was acceptable yesterday, based on one inspector's judgment, is rejected today based on another's opinion.

Those who often excape the brunt of these problems are the various design groups. The *definition* of components and assemblies should be sufficiently communicated so that production and inspection people as well as trainers can work to the same standard. Otherwise, additional open loops will be created.

In modern industry, both inspectors and production operators need all the help they can get. Even under ideal circumstances, the efficiency with which information loops are closed is constantly put to test. The job of the inspector has a built-in adversarial characteristic in that "disapproval" tends to be inherent in the job. Over the years, the term inspector has acquired negative connotations because of this role, giving support to the notion that quality control people hold up progress.

Another kind of communication gap that is usually not identified in this context is the failure of a supervisor or manager to respond to an employee's need for *performance* feedback. Making and communicating performance appraisals is the final link which closes a performance loop. Expectations are communicated to an employee, work is performed, and an informal or formal review or assessment of progress is made. Positive employee attitudes about the job, the superior, and the company can be strengthened through closing this important loop.

Employees want timely, clear, and accurate feedback because it helps them learn about how they compare with others, measure up to established standards, and identify areas where they need to change. Employees will carefully watch nonverbal cues to get this information when verbal or written statements are not provided. And, the conclusions they draw may not always be valid.

Several additional examples are given to illustrate the scope of this closed loop process. The macro system with which most people are familiar is the design-fabrication loop. The design and ancillary specifications represent the plan of action: they are verified as being accurate, released and issued to the respective work centers. Conformance to the plan is attempted by the operator and the inspector appraises conformance to this standard. Inspection reports are the source of feedback to cognizant people.

Based on such results, new decisions and directions are taken. The efficiency with which this cycle is completed is dependent on such factors as: (1) the design must be complete, clear and understandable to those who fabricate and assemble the units, (2) the work must be accomplished according to the design, (3) the appraisal of conformance must be done with integrity and reported accurately, and (4) new decisions are made on the basis of timely and effective feedback of this information. Any breach of information during this MBO cycle will produce one of two outcomes: (1) extra time, money and energy will be required to close the loops, or (2) new decisions will be left up to chance. Either of these circumstances are, of course, undesirable.

Another example which illustrates the importance of this closed loop process is an action memorandum. If a manager issues a memorandum stating his or her wishes that something be done, correspondence is incomplete unless it contains a means by which he or she will gain control. This "plan" should contain a mechanism by which feedback will be received about progress. This may be no more than a statement such as, "Please include the status of this project in your next week's report." Without closing this loop in the action plan, the full message of expectation has not been communicated.

Another kind of communication loop in which upper management believes will somehow result in positive feedback responses is repeatedly issuing generalized directives, believing that these will instill confidence. Instead, they are interpreted as caveats or are not read by those who would have the greatest need to know. The intent of repeated directives, newsletters, and bulletins can be misunderstood if they do not address a need of the employee.

When the plant manager fails to focus on one particular concern at a time, messages to the upper managers can lose their effectiveness. An official who stresses improved quality in production, for example, risks diluting this message when he or she also stresses innovation, higher production rates, and better communications with customers at the same time. While all of these are important, executive energies spread thin to cover all of these areas may result in no concentration in any one of them with eventual compromises being the final result. One quality director complained about his CEO, "Sure he's for quality, but he's for everything else, too. Under pressure to increase output, something will be sacrificed and I'm afraid it's quality."

Management by Objective (MBO)

MBO has become a part of industrial language. The idea is that when objectives are properly set, people will become involved in demonstrating ability to accomplish these objectives. The result is supposed to be greater productivity. Managers usually set the stage for developing objectives through discussion of the company situation, goals, and strategies that are unique to an operational unit. The number of objectives usually vary from four to 10, with the most important ones to be accomplished first. They are normally related, but it may be appropriate to insert a personal development or "stretch" objective— that is typically not a part of the job. They should pertain to the principal areas of concern—cost, quality, or schedule, have target dates for completion, and should be stated in end result terms. This will enable feedback on progress toward their achievement.

Once objectives have been established, the manager and subordinate concentrate on the achievement of the goals. Their work together should focus on the situation and the work being done to achieve the objectives. Discussions should address the problem, not the evaluation of the subordinate's performance. Important feedback on progress should be timely and directly to the subordinate so that both the manager and subordinate are aware of progress being made.

When progress is reviewed employees should not be censured. Achievement of the goals is the primary issue, not the evaluation of the person.

Several rules should be generally followed when setting objectives with employees.

1. Objectives must be measurable. Performances against measurable objectives are not only easier to evaluate, but make the process efficient as well.

2. Employees should participate in setting their own objectives. In allowing employees to participate, performance and job satisfaction tend to increase.

3. Completion times should be established. Individuals who are given excessive time to perform a task may take more time and set easier goals than individuals of comparable ability who are given less time. (In some cases, the opposite occurs, however.)

4. Objectives must be realistic. Goals that are challenging and attainable will provide the opportunity for employees to experience accomplishment.

5. Several primary objectives for each unit or individual are better

than attempting too many. Meeting a few important objectives is better than making a little progress on many. Three general rules can be helpful in dealing with situations in which the desired objective is not being achieved.:

1. Describe the problem in objective terms that avoid personal inferences.

2. Ask for employees' opinions about the problem. Ask questions to establish open dialog which addresses the situation.

3. To conclude the discussion, ask the employee to summarize his or her understanding of the problem and approaches.

Some people find that the benefits from a management-by-objective program are positive but short-term. The approach succeeds at first, but when achieving the objective becomes dulled by repetition, work tends to return to the old level. In all likelihood, lack of success of MBO can be traced to various violations of the aforementioned principles and will be manifested in the following three difficulties:

I.   If one accepts the premise that causes of low productivity are largely attributable to management, one must question the logic of having this "cause" set objectives that could perpetuate the problem. Setting objectives *for* employees by the management hierarchy may only nourish the philosophy and strategies that have caused dysfunction and negative trends. Some managers are unable to allow sufficient participation when setting objectives.

II.   The kinds and intentions of objectives that are originated at high levels may have little correlation with specific people after trickling down through the hierarchy. Advocates of MBO can easily explain that this is not the way it is supposed to happen—but it *does* in many instances. To bridge this gap some companies send managers to work on the shop floor for at least one day a month to gain a better appreciation of the kind of objectives that really need to be established. This again implies that employees have had insufficient inputs in defining objectives.

III.   Meeting an objective may become an end in itself. Sufficient roadblocks to creativity are normally found without sending signals throughout the organization that more paperwork is needed. When *other people* define a measurable quantity or even quality of work, this becomes the target for change. Performance will be measured by the degree to which objectives are met. Those who exceed these levels will be considered excellent, outstanding, etc. But what is the standard? Are targets set in such a way to stretch creativity and provide greater challenge for improvement? Do time and energies spent in filling out reports to "satisfy" others, and judging what went wrong become ends themselves? Or does the quest for *improvement* become the operating philosophy? Meeting a specific objective may overshadow and detract from the real objective, namely improvement.

Power of Expectation

Many managers treat their subordinates in ways that lead to superior performance. Others unintentionally treat subordinates in ways that lead to lower performance than they are capable of achieving. As discussed earlier, managers unknowingly influence their people by what they *expect* of them. Some believe that if a manager's expectations are high, productivity will be high and if expectations are low, productivity will be low.

High expectations without a sound base will lead to results that oppose productivity goals. Illusional expectations raise false hopes and are counter productive. Dr. Mick Ukleja once commented that, "disillusionment is the child of illusion."[3] High expectations stir positive action only if they are undergirded with the training, tools, and environment that make high expectations a viable capability.

Leaders cannot avoid the depressing cycle of events that flow from low expectations by hiding their feelings. The manager who believes that a subordinate will perform poorly, is not likely to be able to mask this expectation; the message is communicated unintentionally, without conscious action.

Managers often communicate most when they believe they are communicating least. For instance, when nothing is said or when a response is cool, this will likely be perceived as a sign that the leader is displeased. The silent treatment communicates negative feelings even more effectively, at times, than a verbal explosion. The communication of expectations may not be what the supervisor says, so much as how he or she behaves. Indifferent and noncommital treatment is much more likely to lead to poor performance than to high performance.

Another way expectations can be communicated is with the use of *situation management*. Situational management means to create a situation which will predetermine an expected outcome. Several examples will serve to illustrate this technique. If housekeeping is poor, the provision of a trash disposal bin may help; if a part can be inverted in a jig or fixture, foolproofing the device with a pin is a preventive situation. If scrap and rework are being proliferated, a cut in the number of scrap bins, or feedback to the perpetrators, may be the needed situations to produce better results. Situational management means either to recognize undesirable situations and implement changes that will lead to more desirable conditions, or recognize desirable conditions and create situations that will assure or re-enforce desired outcomes.

Evidence available from research reveals that, everything else being equal:

1. What a manager expects from subordinates and the way they are treated largely influence employees' performances.

2. A unique characteristic of superior managers is their ability to communicate high performance expectations.

3. Less effective managers fail to develop appropriate expectations, and lower productivity is a result.

Job Enrichment

Utilizing Personnel in Multifunction Roles. From the classic white-collar worker to the operator on the shop floor, more multifunction people are needed. Operators having knowledge and skill in more than one job helps to accomplish at least four important objectives: (1) alleviate boredom which accompanies single function jobs, (2) learning more than one job makes an employee more promotable and challenged by the job, (3) the multifunction concept is an important hedge against absenteeism, (4) employees can be utilized in alternate jobs during period of work slowdown or when flexibility is needed to avoid severe imbalances of work load.

A non-union southern California-based semi-conductor company, for example, is effectively cross-training and employing people extensively in multi-function roles. In the testing department, operators learn to perform environmental tests, as well as conducting both wafer probe and final tests of integrated circuits. Moreover, operators learn how to trouble-shoot equipment and make their own setups. Employees state that they are constantly challenged, never become bored, and establish personal improvement goals. Where job classifications must be highly structured, other options to organize work may need to be investigated.

Flexible Working Hours. Another technique used to provide better overall scheduling and simultaneously enrich employees' jobs, is giving them more of a voice in the choice of the hours they work.

271

Flexible work schedules have several advantages. Alternative scheduling allows workers time to attend to personal matters at the beginning or end of the shift. While some workers may want to change their schedules, the flexible approach allows those who wish to retain their same working hours to do so. Research on flexitime indicates that improvements in performance and quality, increases in job satisfaction, reduced absenteeism, tardiness, and turnover are experienced.

Flexible working hours allows employees to decide when they will start and stop each day with the provision that a given number of hours will be worked within a specified period. For example, companies may define "core" hours between 10:00 a.m. and 3:00 p.m. with 40 minutes for lunch as inflexible, and the remaining hours of the shift as discretionary.

Many variations of this procedure are in use. Data from the U.S. Department of Labor Statistics indicate that more than 10 million Americans work on flexible schedules by which beginning and ending hours of work can vary. Over two million additional employees work compressed work weeks of either three, four, or four and one-half days per week.

Performance Appraisals

Another area in which there is great opportunity to build trust and cooperation (or destroy them) is in the performance appraisal procedure. A performance appraisal is the process by which an organization observes and measures employee accomplishments against job standards and organizational goals over a specific period. Contained in this process is the opportunity to improve employee performance. This entire procedure, however, while carrying strong implication to improvement, can become just another last minute chore that must be accomplished by a superior.

The performance appraisal procedure should be an ongoing process. At a minimum, it entails having adequate job descriptions of the work performed, an incident file on the person involved, and mutually established objectives as criteria for assessment. Job descriptions describe the needed skills and tools for the job; an incident file is a progressive gathering of information about a person's performance between appraisal sessions. This should include both *positive and negative* incidences. The most serious problem in connection with the use of the incident file is that it can turn into a "grudge" file in which only negative evidence is accumulated. Since building such a file is the accepted way to terminate a person, motivation for its use frequently originates from negative objectives. The positive side of the incident file has important values that are inadvertently overlooked. As long as a job is going well, performances are accepted as "normal." Even exceptional performances are sometimes considered usual because a supervisor adjusts to this pattern and expects this level of performance.

Purposes. The principal purposes of the performance appraisal can be summarized in the following ten points.:

1. Provide a mechanism for an employee to discuss his or her performance, achievements and difficulties, and goals and expectations.

2. Establish goals and/or performance standards to be followed until the next evaluation.

3. Clarify mutual expectations.

4. Provide insight into present and potential strengths.

5. Help determine employee potential for advancement.

6. Offer a periodic formal means of gathering employee suggestions for improving methods, procedures, performance, practices, and morale.

7. Offer a periodic formal means of identifying training needs and fostering employee development.

8. Improve employee performance through recognition, encouragement, constructive criticism, or personal counseling.

9. Provide a scheduled, formal opportunity for a supervisor to discuss his or her view of an employee's performance, present standing, and possibilities for improvement or advancement.

10. Deepen the employee's job satisfaction and his or her commitment to the organization.

Conducting Effective Performances Appraisals. The efficacy of these procedures is based on managerial abilities of the supervisor. A great degree of discipline, objectivity and fairness is required. In the final analysis, people evaluate people; those in leadership roles have much the same frailties as those they lead.

Before the performance appraisal is conducted, there are several questions that should be reviewed.

1. What contribution *is* the employee making?
2. What contribution *should* the employee make?
3. What are the employee strengths?
4. What are the employee weaknesses?
5. Is the employee working near his or her potential?
6. What training does the employee need?

Techniques for establishing objectives were described in the previous section. These criteria carry-over to the performance appraisal process. Standards against which performances are appraised should have the following characteristics.

Performance appraisal standards should:

1. Be specific
2. Be practical
3. Be attainable
4. Be measurable
5. Have a targeted attainment date
6. Have stretching properties

Performance *measures* should include quality, quantity, cost and timeliness.

Shown in Figure X-4 is an example of how a performance summary should not be written as opposed to the one described in Figure X-5 which illustrates a more carefully drawn up appraisal. Note in Figure X-4, most phrases are constructed in generalities which are perfunctory criteria, but in Figure X-5, performance is tied to specific and measurable projects or objectives.

Mid-managers and supervisors under crises situations find it very difficult to consistently do a good job of appraising performance of their people.

Common performance appraisal problems which should be addressed between sessions are stated in the following seven statements.

1. Delays in scheduling the evaluation.

2. Evaluate both excellent and poor performances.

3. Sufficient planning for the interview.

4. Sufficient communication with employees, which provides for shared information.

SALARIED/EXEMPT PERFORMANCE SUMMARY

Name _____ Employee No. _____ Dept. Title/No. _____

Position _____ Time in This Position _____ Appraisal Period From 1/1/82 To 1/1/83

Performance Plan Commitments	Actual Performance Achieved	Level of Priority	Agreed Level of Difficulty	Comments
1. INCREASE DEPT OUTPUT PER M/H	OUTPUT INCREASED TO OVER 12 PARTS PER M/H		DIFF	EXCELLENT EFFORT
2. REDUCE SCRAP RATE	SCRAP RATE REDUCED		DIFF	GOOD RESULTS
3. REDUCE EMPLOYEE ABSENTEEISM	ABSENTEEISM REDUCED TO 2.8%		DIFF	SUPERVISORS ARE MONITORING ATTENDENCE DAILY
4. REDUCE LOST TIME INJURIES	LOST TIME INJURIES REDUCED		DIFF	SUPERVISOR CONDUCTED SAFETY TALK EVERY MONTH
5.				

What strengths were demonstrated? MAINTAINS EXCELLENT ATTITUDE.
VERY GOOD PERSONALITY. DEPENDABLE AND ADAPTABLE.
SHOWS GOOD INITIATIVE. A WARM AND SENSITIVE
HUMAN BEING. EXTREMELY PATIENT

What additional development actions are required? NEEDS TO ATTEND
MEANINGFUL SEMINARS

Supervisor's summary statement of employee's performance: EMPLOYEE HAS
HIGH POTENTIAL. OVERALL PERFORMANCE IS OUT-
STANDING. STRONG SENSE OF URGENCY COUPLED WITH
HIS CONTINUED ATTENTION TO DETAIL IDENTIFY HIM
AS ONE OF OUR FINEST SUPERVISORS.

When the overall performance of this employee is considered to be "Outstanding", provide here a descriptive paragraph of the specific performance with examples of the results achieved.

When the overall performance of this employee is considered to be "Less Than Expectations" provide here a paragraph of the specific actions which will be accomplished to strengthen and/or improve capabilities:

Specific actions to be taken by the employee:

Specific actions to be taken by the supervisor:

Employee's Comments: I am happy about this
review but how will it alter progress the
next period?

Signed _Jim Allen_ Date _1-20-82_

Supervisor Signature _V.R. Casey_ Date _11/20/82_

Management Review – Signed _John Jones_ Date _11/20/82_

FIGURE X-4.   POOR EVALUATION OF PERFORMANCE

275

SALARIED/EXEMPT PERFORMANCE SUMMARY

Name _____ Employee No. _____ Dept. Title/No. _____

Position _____ Time in This Position _____ Appraisal Period From 1/1/82 To 1/1/83

Performance Plan Commitments	Actual Performance Achieved	Level of Priority	Agreed Level of Difficulty	Comments
1. INCREASE DEPT. OUTPUT FROM 11.5 PARTS PER M/H TO 12.5 PARTS PER M/H BY JULY 1 (BY JULY 1) WITHOUT SACRIFICING QUALITY	OUTPUT INCREASED TO 12.6 PARTS PER M/H WITH NO LOSS OF QUALITY		V. DIFF	DOUBLE HANDLING MINI-MIZED & MATERIAL FLOW IMPROVED
2. REDUCE DEPT. SCRAP RATE FROM 3.5% TO 2.5% BY SEPT. 1	SCRAP RATE REDUCED TO 3.2% BY DEC. 31		V. DIFF	KEY CAUSES FOR SCRAP NOT ADDRESSED
3. REDUCE EMPLOYEE ABSENTEEISM FROM 3.8% TO 3.0% BY MAY 1	ABSENTEEISM REDUCED TO 2.8% BY APR 1		DIFF.	EXCELLENT APPLICATION OF POLICIES - GOOD FOLLOW-UP
4. REDUCE DEPT. LOST TIME INJURIES FROM 4% TO 2% BY DEC 31	LOST TIME INJURIES REDUCED TO 2.1% BY DEC 31		DIFF.	V. GOOD COMMUNICATION AND FOLLOW-UP ON SAFETY RULES

What strengths were demonstrated? EXCELLENT ORGANIZATIONAL SKILLS SHOWN IN ACCOMPLISHING #1 ABOVE. VERY GOOD COMMUNICATION SKILLS DEMONSTRATED IN #3 & #4. PROVIDED STRONG LEADERSHIP THROUGHOUT.

When the overall performance of this employee is considered to be "Outstanding", provide here a descriptive paragraph of the specific performance with examples of the results achieved

What additional developmental actions are required? A NEED FOR ADDITIONAL QUALITY TRAINING WITH PARTICULAR EMPHASIS ON DEFECT IDENTIFICATION AND PROBLEM SOLVING METHODS IS DEMONSTRATED IN #2 ABOVE.

When the overall performance of this employee is considered to be "Less Than Expectations", provide here a paragraph of the specific actions which will be accomplished to strengthen and/or improve capabilities:

Supervisor's summary statement of employee's performance: EMPLOYEE HAS ACHIEVED ABOVE AVERAGE RESULTS UNDER MOST CIRCUMSTANCES. HE EXHIBITS A WELL ORGANIZED, KNOWLEDGABLE, AND POSITIVE MANAGEMENT STYLE REFLECTED BY MEASURABLE IMPROVEMENTS IN HIS DEPARTMENT. WORKS VERY WELL WITH ALL LEVELS IN ACCOMPLISHING OBJECTIVES.

Specific actions to be taken by the employee: ENROLL EMPLOYEE IN QUALITY TRAINING COURSE WITH EMPHASIS ON IDENTI-FIED NEEDS DURING 1st QTR.

Specific actions to be taken by the supervisor:

Employee's Comments:

Signed _Harvey Reed_ Date 11/10/82

Supervisor Signature _Dale Clark_ Date 11 10 82

Management Review – Signed _Mary Jones_ Date 11-10-82

FIGURE X-5. GOOD EVALUATION OF PERFORMANCE

5. Maintenance of sufficient records on employee performance.

6. Assess one's own contribution to the employee's success or failure.

7. Consistent follow-up on goals set during previous evaluation.

The appraisal session itself requires considerable skill by the supervisor. Typical difficulties that are encountered *during* the interview are listed as follows:

1. Doing too much of the talking.

2. Difficulty in putting the employee at ease.

3. Avoiding discussion of genuine performance problems.

4. Failure to explain the "why" of the rating.

5. Getting sidetracked.

6. Failure to involve the employee adequately in the goal setting process.

7. Forgetting that some "facts" may reflect unconscious assumptions or attitudes toward the employee.

8. Not listening effectively.

9. Failure to build on the employee's strengths.

10. Losing objectivity and becoming opinionated.

11. Making loose comparisons with other employees.

12. Failure to leave the employee with a clear understanding of where he or she stands, what he or she should do to meet standards, and how the supervisor will be of assistance in doing so.

EPILOGUE

A new, unmistakeable vista of quality is taking place in the United States. Consumers increasingly are basing their purchase decisions on the quality of goods and services. They are even willing to pay more for the confidence and assurance of quality features.

This message is being received by producers, but with mixed emotions. Quality apparently is still being treated casually by some manufacturers. But, where quality has been at the forefront of management strategies, the sharper quality focus is an invited challenge.

Dramatic progress is being made by companies which had the foresignt to absorb the quality and productivity message and now continue to assertively transform quality commitments into action. These companies place sufficient emphasis on quality that with each shipment, or negotiation, customer confidence is strengthened. There is good reason for this business strategy. Decades of effort toward building a good company reputation can be negated by a single shipment of defective product.

For many years, the quality-productivity connection was underestimated, and apparently misunderstood by many top executives. While it has been known that "quality" is important, the delivery of *economic* quality has been more abstract, and its influence on productivity and profits eluded many strategic planners. This, too, is changing. Impetus is being placed on the design and vendor aspects of quality as well as manufacturing operations.

In the quest for quality and productivity improvement, most companies face even broader challenges in this era of global competition. Can management and labor figure out better ways to deal with the adversarial climate that tends to exist in industrial cultures? Can top executives be responsive to the needs of the work force? Can teamwork values be developed and sustained in industrial cultures which manifest ambivalent resistance to sharing and participating in goal achievement? Will management be able to convert short-term approaches to business operations into long-term strategies when

278

functioning in economic and industrial systems which expect and reward short-term payoff. How these questions are answered will be measures of success of companies in the years to come.

Many of the most successful firms have internalized the productivity improvement philosophy, and have put it to music. There are four choruses to the productivity song which these companies sing harmoniously: (1) Constancy of purpose, (2) Competency, (3) Efficient process control and conformance, and (4) Competitive position.

Constancy of purpose and active leadership by top executives comprise the first stanza. This begins with the faith that established truths work, and the belief that what is necessary can be accomplished through people. This foundation is essential to the development of teamwork and trust among the work force. Any solution to the "us and them" syndrome that plagues so many U.S. companies will include greater participative efforts by senior managements.

Competency needs to be nurtured and rewarded. A suitably educated and trained work force will reduce errors and their consequences. From the CEO to the assembler, employees should, (1) unleash creative talents, (2) be keenly aware of the importance of customer satisfaction, and (3) experience the pride of success in being contributing members of the productivity team.

Efficient process control and conformance pertain to (1) the full utilization of preventive methods where both systems and processes are found, (2) accurate assessment and communication of changing customer requirements, (3) complete definition of design requirements and (4) conformance of manufacturing procedures, processes and workmanship to all design specifications. With honest criteria, quality and productivity become measurable and manageable entities. Effective achievement of conformance goals always presumes proper leadership and planning, methods and tools, and machines and materials.

Competitive position involves being sensitive to market conditions and conducting proper ongoing research and development work to be a leader in the field. Any goal to achieve a long-term productivity posture will encompass visions and strategies to complete enough product improvement and new product development activities to ensure a strong competitive position.

Best managed companies (evidenced by long-term success) are particularly adept in these four key areas. Firms which have been less successful have chosen the easier passages of the productivity song and have settled for shortsighted goals.

After all has been said and done, the values espoused in this book require an even broader view than a company or even the marketplace. Long-term productivity enhancement will come through the cooperative efforts of management, employees, Government, educational institutions and communities of America. Societal values need to reward and support the economical production of goods and services with high intrinsic value. Familial, religious and educational institutions, need to focus on pride of workmanship and to instill a fundamental value of excellence. The importance of working cooperatively, as a team should also be taught over and above that which is learned through social interaction and sports.

Meanwhile, managements will find it increasingly necessary to deal with the problem of improvement. For some, this step will take the form of upheaval in a society which paradoxically demands high value in its purchases, while its members and institutions tend to be less dedicated to excellence and circumspect performance.

A sound basis for such improvement, nevertheless, exists in the U.S. Individual genius and creativity remain hallmarks of American entrepreneurship. The really new technologies and the inspiration that produces growth and improvement have not come from bureaucratic Government, institutions or even from corporations, per se. They have come and will continue to come from people; from individuals who are passionately committed to excellence and from those who may appear to be a little crazy at times, but are able to overcome the inevitable and uninvited obstacles that hinder progress.

BIBLIOGRAPHY & REFERENCES

CHAPTER I

BIBLIOGRAPHY:

1. Karen W. Arenson, "The Elusive Boom in Productivity," *The New York Times,* April 4, 1984.
2. S.L. Binstock, "Consumers Express Dissatisfaction With Quality of U.S. Products," *Quality Progress,* January 1981, p. 12.
3. Arnold Judson, "The Awkward Truth About Productivity," *Harvard Business Review,* September-October 1982, p. 93.
4. W. Edward Deming, Three-day Seminar on Quality and Productivity, Long Beach, CA, June 1983.
5. John Naisbitt, Megatrends, Warner Books, Inc., 1982.
6. John L. Warne, "Quality and Other Keys to Manufacturing Competitiveness," *Impro 84,* Chicago, Illinois, October 4, 1984.
7. Edgar H. Schein, "Does Japanese Management Style Have A Message for American Managers?" *Sloan Management Review,* Fall 1981, p. 55.
8. Glenn E. Hayes, "A CEO's Responsibilities," *Quality,* Hitchcock Publishing Company, December 1983.
9. Douglas Watson, "Sharp Proves U.S. Workers Thrive Under Japanese Style of Management," *L.A. Times,* June 6, 1983.

REFERENCES:

"Big Steel's Winter of Woes," *Time,* January 24, 1983.

W. Edwards Deming, "If Japan Can, Why Can't We?" *An NBC White Paper,* 1980.

Peter F. Drucker, "Behind Japan's Success," *Harvard Business Review,* p. 83.

Peter F. Drucker, *The Changing World of the Executive,* Truman Talley Book Publishing Co., 1982.

Bruce Horovitz, "Japan's Auto Heyday is Over," *Industry Week,* April 4, 1983, p. 19.

Ann Imse, "A Radical Japanese Ethic: Harmony in the Workplace," *The Register,* Santa Ana, California, January, 1985.

Edward E. Lewler III and Gerald E. Ledford, Jr., "Productivity and the Quality of Work Life," *National Productivity Review,* Vol. I, Winter, 1981-82.

Thomas J. Peters and Robert H. Waterman, Jr., *In Search of Excellence,* Harper and Row, 1982.

Thomas Rosenstiel, "U.S. Productivity Gain—Best Since 1975 Quarter Report Shows," *L.A. Times,* Saturday, August 27, 1983.

Mitatake Yamamoto, "The Japanese—Homogeneity," *Quality Progress,* September, 1980, p. 18.

CHAPTER II

BIBLIOGRAPHY:

1. H. James Harrington, "Quality Education Rides the Crest of the Third Wave," IBM Corporation, San Jose, CA. July 1982.

2.   J. Juran, *Managerial Breakthrough,* McGraw Hill Book Publishing Co., 1964.
3.   Walter Shewhart, *Economic Control of Manufactured Product,* D. Van Nostrand Co., 1931.
4.   H. James Harrington and J. Shaw, "Are You Ready For Integration?" IBM Corporation, San Jose, CA 1973.

REFERENCES:

Robert G. Burns, "Quality Paradoxes Cloud NRC Success," *Quality Progress,* January 1984, p. 29.
Clyde W. Brewer, "Managing the Company-wide Quality Manual," *Quality,* June 1983, p. 49.
Philip Crosby, A.V. Fiegenbaum, and J.M. Juran, "Questions and Answers: A Special Report on Quality," *Quality Progress,* October 1984, p. 32.
Richard L. Engwall, "System Integration and Design-Automating the Factory of the Future," *Industrial Management,* July-August 1984, p. 13.
David A. Garvin, "Product Quality: An Important Strategic Weapon," *Business Horizons,* May/June 1984.
Robert Grenier, "Total Quality Assurance, Part I," *Quality,* January 1985.
Charles C. Harwood, "The View From the Top," *Quality Progress,* October 1984, p. 26.
R.N. Osborn and T.G. Hunt, *Organization Theory: An Integrated Approach,* John Wiley, 1980.
Tom Peters and Perry Pascarella, "Searching for Excellence," *Industry Week,* April 16, 1984.
"The New Industrial Elations," *Special Report Business Week,* May 11, 1981, p. 84.
John L. Warne, "Quality and Other Keys to Manufacturing Competitiveness," *Quality Progress,* January 1985.
Ralph Wurster, "Quality is Applause—After the Performance," *Quality,* January 1985, p. 25.

CHAPTER III

BIBLIOGRAPHY:

1.   Terrence E. Deal and Allan A. Kennedy, *Corporate Cultures,* Addison-Wesley Publishing Co., 1982, p. 22.
2.   Morgan W. McCall and Michael M. Lombardo, "What Makes A Top Executive?" *Psychology Today,* February 1982.
3.   Edgar Magnin, "Wisdom and Practical Idealism," *LA Times,* February 12, 1983.
4.   W. Edwards Deming, Seminar on Quality and Productivity, Long Beach, CA, June, 1983.
5.   John Naisbitt, *Megatrends,* Warner Books Inc.
6.   Lester C. Thurow, "Where Management Fails," *Newsweek,* January 1982.
7.   Mitchell Fein, "Financial Motivation," *Handbook of Industrial Engineers,* John Wiley & Sons, 1982, pp. 1, 2, 3.
8.   "Secrets of America's Best Run Companies," Interview with Peters and Waterman, *Success* Magazine, April 1983, p. 43.

REFERENCES:

James Beggs, "Quality, Productivity and NASA, A Special Report," *Quality Progress,* October 1984.
W. Edwards Deming, "Seven Deadly Diseases Afflicting U.S. Industry," *Manufacturing Engineering,* July 1983, p. 65.
A.V. Feigenbaum, "Quality, Managing a Modern Company," *Quality Progress,* March 1985, p. 18.
Bernard Gendron, "The Great Productivity Scam," *Phi Kappa Phi Journal,* p. 22.

Glenn E. Hayes, "A CEO's Responsibilities," An Interview with Carmelo Santoro, CEO of Silicon Systems Corp., Tustin, CA, *Quality,* January 1984.

Jack Hohengarten, "The Real Challenge—Making it Happen," Productivity Brief, *American Productivity Center,* Houston, Texas, February 1982.

J.M. Juran, "The Quality-Profit Relationship," *Technical Conference Transactions,* American Society for Quality Control, 1976, p. 18.

Carlton P. McNamara, "Productivity is Managements Problem," *Business Horizons,* March/April 1983, p. 55.

Michael T. Midas, "The Productivity-Quality Connection," *Design News,* December 7, 1981, p. 56.

Perry Pascarella, "Can Management Break Out of Its Box?" *Industry Week,* June 1983, p. 53.

Joel Ross, "The Quality Gap: Causes and Cures," *Industrial Management,* September-October 1984, p. 14.

Thomas C. Tuttle, "Measuring Productivity and Quality of Work Life," *Phi Kappa Phi Journal,* Spring 1982.

CHAPTER IV

BIBLIOGRAPHY:

1. Frederick W. Taylor, *Principles of Scientific Management,* Harper and Row, 1911.
2. Joe R. Barnett, "All Work or All Play?" *Upreach,* April 1979, p. 4.
3. K. Davis, "Low Productivity? Try Improving the Social Environment," *Business Horizons,* June 1980, p. 27.
4. Perry Pascarella, "The Corporation Steps in Where Family, Church and Schools Have Failed," *Industry Week,* June 25, 1984.
5. John Brecher, et al., "Taking Drugs on the Job," *Newsweek,* August 22, 1983, p. 53.
6. Daniel D. Cook, "Labor Gets Back to the Basics," *Industry Week,* January 11, 1982, p. 7.
7. Ibid.

REFERENCES:

Jerry Flint, "A New Breed—Professional Union Breakers," *Forbes,* June 25, 1979, p. 29.

J.H. Foegen, "Job Socializing: Endangered Species," *Industrial Management,* July-August 1984, p. 10.

William E. Fulmer, "Step by Step Through a Union Campaign," *Harvard Business Review,* July/August 1981, p. 94.

Gary M. Hanson, "Productivity Gains from the Shopfloor Up," *Production Engineering,* March 1982, p. 82.

Frederick Herzberg, "You Can't Manage People Scientifically," *Industry Week,* September 15, 1980, p. 44.

Steven Lagerfeld, "To Break A Union," *Harpers,* May 1981, p. 16.

Judy Linscott, "Ho Hum: Beating On-the-Job Boredom," *Working Woman,* December 1981, p. 93.

Carlton P. McNamara, "Productivity is Managements Problem," *Business Horizons,* March/April 1983, p. 55.

"Overtime May Mean Inefficient Workers," *Los Angeles Times,* November 27, 1983.

Michael J. Piore, "Why Unions Don't Work Anymore?" *Inc.,* March 1982, p. 17.

Frank H. Squires, *Successful Quality Management,* Hitchcock Publishing Company, Wheaton, IL, 1980.

George A. Steiner and John F. Steiner, *Business, Government and Society: A Managerial Perspective,* Random House Business Division, 1980.

"Taking Aim at Union Busters," *Business Week,* November 12, 1979, p. 98.

"The HP Way," *HP Pamphlet,* #5955-4709, January 1980.

Daniel Yankelovich and Bernard Lefkowitz, "Work and American Expectations," *Phi Kappa Phi Journal,* p. 3.

Richard E. Ward and Terrence J. Stobbe, "Scheduling of Shiftwork in Industry: The Human Factor," *Industrial Management,* July-August 1984, p. 22.

CHAPTER V
BIBLIOGRAPHY:

1. Thomas J. Murrin, "American Strategies for Productivity and International Competitiveness," Harry Sievers Memorial Lecture Series, presented October 14, 1982.
2. "Engineering Supply Gap," *Update,* American Electronics Association, July 1983.
3. Thomas J. Murrin, "An American Challenge: Winning the Global Superbowls," Remarks to the National Security Industrial Association, Washington, D.C., March 16, 1983.
4. Terrell Bell, "America Can't Afford Mediocre Schools," *USA Today,* April 28, 1983.
5. Albert Shanker, "We Must Recruit the Best and the Brightest," *USA Today,* April 29, 1983.
6. J.M. Juran, "Quality's Impact on Productivity and the Economy," *Bottom Line Academia Conference,* Washington, D.C., April 28, 1983.
7. Thomas J. Cartin, "Productivity and Quality: Other Ways to Improve," *Proceedings,* Industrial Engineering Conference, May 1983.
8. Donald N. Frey, "Education is a Prerequisite for Economic Growth," *Industry Week,* February 7, 1983.
9. Jeremy Main, "Why Engineering Deans Worry a Lot," *Fortune,* January 1982, p. 86.
10. "General Education Requirements," Bulletin, 1983-85, California State University, Long Beach, CA, p. 61.

REFERENCES:

Bruce Krauskopf, "The Move From Engineering to Management," *Manufacturing Engineering,* April 1983.

Jeremy Main, "Why Engineering Deans Worry a Lot," *Fortune,* January 1982, p. 86.

Duane P. Schultz, *Psychology and Industry Today,* MacMillan Publishing Co., 1973.

Willis J. Willoughby, Jr., "How Can Academia Positively Impact Quality?" *Bottom Line Academia Conference,* Washington, DC, December 1983.

M.K. Badawy, "What's Wrong With Engineering Management?" *Machine Design,* July 22, 1982, p. 62.

Carot Brown, "MBA Degree No Longer Express Ticket to Success," *LA Times,* August 28, 1983.

Thomas J. Cartin, "Productivity and Quality: Other Ways to Improve," *Proceedings, Industrial Engineers Conference,* May 1983.

John Crosby and David Brandt, "Employee Selection, Placement and Training: Key Terms in the Productivity Equation," *Electronics West,* December 1983, p. 20.

John Crosby and David Brandt, "Management Training and the Bottom Line," *Electronics West,* February 1983.

Navin S. Dedhia, "Education and Training for Quality," *Quality Progress,* January 1985, p. 14.

Laurence Feinberg, "Panel Urges Measures to Halt Decline of Education in America," *Washington Post,* April 27, 1983.

Richard A. Freund, "Education and Training in the Workplace for Statistical Process Control," *Quality Progress,* January 1985, p. 16.

Glenn E. Hayes, "Educations Impact on Quality," *Bottom Line Academia Conference,* Washington, DC, April 28, 1983.

Glenn E. Hayes, "Quality and Productivity: The Education Gap," *Quality,* October 1982, p. 51.

Nancy A. Karabatsos, "Indusry Goes to School," *Quality,* January 1985, p. 57.

CHAPTER VI

BIBLIOGRAPHY:

1. Robert T. Moran and Philip R. Harris, *Managing Cultural Synergy,* Gulf Publishing Company, 1982.
2. J. Juran, "Closing Statements," *IMPRO 1984,* Chicago, IL, October 5, 1984.
3. Beverly A. Potter, *The Way of the Ronin,* American Management Association, AMACOM, 1984.

REFERENCES:

James Braham, "Hazards at the Top," *Industry Week,* January 21, 1985, p. 35.

Chester Burger, *The Chief Executive,* CBI Publishing Co., 1978.

Allan J. Cox, *Corporate Cultures,* Harcourt Press, 1982.

Peter F. Drucker, "The Entrepreneurial Society," *Industry Week,* February 18, 1985, p. 52.

William A. Evans, *Management Ethics,* Martinus Nijhoff Publishing Co., 1981.

Frederick Herzberg, "Productivity Begins with the Individual," *Industry Week,* November 30, 1981, p. 89.

B. Jeanine Hull, "NCR Must Make Top Management Accountable for Quality," *Quality Progress,* January 1984, p. 34.

Tom Kerry, *Workers, Bosses and Bureaucrats,* Pathfinder Press, 1980.

Edward E. Lawler II and Gerald E. Ledrord, Jr., "Productivity and the Quality of Work Life," *National Productivity Review,* Vol I, Winter, 1981-82.

E. A. Locke, "The Nature and Causes of Job Satisfaction," *Handbook of Industrial and Organizational Psychology,* Rand McNally, 1976, p. 104.

John A. McCreight, CMC, "Corporate Culture and Competitive Superiority," *Industrial Management,* July-August 1984, p. 1.

Marshall McDonald, "Commitment to Success," *Quality Progress,* 1984, p. 26.

E. Frank Mead, "Building A Corporate Quality Culture: A Test Cast," *Quality Progress,* March 1985, p. 10.

Jerome M. Rosow, "Quality of Working Life," *National Forum Journal,* Spring 1982, p. 20.

Leonard A. Schlesinger, *Quality of Work Life and the Supervisor,* Praeger Publishers, 1982.

Barry A. Stein and Rosabeth Moss Kanter, "Building the Parallel Organization: Creating Mechanisms for Permanent Quality of Work Life," *Journal of Applied Behavioral Science,* Vol. 16, No. 3, 1980, pp. 371-388.

Barry A. Stein and Rosabeth Moss Kanter, "Productivity Improvement/Personal Satisfaction: A Model Quality of Work Life Project for White-Collar and Professional Workers," Cambridge, MA, Goodmeasure, Inc., 1980.

A.S. Warren, "Quality of Work Life Pays Off in the Auto Industry," *Personnel Journal,* December 1981, p. 930.

CHAPTER VII

BIBLIOGRAPHY:

1. Raymond M. Demeré, Vice President, Manufacturing Sources, Hewlett-Packard,

"The Human Factor in Innovation and Productivity," Statements to House Sub-Committee on Science and Technology, September 16, 1981.

2. Glenn E. Hayes, *Quality Assurance: Management and Technology,* 7th Edition, Charger Productions, Capistrano Beach, CA, 1985.

REFERENCES:

"Advice for Starting Circles: Take It Slow, Be Wary," *Training Today,* January 1982, p. 9.

"American Manufacturers Strive for Quality—Japanese Style," *Business Week,* March 12, 1979.

Richard W. Anderson, General Manager, Hewlitt-Packard Computer Systems Division at HP Press reception, Cupertino, CA, October 21, 1980.

James L. Brown, "Productivity Improvement," *Proceedings: Industrial Engineering Conference,* 1982, p. 371.

Robert E. Cole, "Will QC Circles Work in the U.S.?" *Quality Progress,* July 1980, p. 30.

Michael H. Cook, "Quality Circles—They Really Work, But . . . ," *Training and Development Journal,* January 1982, p. 4.

Joseph D. Gagliardi, "An Alternative to Quality Circles," *Quality,* June 1983, p. 62.

Ben S. Graham, Jr., and Parvin S. Titus, *The Amazing Oversight: Total Participation for Productivity,* New York, AMACOM, 1979.

"How to Win the Quality Circles Game," *Training and Development Journal,* November 1981, p. 7.

Robert R. Irving, "QC Circles Sput Productivity, Improve Product Quality," *Iron Age,* June 5, 1978, p. 61.

J.M. Juran, "International Significance of the QC Movement," *Quality Progress,* November 1980, p. 18.

J.M. Juran, "Japanese and Western Quality—A Contrast," *Quality,* January 1979.

Rosabeth Moss Kanter, "Dilemmas of Participation," *Phi Kappa Phi Journal,* Spring 1982, p. 16.

Robert N. Lehrer, *Participative Productivity and Quality of Work Life,* Prentice Hall, 1982.

Merle O'Donnell and Robert O'Donnell, "Quality Circles: The Latest Fad or a Real Winner?" *Business Horizons,* May/June 1984.

"Quality Circles—Can They Work for Your Company?" *Assembly Engineering,* December 1981, p. 34.

"Quality—The U.S. Drives to Catch Up," Special Report, *Business Week,* November 1982, p. 66.

John Simons and William Mares, *Working Together,* Alfred Knopf Inc., 1983.

D. Scott Sink "Productivity Action Teams: An Alternative Involvement Strategy to Quality Circles," *Proceedings, Industrial Engineering Conference,* 1982, p. 295.

Manfred L. Spangler and Richard F. Hershberger, "Maximizing Operations Productivity Through Team Building—Tapping Employee Creativity."

Gerald E. Swartz and Vivian C. Comstock, "One Firm's Experience with Quality Circles," *Quality Progress,* 1979, p. 14.

John Teresko, "Lincoln Wants to Share Its Productivity Secrets, *Industry Week,* March 7, 1983, p. 75.

Robert C. Wood, "Squaring off on Quality Circles," *Inc.,* August 1982, p. 98.

CHAPTER VIII

REFERENCES:

Leonard Berger and F. Paul Clipp, "The Challenge of the Future for Engineering

Managers," *Industrial Management,* March-April 1983.

Theodore L. Bloomer, "Overstaffing: The Hidden Killer of Productivity," *Program Manager,* September-October 1981, p. 17.

Keith A. Bolte, "Conquering the Administrative Marshmallow," *Industrial Engineer Conference Proceedings,* 1982, p. 719.

Richard A. Calmes, "Improving Salaried Employee Productivity," *Industrial Engineering Conference Proceedings,* 1983.

William F. Christopher, "How to Measure and Improve Productivity in Professional Administrative and Service Organizations," *International Industrial Engineering Conference Proceedings,* 1984.

John J. Connell, "Office of the 80's: Productivity Impact," *Business Week,* February 19, 1980.

Randy J. Goldfield, "The Office Today: The Drive for Productivity," *New York Times Advertising Supplement,* 1981 Annual Issue, pp. 5-6.

Ruth N. Greenwald, "The Industrial Engineer is a Catalyst for Organizational Change," *Fall Industrial Engineering Conference Proceedings,* 1984.

Walter M. Hancock and Jeffery K. Liker, "Improving the Productivity of the White Collar Work Force—New Methods," *Fall Industrial Engineering Conference Proceedings,* 1983.

Stephan Konz, *Work Design,* Grid Publishing Inc., 1979, p. 25.

Fein Mitchell, "Let's Return to Measured Day Work for Incentives," *Industrial Engineering,* January 1979, p. 34.

Marvin E. Mundel, "Productivity Measurement and Improvement," *Industrial Engineering Handbook,* 1983, p. 1.5.1.

Benjamin W. Niebel, *Motion and Time Study,* 7th Ed., Richard D. Irwin, Inc., 1982.

J. Randolph New and Daniel D. Singer, "Understanding Why People Reject New Ideas Helps IEs Convert Resistance Into Acceptance," *Industrial Engineering,* May 1983, p. 81.

Joel E. Ross, *Managing Productivity,* Reston Publishing Co., 1977.

Richard J. Schonberger, "Just-in-Time Production—The Quality Dividend," *Quality Progress,* October 1984.

D. Scott Sink, "Organizational System Performance," *Productivity Management,* Spring 1983, p. 1.

David J. Sumanth, "Implementation Steps for a Productivity Measurement Program in Companies," *Proceedings, Industrial Engineering Conference,* 1982, p. 335.

CHAPTER IX

BIBLIOGRAPHY:

1. D. Scott Sink, Sandra J. DeVries and Thomas C. Tuttle, "An In-Depth Study and Review of State-of-the-Art and Practice Productivity Measurement Techniques," *Industrial Engineering News,* Winter 1985.
2. Edward Sullivan, "Quality Costs: Current Ideas," *Quality Progress,* April 1983, p. 24.

REFERENCES:

Chester L. Brisley and William Fielder, Jr., "Unmeasurable Output of Knowledge/ Office Workers Can and Must be Measured," *Industrial Engineering,* July 1983.

Jack Campanella and Frank J. Corcoran, "Principles of Quality Costs," *Quality Progress,* April 1984, p. 16.

R.A. Cawsey, "A Business Performance Measure of Quality Management," *Technical Transactions,* American Society for Quality Control, 1976.

Richard Dobbins, "Quality Costs: A Place for Decision Making and Corrective Action,"

Technical Transactions, American Society for Quality Control, 1976.

A.V. Feigenbaum, *Total Quality Control,* McGraw Hill Book Company, 1983.

M.R. Goodes, "Dollars and Sense of Productivity: The Human Factor," *Industrial Management,* July-August 1984.

"Japanese Auto Makers Make Heavy Demands on Suppliers," *Quality,* April 1979, p. 16.

J.M. Juran, "The Quality-Profit Relationship," *Technical Conference Transactions,* American Society for Quality Control, 1976, p. 18.

Frank H. Squires, *Successful Quality Management,* Hitchcock Publishing Company, Wheaton, IL, 1980.

Edward Sullivan, "Quality Costs: Current Ideas," *Quality Progress,* April 1984, p. 24.

Joseph J. Tsialsals, "Management Team Seeks Quality Improvement From Quality Costs," *Quality Progress,* April 1983, p. 26.

CHAPTER X
BIBLIOGRAPHY:

1. Glenn E. Hayes and Harry G. Romig, *Modern Quality Control,* Revised Edition, Glencoe Publishing Co., Encino, CA 1983.
2. Douglas McGregor, *The Human Side of Enterprise,* McGraw Hill Book Co., 1960.
3. Mick Ukleja, "Walk, Run and Fly," *Sermon,* January 1, 1984, Grace Community Church, Los Alamitos, CA.

REFERENCES:

Gary L. Benson, "How Employees Assumptions Influence Managerial Behavior," *Supervisory Management,* March 1983.

Charles H. Clark, *Idea Management: How to Motivate Creativity and Innovation,* New York: AMACOM, 1980.

John F. Collins, "How to Motivate Your Employees," *Nation's Business,* December 1982, pp. 48-50.

Richard Davidson, "Motivating the Underachiever," *Supervisory Management,* January 1983, p. 28.

Frederick Herzberg, "One More Time: How Do You Motivate Employees?" *Harbard Business Review,* January/February 1968, p. 53.

Frederick Herzberg, "Productivity Begins with the Individual," *Industry Week,* November 30, 1981, p. 83.

Frederick Herzberg, "Up the Staircase to Productivity Burnout," *Industry Week,* January 10, 1983, p. 65.

Nathan Keyfitz, "Technology and Work in the Late Twentieth Century," *National Forum, The Phi Kappa Phi Journal,* Fall 1978, p. 18.

Brian H. Kleiner, "Integrating Major Motivational Theories," *Journal of Systems Management,* Vol. 34, No. 2, February 1983.

Louis Kraar, "The Japanese Are Coming—With Their Own Style of Management," *Fortune,* March 1975, p. 116.

J. Sterling Livingston, "Pygmalion in Management," *Harvard Business Review,* July/August 1969.

Jay W. Lorsch, "Making Behavorial Science More Useful," *Harvard Business Review,* March/April 1979, p. 171.

William A. Marsh, "Management Theories: Comparing X, Y and Z," *Quality Progress,* December 1982.

Douglas McGregor, *Leadership and Motivation,* Massachusetts: The Massachusetts Institute of Technology, 1966.

William G. Ouchi and Alfred M. Jaeger, "Type Z Organization: Stability in the Midst of Mobility," *Academy of Management Review,* April 1978, p. 305.

Sugar T. Parker, "How the Boys in the Office Mishandle Time," *Iron Age,* March 1, 1982.

Linda J.M. Rott, "IE's Should Examine Impact of Management Style on Motivation and Productivity," *Industry Engineering,* January 1984.

Bob J. Roth, "New Approach to Quality at the UAW," *Quality Progress,* October 1983, p. 19.

Erwin S. Stanton, "A Critical Reevaluation of Motivation, Management, and Productivity," *Personnel Journal,* March 1983.

John Teresko, "Lincoln Wants to Share Its Productivity Secrets," *Industry Week,* March 7, 1983, p. 75.

"The New Industrial Elations," Special Report, *Business Week,* May 11, 1981, p. 84.

Harold Richard Walt, "Managers for the Year 2000," *Industrial Management, Institute of Industrial Engineers,* p. 3.

R.A. Zawacki and J.S. Johnson, "Alternative Worksheet Schedules: One Company's Experience with Flextime," *Supervisory Management,* Vol. 21, June 1976, pp. 15-19.

INDEX